Sean O'Casey

by the same author

SEAN O'CASEY: PLAYS ONE

Juno and the Paycock
Within the Gates
Red Roses for Me
Cock-A-Doodle Dandy

SEAN O'CASEY

Plays Two

The Shadow of a Gunman

The Plough and the Stars

The Silver Tassie

Purple Dust

Hall of Healing

Introduced by
Arthur Miller

faber and faber

The Shadow of a Gunman, The Plough and the Stars
and *The Silver Tassie* were first published in 1949 by
Macmillan London Ltd.
Purple Dust and *Hall of Healing* were first published
in 1951 by Macmillan London Ltd.
First published in this edition in 1998 by
Faber and Faber Limited
3 Queen Square London WC1N 3AU

Photoset by Parker Typesetting Service, Leicester
Printed in England by Mackays of Chatham plc, Chatham, Kent

All rights whatsoever in these plays are strictly reserved.
Applications for permission for any use whatsoever including performance
rights must be made in advance, prior to any such proposed use to
MacNaughton Lord Representation, 200 Fulham Road, London SW10 9PN.
No performance may be given unless a licence has first been obtained.

A CIP record for this book
is available from the British Library
ISBN 0-571-19182-7

2 4 6 8 10 9 7 5 3 1

Contents

Introduction, vii

The Shadow of a Gunman, 1

The Plough and the Stars, 63

The Silver Tassie, 163

Purple Dust, 271

Hall of Healing, 391

Introduction

Since at least the turn of the century – probably much longer – playwrights have been wandering in the desert searching for a convincing way of poeticizing dialogue without sounding arty. In a letter to O'Casey about his latest play, Eugene O'Neill cried out, 'Oh, if I could write like that!' J. M. Synge, in the earlier generation, had long before described the problem. Synge was in a supremely conscious revolt against the banality of most theatre language. He hated Ibsen's prosaic language and Zola's dead level reportage. In Ireland, however, Synge believed things were different: the popular imagination was still 'fiery and magnificent, and tender; so that those of us who wish to write start with a chance that is not given to writers in places where the springtime of local life has been forgotten, and the harvest is a memory only, and the straw has been turned into bricks'.

In the next generation, O'Casey was among those, Yeats most prominently, who were bent on making the bricks. What distinguishes O'Casey's approach, I think, from the Yeats people was the absence of any antiquarian interest; his art was demotic, aimed at the people talking their heads off in the pubs and street corners, people with minds saturated with Ireland's struggle. Even in the most mundane of conversational exchanges O'Casey sought and as often as not found the lift of poetry. Indeed, that was the whole point – that the significantly poetic sprang from the raw and real experience of ordinary people rather than the manipulation of the legendary icons. Whether this demotic tendency had an extra-literary root one cannot say, but given O'Casey's passionate revolt against not only

vii

the British domination of his country but capitalism itself, one can believe with some confidence that O'Casey the poet and O'Casey the political rebel was all of a piece. Thus, his revelling in the language of common people worked in part to celebrate their immortal creative powers, powers that were fated one day to remake the world.

I came of age in the Fascist-threatened thirties of the Great Depression. Many a writer, myself among them, felt beleaguered as the democracies feigned or felt paralysis before the rising militarism of Germany, Italy and Japan, who in turn were promising to bring down the heart of darkness itself, the Communist Soviets. In America for a little while we had a voice of the left in Clifford Odets, but he was swallowed up in the Hollywood sea before his artistic maturity had taken place. From my youthful vantage, partisan as it surely was, the only steady-on democratic conscience was O'Casey's, a beam of light searching the darkness ahead for a sign of a humane polity.

To be sure, his Irish dialect was light years away from New York speech and temperament, but to those of us who were alienated from Broadway theatre he spoke to our hearts. To put it in a nutshell, in play after Broadway play it was impossible to know how the characters made a living: either they had no conceivable existence off the stage or it was too comfortable a one to reflect our Depression psychology. And so our problem was the age-old problem of all the arts – to find not so much the direction but the indirection through which our time might be illuminated. O'Casey, because he was a real poet, had found his path, a path lit up by wit and humour that reached out to audiences who might otherwise have dug in their heels against a strictly sombre confrontation with the social realities he was bent on setting forth.

O'Casey's uniqueness for young writers of the thirties

was not so much that he had a style, but that he was a style. His personality shone through his plays in a time when it was hard to tell which playwright might have authored a play, so conventional and objective was the reigning theatre custom. There was no problem whatever in being able to tell whether O'Casey had written a play. It was primarily his language that fascinated and challenged. The tongue of his dialogue could crack like a whip or it could kiss; his arsenal of words, his wit and his dirges made the rest of the English-speaking stage seem palid and worn out. Where most Broadway plays were terribly controlled and plotted, O'Casey's were lavish and careless and their gaze was broad enough to take in the pit and the horizon.

Inevitably, with the onset of the Cold War, caution set in among critics and commentators toward the work of a man who, it was said, still wore a hammer-and-sickle badge on his lapel. Those who were not outraged put him down as a crank. The only pride I have ever taken in American critics was evoked by the stubborn praise for O'Casey in the *New York Times* columns of Brooks Atkinson who, even against the right-wing gale that seemed to be quashing admiration for the self-described Communist, never wavered in his declarations of love for the Irish maverick.

My first experience with O'Casey was, I think, in 1939 when *Juno* came to New York with Sarah Algood, Barry Fitzgerald and F. J. McCormick, and to this day almost half a century later I believe I could easily restage its main scenes, so vivid was their impression. I will never forget the expression on Algood's face when she returns home to find her husband the Paycock and his pal Joxer on hands and knees looking under the furniture for a hidden bottle; caught *in flagrante* by his wife's sudden appearance, the Paycock blithely explains that what they were so desperately searching for was a *book*! (The scene does not appear in the published version.) I can still see Algood's face, the sorrow that overwhelmed her anger as she stood there in silence for a long, long moment emitting a kind of metaphorical sigh that was broad enough to cover Ireland and the balcony together. And then the hilarity that greeted Joxer's 'Oh, it was a darlin' book!' In a lesser actress, the laughter that burst forth at that lovely and pathetic line could have trivialized the tragic waste of her life, but Algood made it frame and set off her anguish.

That was the thing about O'Casey, his gift of laughter that left you in tears for the human race. What high seriousness that was, to be able to release simultaneously his wrath at injustice, his wild joy in the language he was blessed with, and all of it wreathed in ironical wit and the deepest sorrow.

He seems to have loved America and New York, and so it was doubly hurtful, at least to me, when in the early fifties his last play was denied a scheduled production on Broadway because of threatened attacks by veterans' groups and other right-wing hysterics who warned of picket lines before the theatre if the play ever opened. I was at the time on the Board of the Dramatists Guild and offered a resolution stating that we, American playwrights, insisted on O'Casey's right to be heard on the Broadway stage, and would mount a counter-picket line if necessary to help secure that right. The anti-Communist flood-tide was at its height then, and one of our most faithful members took the floor to threaten to resign from the Guild and to take as many members as he could with him should a penny of Guild funds be spent defending this Communist. Oscar Hammerstein was the Guild President, and I know his heart was with O'Casey, but such were the times that this greatest of playwrights could not find his defence among American playwrights. His play's backers withdrew their money and with it, I thought, the illusion that America was somehow different, and unlike other countries could not be confused and stampeded into giving away liberty to the nasties, the frightened and angry little men who are always and everywhere eager to destroy it.

It is a special pleasure in knowing that O'Casey's plays still hold the stage after so many decades have passed and so much unexpected history has changed tastes and conditions of production. If there is any grandeur at all in the temple of the arts of the twentieth century, surely more than his share of the hods that went into the building of it were carried up on O'Casey's shoulder. And it is a most satisfying thought that a new collection of his work will now go out to the world. Lucky world!

Arthur Miller
September 1997

THE SHADOW OF A GUNMAN

A TRAGEDY IN TWO ACTS

Characters

Donal Davoren
Seumas Shields, a pedlar
Tommy Owens   } Residents in
Adolphus Grigson   the Tenement
Mrs Grigson
Minnie Powell
Mr Mulligan, the landlord
Mr Maguire, soldier of the IRA
Mrs Henderson   } Residents of an
Mr Gallogher   adjoining Tenement
An Auxiliary

The period of the play is May 1920.

Act One

A return-room in a tenement house in Hilljoy Square. At the back two large windows looking out into the yard; they occupy practically the whole of the back wall space. Between the windows is a cupboard, on the top of which is a pile of books. The doors are open, and on these are hanging a number of collars and ties. Running parallel with the windows is a stretcher bed; another runs at right angles along the wall at right. At the head of this bed is a door leading to the rest of the house. The wall on the left runs diagonally, so that the fireplace – which is in the centre – is plainly visible. On the mantelshelf to the right is a statue of the Virgin, to the left a statue of the Sacred Heart, and in the centre a crucifix. Around the fireplace are a few common cooking utensils. In the centre of the room is a table, on which are a typewriter, a candle and candlestick, a bunch of wild flowers in a vase, writing materials and a number of books. There are two chairs, one near the fireplace and one at the table. The aspect of the place is one of absolute untidiness, engendered on the one hand by the congenital slovenliness of Seumas Shields, and on the other by the temperament of Donal Davoren, making it appear impossible to effect an improvement in such a place.

Davoren is sitting at the table typing. He is about thirty. There is in his face an expression that seems to indicate an eternal war between weakness and strength; there is in the lines of the brow and chin an indication of a desire for activity, while in his eyes there is visible an unquenchable tendency towards rest. His struggle through life has been a hard one, and his efforts have been handicapped by an

3

inherited and self-developed devotion to 'the might of design, the mystery of colour, and the belief in the redemption of all things by beauty everlasting'. His life would drive him mad were it not for the fact that he never knew any other. He bears upon his body the marks of the struggle for existence and the efforts towards self-expression.

Seumas Shields, who is in the bed next to the wall to the right, is a heavily built man of thirty-five; he is dark-haired and sallow-complexioned. In him is frequently manifested the superstition, the fear and the malignity of primitive man.

Davoren (*lilting an air as he composes*)
Or when sweet Summer's ardent arms outspread,
Entwined with flowers,
Enfold us, like two lovers newly wed,
Thro' ravish'd hours –
Then sorrow, woe and pain lose all their powers,
For each is dead, and life is only ours.

A Woman's figure appears at the window and taps loudly on one of the panes; at the same moment there is loud knocking at the door.

Voice of Woman at window Are you awake, Mr Shields – Mr Shields, are you awake? Are you goin' to get up today at all, at all?

Voice at the door   Mr Shields, is there any use of callin' you at all? This is a nice nine o'clock, do you know what time it is, Mr Shields?

Seumas (*loudly*) Yus!

Voice at the door Why don't you get up, then, an' not have the house turned into a bedlam tryin' to waken you?

Seumas (*shouting*) All right, all right, all right! The way

4

these oul' ones bawl at a body! Upon my soul! I'm beginnin' to believe that the Irish People are still in the stone age. If they could they'd throw a bomb at you.

Davoren A land mine exploding under the bed is the only thing that would lift you out of it.

Seumas (*stretching himself*) Oh-h-h. I was fast in the arms of Morpheus – he was one of the infernal deities, son of Somnus, wasn't he?

Davoren I think so.

Seumas The poppy was his emblem, wasn't it?

Davoren Ah, I don't know.

Seumas It's a bit cold this morning, I think, isn't it?

Davoren It's quite plain I'm not going to get much quietness in this house.

Seumas (*after a pause*) I wonder what time is it?

Davoren The Angelus went some time ago.

Seumas (*sitting up in bed suddenly*) The Angelus! It couldn't be that late, could it? I asked them to call me at nine so that I could get Mass before I went on my rounds. Why didn't you give us a rap?

Davoren Give you a rap! Why, man, they've been thundering at the door and hammering at the window for the past two hours, till the house shook to its very foundations, but you took less notice of the infernal din than I would take of the strumming of a grasshopper.

Seumas There's no fear of you thinking of anyone else when you're at your poetry. The land of Saints and Scholars 'ill shortly be a land of bloody poets. (*Anxiously*) I suppose Maguire has come and gone?

Davoren Maguire? No, he hasn't been here – why, did you expect him?

Seumas (*in a burst of indignation*) He said he'd be here at nine. 'Before the last chime has struck,' says he, 'I'll be coming in on the door,' and it must be – what time is it now?

Davoren Oh, it must be half-past twelve.

Seumas Did anybody ever see the like of the Irish People? Is there any use of tryin' to do anything in this country? Have everything packed and ready, have everything packed and ready, have . . .

Davoren And have you everything packed and ready?

Seumas What's the use of having anything packed and ready when he didn't come? (*He rises and dresses himself.*) No wonder this unfortunate country is as it is, for you can't depend upon the word of a single individual in it. I suppose he was too damn lazy to get up; he wanted the streets to be well aired first – Oh, Kathleen ni Houlihan, your way's a thorny way.

Davoren Ah me! alas, pain, pain ever, for ever!

Seumas That's from Shelley's *Prometheus Unbound*. I could never agree with Shelley, not that there's anything to be said against him as a poet – as a poet – but . . .

Davoren He flung a few stones through stained-glass windows.

Seumas He wasn't the first nor he won't be the last to do that, but the stained-glass windows – more than ever of them – are here still, and Shelley is doing a jazz dance down below. (*He gives a snarling laugh of pleasure.*)

Davoren (*shocked*) And you actually rejoice and are exceedingly glad that, as you believe, Shelley, the sensitive, high-minded, noble-hearted Shelley, is suffering the tortures of the damned.

Seumas I rejoice in the vindication of the Church and Truth.

Davoren Bah. You know as little about truth as anybody else, and you care as little about the Church as the least of those that profess her faith; your religion is simply the state of being afraid that God will torture your soul in the next world as you are afraid the Black and Tans will torture your body in this.

Seumas Go on, me boy; I'll have a right laugh at you when both of us are dead.

Davoren You're welcome to laugh as much as you like at me when both of us are dead.

Seumas (*as he is about to put on his collar and tie*) I don't think I need to wash meself this morning; do I look all right?

Davoren Oh, you're all right; it's too late now to start washing yourself. Didn't you wash yourself yesterday morning?

Seumas I gave meself a great rub yesterday. (*He proceeds to pack various articles into an attaché case – spoons, forks, laces, thread, etc.*) I think I'll bring out a few of the braces too; damn it, they're well worth sixpence each; there's great stuff in them – did you see them?

Davoren Yes, you showed them to me before.

Seumas They're great value; I only hope I'll be able to get enough o' them. I'm wearing a pair of them meself – they'd do Cuchullian, they're so strong. (*Counting the spoons*) There's a dozen in each of these parcels – three, six, nine – damn it, there's only eleven in this one. I better try another. Three, six, nine – my God, there's only eleven in this one too, and one of them bent! Now I suppose I'll have to go through the whole bloody lot of them, for I'd never be easy in me mind thinkin' there'd be more than a dozen in some o' them. And still we're looking for freedom – ye gods, it's a glorious country! (*He lets one fall, which he stoops to pick up.*) Oh, my God, there's the braces after breakin'.

Davoren That doesn't look as if they were strong enough for Cuchullian.

Seumas I put a heavy strain on them too sudden. There's that fellow Maguire never turned up, either; he's almost too lazy to wash himself.

As he is struggling with the braces the door is hastily shoved in and Maguire rushes in with a handbag.

This is a nice nine o'clock. What's the use of you coming at this hour o' the day? Do you think we're going to work be moonlight? If you weren't goin' to come at nine couldn't you say you weren't . . .

Maguire Keep your hair on; I just blew in to tell you that I couldn't go today at all. I have to go to Knocksedan.

Seumas Knocksedan! An' what, in the name o' God, is bringin' you to Knocksedan?

Maguire Business, business. I'm going out to catch butterflies.

Seumas If you want to make a cod of anybody, make a cod of somebody else, an' don't be tryin' to make a cod o' me. Here I've had everything packed an' ready for hours; you were to be here at nine, an' you wait till just one o'clock to come rushin' in like a mad bull to say you've got to go to Knocksedan! Can't you leave Knocksedan till tomorrow?

Maguire Can't be did, can't be did, Seumas; if I waited till tomorrow all the butterflies might be dead. I'll leave this bag here till this evening. (*He puts the bag in a corner of the room.*) Goodbye . . . ee. (*He is gone before Seumas is aware of it.*)

Seumas (*with a gesture of despair*) Oh, this is a hopeless country! There's a fellow that thinks that the four cardinal virtues are not to be found outside an Irish Republic. I don't want to boast about myself – I don't want to boast about myself, and I suppose I could call meself as good a Gael as some of those that are knocking about now – knocking about now – as good a Gael as some that are knocking about now, – but I remember the time when I taught Irish six nights a week, when in the Irish Republican Brotherhood I paid me rifle levy like a man, an' when the Church refused to have anything to do with James Stephens, I tarred a prayer for the repose of his soul on the steps of the Pro-Cathedral. Now, after all me work for Dark Rosaleen, the only answer you can get from a roarin' Republican to a simple question is 'goodbye . . . ee'. What, in the name o' God, can be bringin' him to Knocksedan?

Davoren Hadn't you better run out and ask him?

Seumas That's right, that's right – make a joke about it! That's the Irish People all over – they treat a joke as a serious thing and a serious thing as a joke. Upon me soul, I'm beginning to believe that the Irish People aren't, never were, an' never will be fit for self-government. They've made Balor of the Evil Eye King of Ireland, an' so signs on it there's neither conscience nor honesty from one end of the country to the other. Well, I hope he'll have a happy day in Knocksedan. (*A knock at the door.*) Who's that?

Another knock.

(*Irritably*) Who's that; who's there?

Davoren (*more irritably*) Halt and give the countersign – damn it, man, can't you go and see?

Seumas goes over and opens the door. A man of about sixty is revealed, dressed in a faded blue serge suit; a half-tall hat is on his head. It is evident that he has no love for Seumas, who denies him the deference he believes is due from a tenant to a landlord. He carries some papers in his hand.

The Landlord (*ironically*) Good-day, Mr Shields; it's meself that hopes you're feelin' well – you're lookin' well, anyhow – though you can't always go be looks nowadays.

Seumas It doesn't matter whether I'm lookin' well or feelin' well; I'm all right, thanks be to God.

The Landlord I'm very glad to hear it.

Seumas It doesn't matter whether you're glad to hear it or not, Mr Mulligan.

The Landlord You're not inclined to be very civil, Mr Shields.

Seumas Look here, Mr Mulligan, if you come here to raise an argument, I've something to do – let me tell you that.

The Landlord I don't come here to raise no argument; a person ud have small gains argufyin' with you – let me tell you that.

Seumas I've no time to be standin' here gostherin' with you – let me shut the door, Mr Mulligan.

The Landlord You'll not shut no door till you've heard what I've got to say.

Seumas Well, say it then, an' go about your business.

The Landlord You're very high an' mighty, but take care

you're not goin' to get a drop. What a baby you are not to know what brings me here! Maybe you thought I was goin' to ask you to come to tea.

Davoren Ah me! alas, pain, pain ever, for ever!

Seumas Are you goin' to let me shut the door, Mr Mulligan?

The Landlord I'm here for me rent; you don't like the idea of bein' asked to pay your just an' lawful debts.

Seumas You'll get your rent when you learn to keep your rent-book in a proper way.

The Landlord I'm not goin' to take any lessons from you, anyhow.

Seumas I want to have no more talk with you, Mr Mulligan.

The Landlord Talk or no talk, you owe me eleven weeks' rent, an' it's marked down again' you in black an' white.

Seumas I don't care a damn if it was marked down in green, white, an' yellow.

The Landlord You're a terribly independent fellow, an' it ud be fitter for you to be less funny an' stop tryin' to be billickin' honest an' respectable people.

Seumas Just you be careful what you're sayin', Mr Mulligan. There's law in the land still.

The Landlord Be me sowl there is, an' you're goin' to get a little of it now. (*He offers the papers to Seumas.*) Them's for you.

Seumas (*hesitating to take them*) I want to have nothing to do with you, Mr Mulligan.

The Landlord (*throwing the papers in the centre of the room*) What am I better? It was the sorry day I ever let you come into this house. Maybe them notices to quit will stop your writin' letters to the papers about me an' me house.

Davoren For goodness' sake, bring the man in, and don't be discussing the situation like a pair of primitive troglodytes.

Seumas (*taking no notice*) Writing letters to the papers is my business, an' I'll write as often as I like, when I like, an' how I like.

The Landlord You'll not write about this house at all events. You can blow about the state of the yard, but you took care to say nothin' about payin' rent: oh no, that's not in your line. But since you're not satisfied with the house, you can pack up an' go to another.

Seumas I'll go, Mr Mulligan, when I think fit, an' no sooner.

The Landlord Not content with keeping the rent, you're startin' to bring in lodgers – (*to Davoren*) not that I'm sayin' anythin' again' you, sir. Bringin' in lodgers without as much as be your leave – what's the world comin' to at all that a man's house isn't his own? But I'll soon put a stop to your gallop, for on the twenty-eight of the next month out you go, an' there'll be few sorry to see your back.

Seumas I'll go when I like.

The Landlord I'll let you see whether you own the house or no.

Seumas I'll go when I like!

The Landlord We'll see about that.

Seumas We'll see.

The Landlord Ay, we'll see.

The Landlord goes out and Seumas shuts the door.

(*Outside*) Mind you, I'm in earnest; you'll not stop in this house a minute longer than the twenty-eight.

Seumas (*with a roar*) Ah, go to hell!

Davoren (*pacing the room as far as the space will permit*) What in the name of God persuaded me to come to such a house as this?

Seumas It's nothing when you're used to it; you're too thin-skinned altogether. The oul' sod's got the wind up about you, that's all.

Davoren Got the wind up about me!

Seumas He thinks you're on the run. He's afraid of a raid, and that his lovely property'll be destroyed.

Davoren But why, in the name of all that's sensible, should he think that I'm on the run?

Seumas Sure they all think you're on the run. Mrs Henderson thinks it, Tommy Owens thinks it, Mrs an' Mr Grigson think it, an' Minnie Powell thinks it too. (*Picking up his attaché case*) I'd better be off if I'm goin' to do anything today.

Davoren What are we going to do with these notices to quit?

Seumas Oh, shove them up on the mantelpiece behind one of the statues.

Davoren Oh, I mean what action shall we take?

Seumas I haven't time to stop now. We'll talk about them when I come back . . . . I'll get me own back on that oul' Mulligan yet. I wish to God they would come an' smash his rookery to pieces, for it's all he thinks of, and, mind you, oul' Mulligan would call himself a descendant of the true Gaels of Banba – (*as he goes out*)

Oh, proud were the chieftains of famed Inisfail.
Is truagh gan oidher 'na Vfarradh.
The stars of our sky an' the salt of our soil –

Oh, Kathleen ni Houlihan, your way's a thorny way! (*He goes out.*)

Davoren (*returning to the table and sitting down at the typewriter*) Oh, Donal Og O'Davoren, your way's a thorny way. Your last state is worse than your first. Ah me, alas! Pain, pain ever, for ever. Like thee, Prometheus, no change, no pause, no hope. Ah, life, life, life! (*There is a gentle knock at the door.*) Another Fury come to plague me now! (*Another knock, a little louder.*) You can knock till you're tired.

> *The door opens and Minnie Powell enters with an easy confidence one would not expect her to possess for her gentle way of knocking. She is a girl of twenty-three, but the fact of being forced to earn her living, and to take care of herself, on account of her parents' early death, has given her a force and an assurance beyond her years. She has lost the sense of fear (she does not know this), and, consequently, she is at ease in all places and before all persons, even those of a superior education, so long as she meets them in the atmosphere that surrounds the members of her own class. Her hair is brown, neither light nor dark, but partaking of both tints according to the light or shade she may happen to be in. Her well-shaped figure – a rare thing in a city girl – is charmingly dressed in a brown tailor-made costume, her stockings and shoes are a darker brown tint than the costume, and all are crowned by a silk tam-o'-shanter of a rich blue tint.*

Minnie Are you in, Mr Shields?

Davoren (*rapidly*) No, he's not, Minnie; he's just gone out

– if you run out quickly you're sure to catch him.

Minnie Oh, it's all right, Mr Davoren, you'll do just as well; I just come in for a drop o' milk for a cup o' tea; I shouldn't be troublin' you this way, but I'm sure you don't mind.

Davoren (*dubiously*) No trouble in the world; delighted, I'm sure. (*Giving her the milk*) There, will you have enough?

Minnie Plenty, lashins, thanks. Do you be all alone all the day, Mr Davoren?

Davoren No, indeed; I wish to God I was.

Minnie It's not good for you then. I don't know how you like to be by yourself – I couldn't stick it long.

Davoren (*wearily*) No?

Minnie No, indeed; (*with rapture*) there's nothin' I'm more fond of than a Hooley. I was at one last Sunday – I danced rings round me! Tommy Owens was there – you know Tommy Owens, don't you?

Davoren I can't say I do.

Minnie D'ye not? The little fellow that lives with his mother in the two-pair back – (*ecstatically*) he's a gorgeous melodeon player!

Davoren A gifted son of Orpheus, eh?

Minnie (*who never heard of Orpheus*) You've said it, Mr Davoren: the son of poor oul' Battie Owens, a weeshy, dawny, bit of a man that was never sober an' was always talkin' politics. Poor man, it killed him in the long run.

Davoren A man should always be drunk, Minnie, when he talks politics – it's the only way in which to make them important.

Minnie Tommy takes after the oul' fellow, too; he'd talk from morning till night when he has a few jars in him. (*Suddenly; for like all her class, Minnie is not able to converse very long on the one subject, and her thoughts spring from one thing to another*) Poetry is a grand thing, Mr Davoren, I'd love to be able to write a poem – a lovely poem on Ireland an' the men o' '98.

Davoren Oh, we've had enough of poems, Minnie, about '98, and of Ireland, too.

Minnie Oh, there's a thing for a Republican to say! But I know what you mean: it's time to give up the writing an' take to the gun. (*Her roving eye catches sight of the flowers in the vase.*) What's Mr Shields doin' with the oul' weeds?

Davoren Those aren't Shields', they're mine. Wild flowers is a kindlier name for them, Minnie, than weeds. These are wild violets, this is an *Arum maculatum*, or Wake Robin, and these are Celandines, a very beautiful flower related to the buttercups. (*He quotes.*)

One day, when Morn's half-open'd eyes
Were bright with Spring sunshine –
My hand was clasp'd in yours, dear love,
And yours was clasp'd in mine –
We bow'd as worshippers before
The Golden Celandine.

Minnie Oh, aren't they lovely, an' isn't the poem lovely, too! I wonder, now, who she was.

Davoren (*puzzled*) She, who?

Minnie Why, the . . . (*roguishly*) Oh, be the way you don't know.

Davoren Know? I'm sure I don't know.

Minnie It doesn't matter, anyhow – that's your own business; I suppose I don't know her.

Davoren Know her – know whom?

Minnie (*shyly*) Her whose hand was clasped in yours, an' yours was clasped in hers.

Davoren Oh, that – that was simply a poem I quoted about the Celandine, that might apply to any girl – to you, for instance.

Minnie (*greatly relieved, coming over and sitting beside Davoren*) But you have a sweetheart, all the same, Mr Davoren, haven't you?

Davoren I? No, not one, Minnie.

Minnie Oh, now, you can tell that to someone else; aren't you a poet an' aren't all the girls fond o' poets?

Davoren That may be, but all the poets aren't fond of girls.

Minnie They are in the story-books, ay, and fond of more than one, too. (*With a questioning look*) Are you fond of them, Mr Davoren?

Davoren Of course I like girls, Minnie, especially girls who can add to their charms by the way in which they dress, like you, for instance.

Minnie Oh, now, you're on for coddin' me, Mr Davoren.

Davoren No, really, Minnie, I'm not; you are a very charming little girl indeed.

Minnie Then if I'm a charmin' little girl, you ought to be able to write a poem about me.

Davoren (*who has become susceptible to the attractiveness of Minnie, catching her hand*) And so I will, so I will,

17

Minnie; I have written them about girls not half so pretty as yourself.

Minnie Ah, I knew you had one, I knew you had one now.

Davoren Nonsense. Every girl a poet writes about isn't his sweetheart; Annie Laurie wasn't the sweetheart of Bobbie Burns.

Minnie You needn't tell me she wasn't; 'An' for bonnie Annie Laurie I'd lay me down an' die'. No man ud lay down an' die for any but a sweetheart, not even for a wife.

Davoren No man, Minnie, willingly dies for anything.

Minnie Except for his country, like Robert Emmet.

Davoren Even he would have lived on if he could; he died not to deliver Ireland. The British Government killed him to save the British nation.

Minnie You're only jokin' now; you'd die for your country.

Davoren I don't know so much about that.

Minnie You would, you would, you would – I know what you are.

Davoren What am I?

Minnie (*in a whisper*) A gunman on the run!

Davoren (*too pleased to deny it*) Maybe I am, and maybe I'm not.

Minnie Oh, I know, I know, I know. Do you never be afraid?

Davoren Afraid! Afraid of what?

Minnie Why, the ambushes of course; *I'm* all of a tremble when I hear a shot go off, an' what must it be in the middle of the firin'?

Davoren (*delighted at Minnie's obvious admiration; leaning back in his chair, and lighting a cigarette with placid affectation*) I'll admit one does be a little nervous at first, but a fellow gets used to it after a bit, till, at last, a gunman throws a bomb as carelessly as a schoolboy throws a snowball.

Minnie (*fervently*) I wish it was all over, all the same. (*Suddenly, with a tremor in her voice*) You'll take care of yourself, won't you, won't you, Donal – I mean, Mr Davoren?

Davoren (*earnestly*) Call me Donal, Minnie; we're friends, great friends now – (*putting his arm around her*) go on, Minnie, call me Donal, let me hear you say Donal.

Minnie The place badly needs a tidyin' up . . . Donal – there now, are you satisfied? (*Rapidly, half afraid of Davoren's excited emotions*) But it really does, it's in an awful state. Tomorrow's a half-day, an' I'll run in an' straighten it up a bit.

Davoren (*frightened at the suggestion*) No, no, Minnie, you're too pretty for that sort of work; besides, the people of the house would be sure to start talking about you.

Minnie An' do you think Minnie Powell cares whether they'll talk or no? She's had to push her way through life up to this without help from anyone, an' she's not goin' to ask their leave, now, to do what she wants to do.

Davoren (*forgetting his timidity in the honest joy of appreciating the independent courage of Minnie*) My soul within art thou, Minnie! A pioneer in action as I am a pioneer in thought. The two powers that shall 'grasp this sorry scheme of things entire, and mould life nearer to the heart's desire'. Lovely little Minnie, and brave as well; brave little Minnie, and lovely as well!

His disengaged hand lifts up her bent head, and he looks earnestly at her; he is stooping to kiss her, when Tommy Owens appears at the door, which Minnie has left partially open. Tommy is about twenty-five years of age. He is small and thin; his words are uttered in a nasal drawl; his voice is husky, due to frequent drinks and perpetual cigarette-smoking. He tries to get rid of the huskiness by an occasional cough. Tommy is a hero-worshipper, and, like many others, he is anxious to be on familiar terms with those who he thinks are braver than he is himself, and whose approbation he tries to win by an assumption equal to their own. He talks in a staccato manner. He has a few drinks taken – it is too early to be drunk – that make him talkative. He is dressed in a suit of dungarees, and gives a gentle cough to draw attention to his presence.

Tommy I seen nothin' – honest – thought you was learnin' to typewrite – Mr Davoren teachin' you. I seen nothin' else – s'help me God!

Minnie We'd be hard put to it if we minded what you seen, Tommy Owens.

Tommy Right, Minnie, Tommy Owens has a heart – Evenin', Mr Davoren – don't mind me comin' in – I'm Tommy Owens – live up in the two-pair back, workin' in Ross an' Walpole's – Mr Shields knows me well; you needn't be afraid o' me, Mr Davoren.

Davoren Why should I be afraid of you, Mr Owens, or of anybody else?

Tommy Why should you, indeed? We're all friends here – Mr Shields knows me well – all you've got to say is, 'Do you know Tommy Owens?' an' he'll tell you the sort of a man Tommy Owens is. There's no flies on Tommy – got me?

Minnie For goodness' sake, Tommy, leave Mr Davoren alone – he's got enough burgeons on him already.

Tommy Not a word, Minnie, not a word – Mr Davoren understands me well, as man to man. It's 'Up the Republic' all the time – eh, Mr Davoren?

Davoren I know nothing about the Republic; I have no connection with the politics of the day, and I don't want to have any connection.

Tommy You needn't say no more – a nod's as good as a wink to a blind horse – you've no meddlin' or makin' with it, good, bad, or indifferent, pro nor con; I know it an' Minnie knows it – give me your hand. (*He catches Davoren's hand.*) Two firm hands clasped together will all the power outbrave of the heartless English tyrant, the Saxon coward an' knave. That's Tommy Owens' hand, Mr Davoren, the hand of a man, a man – Mr Shields knows me well. (*He breaks into song.*)

> High upon the gallows tree stood the noble-hearted
>   three,
> By the vengeful tyrant stricken in their bloom;
> But they met him face to face with the spirit of their
>   race,
> And they went with souls undaunted to their doom!

Minnie (*in an effort to quell his fervour*) Tommy Owens, for goodness' sake . . .

Tommy (*overwhelming her with a shout*)
> God save Ireland ses the hayros, God save Ireland ses
>   we all,
> Whether on the scaffold high or the battle-field we die,
> Oh, what matter when for Ayryinn dear we fall!

(*Tearfully*) Mr Davoren, I'd die for Ireland!

Davoren I know you would, I know you would, Tommy.

Tommy I never got a chance – they never gave me a chance – but all the same I'd be there if I was called on – Mr Shields knows that – ask Mr Shields, Mr Davoren.

Davoren There's no necessity, Tommy; I know you're the right stuff if you got the chance, but remember that 'he also serves who only stands and waits'.

Tommy (*fiercely*) I'm bloody well tired o' waitin' – we're all tired o' waitin'. Why isn't every man in Ireland out with the IRA? Up with the barricades, up with the barricades; it's now or never, now an' for ever, as Sarsfield said at the battle o' Vinegar Hill. Up with the barricades – that's Tommy Owens – an' a penny buys a whistle. Let them as thinks different say different – what do you say, Mr Davoren?

Davoren I say, Tommy, you ought to go up and get your dinner, for if you wait much longer it won't be worth eating.

Tommy Oh, damn the dinner; who'd think o' dinner an' Ireland fightin' to be free? – not Tommy Owens, anyhow. It's only the Englishman who's always thinkin' of his belly.

Minnie Tommy Owens!

Tommy Excuse me, Miss Powell, in the ardure ov me anger I disremembered there was a lady present.

Voices are heard outside, and presently Mrs Henderson comes into the room, followed by Mr Gallogher, who, however, lingers at the door, too timid to come any farther. Mrs Henderson is a massive woman in every way; massive head, arms, and body; massive voice, and a massive amount of self-confidence. She is a mountain

of good nature, and during the interview she behaves
towards Davoren with deferential self-assurance. She
dominates the room, and seems to occupy the whole of
it. She is dressed poorly but tidily, wearing a white
apron and a large shawl. Mr Gallogher, on the other
hand, is a spare little man with a spare little grey beard
and a thin, nervous voice. He is dressed as well as a
faded suit of blue will allow him to be. He is obviously
ill at ease during his interview with Davoren. He carries
a hard hat, much the worse for wear, under his left arm,
and a letter in his right hand.

Mrs Henderson (*entering the room*) Come along in, Mr
Gallicker, Mr Davoren won't mind; it's him as can put you
in the way o' havin' your wrongs righted; come on in,
man, an' don't be so shy – Mr Davoren is wan ov
ourselves that stands for govermint ov the people with the
people by the people. You'll find you'll be as welcome as
the flowers in May. Good evenin', Mr Davoren, an' God
an' His holy angels be between you an' all harm.

Tommy (*effusively*) Come on, Mr Gallicker, an' don't be a
stranger – we're all friends here – anything special to be
done or particular advice asked, here's your man here.

Davoren (*subconsciously pleased, but a little timid of the*
belief that he is connected with the gunmen) I'm very busy
just now, Mrs Henderson, and really . . .

Mrs Henderson (*mistaking the reason of his embarrass-*
ment) Don't be put out, Mr Davoren, we won't keep you
more nor a few minutes. It's not in me or in Mr Gallicker
to spoil sport. Him an' me was young once, an' knows
what it is to be strolling at night in the pale moonlight,
with arms round one another. An' I wouldn't take much
an' say there's game in Mr Gallicker still, for I seen,
sometimes, a dangerous cock in his eye. But we won't keep
you an' Minnie long asunder; he's the letter an' all written.

You must know, Mr Davoren – excuse me for not introducin' him sooner – this is Mr Gallicker, that lives in the front drawin'-room ov number fifty-five, as decent an' honest an' quiet a man as you'd meet in a day's walk. An' so signs on it, it's them as 'ill be imposed upon – read the letter, Mr Gallicker.

Tommy Read away, Mr Gallicker, it will be attended to, never fear; we know our own know, eh, Mr Davoren?

Minnie Hurry up, Mr Gallicker, an' don't be keeping Mr Davoren.

Mrs Henderson Give him time, Minnie Powell. Give him time. You must know in all fairity, Mr Davoren, that the family livin' in the next room to Mr Gallicker – the back drawin'-room, to be particular – am I right or am I wrong, Mr Gallicker?

Mr Gallogher You're right, Mrs Henderson, perfectly right, indeed – that's the very identical room.

Mrs Henderson Well, Mr Davoren, the people in the back drawin'-room, or, to be more particular, the residents – that's the word that's writ in the letter – am I right or am I wrong, Mr Gallicker?

Mr Gallogher You're right, Mrs Henderson, perfectly accurate – that's the very identical word.

Mrs Henderson Well, Mr Davoren, the residents in the back drawin'-room, as I aforesaid, is nothin' but a gang o' tramps that oughtn't to be allowed to associate with honest, decent, quiet, respectable people. Mr Gallicker has tried to reason with them, and make them behave themselves – which in my opinion they never will – however, that's only an opinion, an' not legal – ever since they have made Mr Gallicker's life a HELL! Mr Gallicker, am I right or am I wrong?

Mr Gallogher I'm sorry to say you're right, Mrs Henderson, perfectly right – not a word of exaggeration.

Mrs Henderson Well, now, Mr Gallicker, seein' as I have given Mr Davoren a fair account ov how you're situated, an' ov these tramps' cleverality, I'll ask you to read the letter, which I'll say, not because you're there, or that you're a friend o' mine, is as good a letter as was decomposed by a scholar. Now, Mr Gallicker, an' don't forget the top sayin'.

> *Mr Gallogher prepares to read; Minnie leans forward to listen; Tommy takes out a well-worn note-book and a pencil stump, and assumes a very important attitude.*

Tommy One second. Mr Gallicker, is this the twenty-first or twenty-second?

Mr Gallogher The twenty-first, sir.

Tommy Thanks; proceed, Mr Gallicker.

Mr Gallogher (*with a few preliminary tremors, reads the letter. Reading*)

  'To all to Whom These Presents Come, Greeting

  'Gentlemen of the Irish Republican Army . . .'

Mrs Henderson There's a beginnin' for you, Mr Davoren.

Minnie That's some swank.

Tommy There's a lot in that sayin', mind you; it's a hard wallop at the British Empire.

Mrs Henderson (*proudly*) Go on, Mr Gallicker.

Mr Gallogher (*reading*)
  'I wish to call your attention to the persecution me and my family has to put up with in respect of and appertaining to the residents of the back drawing-room

of the house known as fifty-five, Saint Teresa Street, situate in the Parish of St Thomas, in the Borough and City of Dublin. This persecution started eighteen months ago – or to be precise – on the tenth day of the sixth month, in the year nineteen hundred and twenty.'

Mrs Henderson That's the word I was trying to think ov – precise – it cuts the ground from under their feet – so to speak.

Mr Gallogher (*reading*)
'We, the complainants, resident on the ground floor, deeming it disrespectable . . .'

Mrs Henderson (*with an emphatic nod*) Which it was.

Mr Gallogher (*reading*)
'Deeming it disrespectable to have an open hall, door, and to have the hall turned into a playground, made a solemn protest, and, in consequence, we the complainants aforesaid has had no peace ever since. Owing to the persecution, as aforesaid specified, we had to take out a summons again them some time ago as there was no Republican Courts then; but we did not proceed again them as me and my wife – to wit, James and Winifred Gallogher – has a strong objection to foreign Courts as such. We had peace for some time after that, but now things have gone from bad to worse. The name calling and the language is something abominable . . .'

Mrs Henderson (*holding out her hand as a constable would extend his to stop a car that another may pass*) Excuse me, Mr Gallicker, but I think the word 'shockin'' should be put in there after abominable; for the language used be these tramps has two ways o' bein' looked at – for it's abominable to the childer an' shockin' to your wife – am I right or am I wrong, Mr Davoren?

Tommy (*judicially*) Shockin' is a right good word, with a great deal o' meanin', an' . . .

Mrs Henderson (*with a deprecating gesture that extinguishes Tommy*) Tommy, let Mr Davoren speak; whatever Mr Davoren ses, Julia Henderson'll abide be.

Davoren (*afraid to say anything else*) I think the word might certainly be introduced with advantage.

Mrs Henderson Go over there, Mr Gallicker, an' put in the word shockin', as aforesaid.

Gallogher goes over to the table, and with a great deal of difficulty enters the word.

Tommy (*to Mr Gallogher as he writes*) Ey, there's two k's in shockin'!

Mr Gallogher (*reading*):
'The language is something abominable and shocking. My wife has often to lock the door of the room to keep them from assaulting her. If you would be so kind as to send some of your army or police down to see for themselves we would give them full particulars. I have to be always from home all day, as I work with Mr Hennessy, the harness maker of the Coombe, who will furnish all particulars as to my unvarnished respectability, also my neighbours. The name of the resident-tenant who is giving all this trouble and who, pursuant to the facts of the case aforesaid, mentioned, will be the defendant, is Dwyer. The husband of the aforesaid Mrs Dwyer, or the aforesaid defendant, as the case may be, is a seaman, who is coming home shortly, and we beg The Irish Republican Army to note that the said Mrs Dwyer says he will settle us when he comes home. While leaving it entirely in the hands of the gentlemen of The Republican Army, the defendant, that is to say, James Gallogher of fifty-five St Teresa Street,

ventures to say that he thinks he has made out a Primmy
Fashy Case against Mrs Dwyer and all her heirs, male
and female as aforesaid mentioned in the above written
schedule.

'*N.B.* – If you send up any of your men, please tell
them to bring their guns. I beg to remain the humble
servant and devoted admirer of the Gentlemen of the
Irish Republican Army.

'Witness my hand this tenth day of the fifth month of
the year nineteen hundred and twenty.

'James Gallogher.'

(*With a modest cough*) Ahem.

Mrs Henderson There's a letter for you, Mr Davoren!

Tommy It's the most powerfullest letter I ever heard read.

Minnie It wasn't you, really, that writ it, Mr Gallicker?

Mrs Henderson Sinn Fein Amhain: him an' him only,
Minnie. I seen him with me own two eyes when me an'
Winnie – Mrs Gallicker, Mr Davoren, aforesaid as appears
in the letter – was havin' a chat be the fire.

Minnie You'd never think it was in him to do it.

Mrs Henderson An' to think that the likes ov such a man
is to have the sowl-case worried out ov him by a gang o'
tramps; but it's in good hands now, an' instead ov them
settlin' yous, Mr Gallicker, it's yous 'ill settle them. Give
the letter to Mr Davoren, an' we'll be goin'.

Gallogher gives the letter to Davoren.

(*Moving towards the door*) I hope you an' Mr Shields is
gettin' on all right together, Mr Davoren.

Davoren Fairly well, thanks, Mrs Henderson. We don't
see much of each other. He's out during the day, and I'm
usually out during the evening.

Mrs Henderson I'm afraid he'll never make a fortune out ov what he's sellin'. He'll talk above an hour over a pennorth o' pins. Every time he comes to our place I buy a package o' hairpins from him to give him a little encouragement. I 'clare to God I have as many pins now as ud make a wire mattress for a double bed. All the young divils about the place are beginnin' to make a jeer ov him, too; I gave one ov them a mallavogin' the other day for callin' him oul' hairpins!

Mr Gallogher (*venturing an opinion*) Mr Shields is a man of exceptional mental capacity, and is worthy of a more dignified position.

Mrs Henderson Them words is true, Mr Gallicker, and they aren't. For to be wise is to be a fool, an' to be a fool is to be wise.

Mr Gallogher (*with deprecating tolerance*) Oh, Mrs Henderson, that's a parrotox.

Mrs Henderson It may be what a parrot talks, or a blackbird, or, for the matter of that, a lark – but it's what Julia Henderson thinks, any . . . whisht, is that a *Stop Press*?

> *Outside is heard the shriek of a newsboy calling 'Stop Press'.*

Run out, Tommy, an' get it till we see what it is.

Tommy I haven't got a make.

Mrs Henderson I never seen you any other way, an' you'll be always the same if you keep follyin' your Spearmints, an' your Bumble Bees an' your Night Patrols. (*Shouting to someone outside*) Is that a *Stop Press*, Mrs Grigson?

Voice (*outside*) Yis; an ambush out near Knocksedan.

Mrs Henderson That's the stuff to give them. (*Loudly*) Was there anybody hurted?

Voice (*outside*) One poor man killed – some chap named Maguire, the paper says.

Davoren (*agitated*) What name did she say?

Minnie Maguire; did you know him, Mr Davoren?

Davoren Yes – no, no; I didn't know him, no, I didn't know him, Minnie.

Minnie I wonder is it the Maguire that does be with Mr Shields?

Davoren Oh no, not at all, it couldn't be.

Mrs Henderson Knocksedan? That's in the County Sligo, now, or I'm greatly mistaken – am I right, Mr Gallicker, or am I wrong?

Mr Gallogher (*who knows perfectly well that it is in the County Dublin, but dare not correct Mrs Henderson*) That's where it is – Knocksedan, that's the very identical county.

Mrs Henderson Well, I think we better be makin' a move, Mr Gallicker; we've kep' Mr Davoren long enough, an' you'll find the letter'll be in good hans.

Mr Gallogher and Mrs Henderson move towards the door, which when he reaches it Mr Gallogher grips, hesitates, buttons his coat, and turns to Davoren.

Mr Gallogher Mr Davoren, sir, on behalf ov meself, James Gallicker, an' Winifred, Mrs Gallicker, wife ov the said James, I beg to offer, extend an' furnish our humble an' hearty thanks for your benevolent goodness in interferin' in the matter specified, particularated an' expanded upon in the letter, mandamus or schedule, as the case may be.

An' let me interpretate to you on behalf ov meself an'
Winifred Gallicker, that whenever you visit us you will be
supernally positive ov a hundred thousand welcomes –
ahem.

Mrs Henderson (*beaming with pride for the genius of her
friend*) There's a man for you, Mr Davoren! You forgot to
mention Biddy and Shaun, Mr Gallicker – (*to Davoren*)
his two children – it's himself has them trained well. It ud
make your heart thrill like an alarm clock to hear them
singin' 'Faith ov Our Fathers' an' 'Wrap the Green Flag
Roun' Me'.

Mr Gallogher (*half apologetically and half proudly*) Faith
an' Fatherland, Mrs Henderson, Faith and Fatherland.

Mrs Henderson Well, good-day, Mr Davoren, an' God
keep you an' strengthen all the men that are fightin' for
Ireland's freedom.

She and Gallogher go out.

Tommy I must be off too; so-long, Mr Davoren, an'
remember that Tommy Owens only waits the call. (*He
goes out too.*)

Davoren Well, Minnie, we're by ourselves once more.

Minnie Wouldn't that Tommy Owens give you the sick –
only waitin' to hear the call! Ah, then it'll take all the brass
bands in the country to blow the call before Tommy
Owens ud hear it. (*She looks at her wristlet watch.*) Sacred
Heart, I've only ten minutes to get back to work! I'll have
to fly! Quick, Mr Davoren, write me name in typewritin'
before I go – just 'Minnie'.

Davoren types the name.

(*Shyly but determinedly*) Now yours underneath – just
'Donal'.

Davoren does so.

Minnie, Donal; Donal, Minnie; goodbye now.

Davoren Here, what about your milk?

Minnie I haven't time to take it now. (*Slyly*) I'll come for it this evening.

They both go towards the door.

Davoren Minnie, the kiss I didn't get.

Minnie What kiss?

Davoren When we were interrupted; you know, you little rogue, come, just one.

Minnie Quick, then.

Davoren kisses her and she runs out. Davoren returns thoughtfully to the table.

Davoren Minnie, Donal; Donal, Minnie. Very pretty, but very ignorant. A gunman on the run! Be careful, be careful, Donal Davoren. But Minnie is attracted to the idea, and I am attracted to Minnie. And what danger can there be in being the shadow of a gunman?

Curtain.

Act Two

The same as in Act One. But it is now night. Seumas is in the bed that runs along the wall at back. Davoren is seated near the fire, to which he has drawn the table. He has a fountain-pen in his hand, and is attracted in thought towards the moon, which is shining in through the windows. An open writing-pad is on the table at Davoren's elbow. The bag left by Maguire is still in the same place.

Davoren

  The cold chaste moon, the Queen of Heaven's bright
    isles,
  Who makes all beautiful on which she smiles;
  That wandering shrine of soft yet icy flame,
  Which ever is transformed yet still the same.

Ah, Shelley, Shelley, you yourself were a lovely human orb shining through clouds of whirling human dust. 'She makes all beautiful on which she smiles.' Ah, Shelley, she couldn't make this thrice accursed room beautiful. Her beams of beauty only make its horrors more full of horrors still. There is an ugliness that can be made beautiful, and there is an ugliness that can only be destroyed, and this is part of that ugliness. Donal, Donal, I fear your last state is worse than your first. (*He lilts a verse, which he writes on the pad before him.*)

  When night advances through the sky with slow
    And solemn tread,
  The queenly moon looks down on life below,
    As if she read

33

Man's soul, and in her scornful silence said:
　All beautiful and happiest things are dead.

Seumas (*sleepily*) Donal, Donal, are you awake? (*Pause.*)
Donal, Donal, are you asleep?

Davoren I'm neither awake nor asleep: I'm thinking.

Seumas I was just thinkin', too – I was just thinkin', too,
that Maguire is sorry now that he didn't come with me
instead of going to Knocksedan. He caught something
besides butterflies – two of them he got, one through each
lung.

Davoren The Irish people are very fond of turning a
serious thing into a joke; that was a serious affair – for
poor Maguire.

Seumas (*defensively*) Why didn't he do what he arranged
to do? Did he think of me when he was goin' to
Knocksedan? How can he expect me to have any
sympathy with him now?

Davoren He can hardly expect that now that he's dead.

Seumas The Republicans 'll do a lot for him, now. How
am I goin' to get back the things he has belongin' to me,
either? There's some of them in that bag over there, but
that's not quarter of what he had; an' I don't know where
he was stoppin', for he left his old digs a week or so ago –
I suppose there's nothing to be said about my loss; I'm to
sing dumb.

Davoren I hope there's nothing else in the bag, besides
thread and hairpins.

Seumas What else ud be in it? . . . I can't sleep properly
ever since they put on this damned curfew. A minute ago I
thought I heard some of the oul' ones standin' at the door;
they won't be satisfied till they bring a raid on the house;

an' they never begin to stand at the door till after curfew
. . . Are you gone to bed, Donal?

Davoren No; I'm trying to finish this poem.

Seumas (*sitting up in bed*) If I was you I'd give that game
up; it doesn't pay a working-man to write poetry. I don't
profess to know much about poetry – I don't profess to
know much about poetry – about poetry – I don't know
much about the pearly glint of the morning dew, or the
damask sweetness of the rare wild rose, or the subtle
greenness of the serpent's eye – but I think a poet's claim to
greatness depends upon his power to put passion in the
common people.

Davoren Ay, passion to howl for his destruction. The
People! Damn the people! They live in the abyss, the poet
lives on the mountain-top; to the people there is no
mystery of colour: it is simply the scarlet coat of the
soldier; the purple vestments of a priest; the green banner
of a party; the brown or blue overalls of industry. To
them the might of design is a three-roomed house or a
capacious bed. To them beauty is for sale in a butcher's
shop. To the people the end of life is the life created for
them; to the poet the end of life is the life that he creates
for himself; life has a stifling grip upon the people's
throat – it is the poet's musician. The poet ever strives to
save the people; the people ever strive to destroy the poet.
The people view life through creeds, through customs,
and through necessities; the poet views creeds, customs,
and necessities through life. The people . . .

Seumas (*suddenly, and with a note of anxiety in his voice*)
Whisht! What's that? Is that the tappin' again?

Davoren Tappin'. What tappin'?

Seumas (*in an awed whisper*) This is the second night I
heard that tappin'! I believe it bodes no good to me. There,

do you hear it again – a quiet, steady, mysterious tappin' on the wall.

Davoren I hear no tappin'.

Seumas It ud be better for me if you did. It's a sure sign of death when nobody hears it but meself.

Davoren Death! What the devil are you talking about, man?

Seumas I don't like it at all; there's always something like that heard when one of our family dies.

Davoren I don't know about that; but I know there's a hell of a lot of things heard when one of your family lives.

Seumas God between us an' all harm! Thank God I'm where I ought to be – in bed . . . It's always best to be in your proper place when such things happen – Sacred Heart! There it is again; do you not hear it now?

Davoren Ah, for God's sake go asleep.

Seumas Do you believe in nothing?

Davoren I don't believe in tappin'.

Seumas Whisht, it's stopped again; I'll try to go asleep for fear it ud begin again.

Davoren Ay, do; and if it starts again I'll be sure to waken you up.

Pause.

Seumas It's very cold tonight. Do you feel cold?

Davoren I thought you were goin' asleep?

Seumas The bloody cold won't let me . . . You'd want a pair of pyjamas on you. (*Pause.*) Did you ever wear pyjamas, Donal?

36

Davoren No, no, no.

Seumas What kind of stuff is in them?

Davoren (*angrily*) Oh, it depends on the climate; in India, silk; in Italy, satin; and the Eskimo wears them made from the skin of the Polar bear.

Seumas (*emphatically*) If you take my advice you'll get into bed – that poem is beginnin' to get on your nerves.

Davoren (*extinguishing the candle with a vicious blow*) Right; I'm going to bed now, so you can shut up.

Visibility is still maintained from the light of the moon.

Seumas I was goin' to say something when you put out the light – what's this it was? – um, um, oh, ay: when I was comin' in this evenin' I saw Minnie Powell goin' out. If I was you I wouldn't have that one comin' in here.

Davoren She comes in; I don't bring her in, do I?

Seumas The oul' ones'll be talkin', an' once they start you don't know how it'll end. Surely a man that has read Shelley couldn't be interested in an ignorant little bitch that thinks of nothin' but jazz dances, fox-trots, picture theatres an' dress.

Davoren Right glad I am that she thinks of dress, for she thinks of it in the right way, and makes herself a pleasant picture to the eye. Education has been wasted on many persons, teaching them to talk only, but leaving them with all their primitive instincts. Had poor Minnie received an education she would have been an artist. She is certainly a pretty girl. I'm sure she is a good girl, and I believe she is a brave girl.

Seumas A Helen of Troy come to live in a tenement! You think a lot about her simply because she thinks a lot about you, an' she thinks a lot about you because she looks upon

you as a hero – a kind o' Paris . . . she'd give the world an'
all to be gaddin' about with a gunman. An' what ecstasy it
ud give her if after a bit you were shot or hanged; she'd be
able to go about then – like a good many more – singin', 'I
do not mourn me darlin' lost, for he fell in his Jacket
Green'. An' then, for a year an' a day, all round her hat
she'd wear the Tricoloured Ribbon O, till she'd pick up an'
marry someone else – possibly a British Tommy with a
Mons Star. An' as for bein' brave, it's easy to be that when
you've no cause for cowardice; I wouldn't care to have me
life dependin' on brave little Minnie Powell – she wouldn't
sacrifice a jazz dance to save it.

Davoren (*sitting on the bed and taking off his coat and
vest, preparatory to going to bed*) There; that's enough
about Minnie Powell. I'm afraid I'll soon have to be on the
run out of this house, too; it is becoming painfully obvious
that there is no peace to be found here.

Seumas Oh, this house is all right; barrin' the children, it
does be quiet enough. Wasn't there children in the last
place you were in too?

Davoren Ay, ten; (*viciously*) and they were all over forty.
(*A pause as Davoren is removing his collar and tie.*)

Seumas Everything is very quiet now; I wonder what time
is it?

Davoren The village cock hath thrice done salutation to
the morn.

Seumas Shakespeare, *Richard the III*, Act Five, Scene III.
It was Ratcliffe said that to Richard just before the battle
of Bosworth . . . How peaceful the heavens look now with
the moon in the middle; you'd never think there were men
prowlin' about tryin' to shoot each other. I don't know
how a man who has shot anyone can sleep in peace at
night.

Davoren There's plenty of men can't sleep in peace at night now unless they know that they have shot somebody.

Seumas I wish to God it was all over. The country is gone mad. Instead of counting their beads now they're countin' bullets; their Hail Marys and paternosters are burstin' bombs – burstin' bombs, an' the rattle of machine-guns; petrol is their holy water; their Mass is a burnin' buildin'; their De Profundis is 'The Soldiers' Song', an' their creed is, I believe in the gun almighty, maker of heaven an' earth – an' it's all for 'the glory o' God an' the honour o' Ireland'.

Davoren I remember the time when you yourself believed in nothing but the gun.

Seumas Ay, when there wasn't a gun in the country; I've a different opinion now when there's nothin' but guns in the country . . . An' you daren't open your mouth, for Kathleen ni Houlihan is very different now to the woman who used to play the harp an' sing 'Weep on, weep on, your hour is past', for she's a ragin' divil now, an' if you only look crooked at her you're sure of a punch in th' eye. But this is the way I look at it – I look at it this way: You're not goin' – you're not goin' to beat the British Empire – the British Empire, by shootin' an occasional Tommy at the corner of an occasional street. Besides, when the Tommies have the wind up – when the Tommies have the wind up they let bang at everything they see – they don't give a God's curse who they plug.

Davoren Maybe they ought to get down off the lorry and run to the Records Office to find out a man's pedigree before they plug him.

Seumas It's the civilians that suffer; when there's an

ambush they don't know where to run. Shot in the back to save the British Empire, an' shot in the breast to save the soul of Ireland. I'm a Nationalist meself, right enough – a Nationalist right enough, but all the same – I'm a Nationalist right enough; I believe in the freedom of Ireland, an' that England has no right to be here, but I draw the line when I hear the gunmen blowin' about dyin' for the people, when it's the people that are dyin' for the gunmen! With all due respect to the gunmen, I don't want them to die for me.

Davoren Not likely; you object to any one of them deliberately dying for you for fear that one of these days you might accidentally die for one of them.

Seumas You're one of the brave fellows that doesn't fear death.

Davoren Why should I be afraid of it? It's all the same to me how it comes, where it comes, or when it comes. I leave fear of death to the people that are always praying for eternal life; 'Death is here and death is there, death is busy everywhere'.

Seumas Ay, in Ireland. Thanks be to God I'm a daily communicant. There's a great comfort in religion; it makes a man strong in time of trouble an' brave in time of danger. No man need be afraid with a crowd of angels round him; thanks to God for His Holy religion!

Davoren You're welcome to your angels; philosophy is mine; philosophy that makes the coward brave; the sufferer defiant; the weak strong; the . . .

A volley of shots is heard in a lane that runs parallel with the wall of the back-yard. Religion and philosophy are forgotten in the violent fear of a nervous equality.

Seumas Jesus, Mary, an' Joseph, what's that?

Davoren My God, that's very close.

Seumas Is there no Christianity at all left in the country?

Davoren Are we ever again going to know what peace and security are?

Seumas If this continues much longer I'll be nothing but a galvanic battery o' shocks.

Davoren It's dangerous to be in and it's equally dangerous to be out.

Seumas This is a dangerous spot to be in with them windows; you couldn't tell the minute a bullet ud come in through one of them – through one of them, an' hit the – hit the – an' hit the . . .

Davoren (*irritably*) Hit the what, man?

Seumas The wall.

Davoren Couldn't you say that at first without making a song about it?

Seumas (*suddenly*) I don't believe there's horses in the stable at all.

Davoren Stable! What stable are you talking about?

Seumas There's a stable at the back of the house with an entrance from the yard; it's used as a carpenter's shop. Didn't you often hear the peculiar noises at night? They give out that it's the horses shakin' their chains.

Davoren And what is it?

Seumas Oh, there I'll leave you!

Davoren Surely you don't mean . . .

Seumas But I do mean it.

Davoren You do mean what?

Seumas I wouldn't – I wouldn't be surprised – wouldn't be surprised – surprised . . .

Davoren Yes, yes, surprised – go on.

Seumas I wouldn't be surprised if they were manufacturin' bombs there.

Davoren My God, that's a pleasant contemplation! The sooner I'm on the run out of this house the better. How is it you never said anything about this before?

Seumas Well – well, I didn't want – I didn't want to – to . . .

Davoren You didn't want to what?

Seumas I didn't want to frighten you.

Davoren (*sarcastically*) You're bloody kind!

A knock at the door; the voice of Mrs Grigson heard.

Mrs Grigson Are you asleep, Mr Shields?

Seumas What the devil can she want at this hour of the night? (*To Mrs Grigson*) No, Mrs Grigson, what is it?

Mrs Grigson opens the door and stands at the threshold. She is a woman about forty, but looks much older. She is one of the cave-dwellers of Dublin, living as she does in a tenement kitchen, to which only an occasional sickly beam of sunlight filters through a grating in the yard; the consequent general dimness of her abode has given her a habit of peering through half-closed eyes. She is slovenly dressed in an old skirt and bodice; her face is grimy, not because her habits are dirty – for, although she is untidy, she is a clean woman – but because of the smoky atmosphere of her room. Her hair is constantly falling over her face, which she is as frequently removing by rapid movements of her right hand.

Mrs Grigson He hasn't turned up yet, an' I'm stiff with the cold waitin' for him.

Seumas Mr Grigson, is it?

Mrs Grigson Adolphus, Mr Shields, after takin' his tea at six o'clock – no, I'm tellin' a lie – it was before six, for I remember the Angelus was ringin' out an' we sittin' at the table – after takin' his tea he went out for a breath o' fresh air, an' I haven't seen sign or light of him since. 'Clare to God me heart is up in me mouth, thinkin' he might be shot be the Black an' Tans.

Seumas Aw, he'll be all right, Mrs Grigson. You ought to go to bed an' rest yourself; it's always the worst that comes into a body's mind; go to bed, Mrs Grigson, or you'll catch your death of cold.

Mrs Grigson I'm afraid to go to bed, Mr Shields, for I'm always in dread that some night or another, when he has a sup taken, he'll fall down the kitchen stairs an' break his neck. Not that I'd be any the worse if anything did happen to him, for you know the sort he is, Mr Shields; sure he has me heart broke.

Seumas Don't be downhearted, Mrs Grigson; he may take a thought one of these days an' turn over a new leaf.

Mrs Grigson Sorra leaf Adolphus 'll ever turn over, he's too far gone in the horns for that now. Sure no one ud mind him takin' a pint or two, if he'd stop at that, but he won't; nothin' could fill him with beer, an' no matter how much he may have taken, when he's taken more he'll always say, 'Here's the first today'.

Davoren (*to Seumas*) Christ! Is she going to stop talking there all the night?

Seumas 'Sh, she'll hear you; right enough, the man has the poor woman's heart broke.

Davoren And because he has her heart broken, she's to have the privilege of breaking everybody else's.

Mrs Grigson Mr Shields.

Seumas Yes?

Mrs Grigson Do the insurance companies pay if a man is shot after curfew?

Seumas Well, now, that's a thing I couldn't say, Mrs Grigson.

Mrs Grigson (*plaintively*) Isn't he a terrible man to be takin' such risks, an' not knowin' what'll happen to him. He knows them Societies only want an excuse to do people out of their money – is it after one, now, Mr Shields?

Seumas Aw, it must be after one, Mrs Grigson.

Mrs Grigson (*emphatically*) Ah, then, if I was a young girl again I'd think twice before gettin' married. Whisht! There's somebody now – it's him, I know be the way he's fumblin'.

She goes out a little way. Stumbling steps are heard in the hall.

(*Outside*) Is that you, Dolphie, dear?

After a few moments Adolphus, with Mrs Grigson holding his arm, stumbles into the room. He is a man of forty-five, but looks, relatively, much younger than Mrs Grigson. His occupation is that of a solicitor's clerk. He has all the appearance of being well fed; and, in fact, he gets most of the nourishment, Mrs Grigson getting just enough to give her strength to do the necessary work of the household. On account of living most of his life out of the kitchen, his complexion is fresh, and his movements, even when sober, are livelier than those of his wife. He is comfortably dressed; heavy top-coat, soft trilby hat, a fancy coloured scarf about his neck, and he carries an umbrella.

Mrs Grigson Dolphie, dear, mind yourself.

Adolphus Grigson I'm all right; do you see anything wrong with me?

Mrs Grigson Of course you're all right, dear; there's no one mindin' you.

Adolphus Grigson Mindin' me, is it, mindin' me? He'd want to be a good thing that ud mind me. There's a man here – a man, mind you, afraid av nothin' – not in this bloody house anyway.

Mrs Grigson (*imploringly*) Come on downstairs, Dolphie, dear; sure there's not one in the house ud say a word to you.

Adolphus Grigson Say a word to me, is it? He'd want to be a good thing that ud say anything to Dolphus Grigson. (*Loudly*) Is there anyone wants to say anything to Dolphus Grigson? If there is, he's here – a man, too – there's no blottin' it out – a man.

Mrs Grigson You'll wake everybody in the house; can't you speak quiet.

Adolphus Grigson (*more loudly still*) What do I care for anybody in the house? Are they keepin' me; are they givin' me anything? When they're keepin' Grigson it'll be time enough for them to talk. (*With a shout*) I can tell them Adolphus Grigson wasn't born in a bottle!

Mrs Grigson (*tearfully*) Why do you talk like that, dear? We all know you weren't born in a bottle.

Adolphus Grigson There's some of them in this house think that Grigson was born in a bottle.

Davoren (*to Seumas*) A most appropriate place for him to be born in.

Mrs Grigson Come on down to bed, now, an' you can talk about them in the mornin'.

Adolphus Grigson I'll talk about them, now; do you think I'm afraid of them? Dolphus Grigson's afraid av nothin', creepin' or walkin', – if there's anyone in the house thinks he's fit to take a fall out av Adolphus Grigson, he's here – a man; they'll find that Grigson's no soft thing.

Davoren Ah me, alas! Pain, pain ever, for ever.

Mrs Grigson Dolphie, dear, poor Mr Davoren wants to go to bed.

Davoren Oh, she's terribly anxious about poor Mr Davoren, all of a sudden.

Adolphus Grigson (*stumbling towards Davoren, and holding out his hand*) Davoren! He's a man. Leave it there, mate. You needn't be afraid av Dolphus Grigson; there never was a drop av informer's blood in the whole family av Grigson. I don't know what you are or what you think, but you're a man, an' not like some of the goughers in this house, that ud hang you. Not referrin' to you, Mr Shields.

Mrs Grigson Oh, you're not deluding to Mr Shields.

Seumas I know that, Mr Grigson; go on down, now, with Mrs Grigson, an' have a sleep.

Adolphus Grigson I tie meself to no woman's apron strings, Mr Shields; I know how to keep Mrs Grigson in her place; I have the authority of the Bible for that. I know the Bible from cover to cover, Mr Davoren, an' that's more than some in this house could say. And what does the Holy Scripture say about woman? It says, 'The woman shall be subject to her husband', an' I'll see that Mrs

Grigson keeps the teachin' av the Holy Book in the letter an' in the spirit. If you're ever in trouble, Mr Davoren, an' Grigson can help – I'm your man – have you me?

Davoren I have you, Mr Grigson, I have you.

Adolphus Grigson Right; I'm an Orangeman, an' I'm not ashamed av it, an' I'm not afraid av it, but I can feel for a true man, all the same – have *you* got me, Mr Shields?

Seumas Oh, we know you well, Mr Grigson; many a true Irishman was a Protestant – Tone, Emmet an' Parnell.

Adolphus Grigson Mind you, I'm not sayin' as I agree with them you've mentioned, Mr Shields, for the Bible forbids it, an' Adolphus Grigson 'll always abide be the Bible. Fear God an' honour the King – that's written in Holy Scripture, an' there's no blottin' it out. (*Pulling a bottle out of his pocket*) But here, Mr Davoren, have a drink, just to show there's no coolness.

Davoren No, no, Mr Grigson, it's too late now to take anything. Go on down with Mrs Grigson, and we can have a chat in the morning.

Adolphus Grigson Sure you won't have a drink?

Davoren Quite sure – thanks all the same.

Adolphus Grigson (*drinking*) Here's the first today! To all true men, even if they were born in a bottle. Here's to King William, to the battle av the Boyne; to the Hobah Black Chapter – that's my Lodge, Mr Davoren; an' to The Orange Lily O. (*Singing in a loud shout*)

An' dud ya go to see the show, each rose an' pinkadilly O,
To feast your eyes an' view the prize won be the Orange Lily O.

The Vic'roy there, so debonair, just like a daffadilly O,
With Lady Clarke, blithe as a lark, approached the
    Orange Lily O.
      Heigh Ho the Lily O,
      The Royal, Loyal Lily O,
Beneath the sky what flower can vie with Erin's Orange
    Lily O!

Davoren Holy God, isn't this terrible!

Adolphus Grigson (*singing*)
The elated Muse, to hear the news, jumped like a
    Connaught filly O,
As gossip Fame did loud proclaim the triumph av the
    Lily O.
The Lowland field may roses yield, gay heaths the
    Highlands hilly O;
But high or low no flower can show like Erin's Orange
    Lily O.
      Heigh Ho the Lily O,
      The Royal, Loyal Lily O,
Beneath the sky what flower can vie with Erin's Or . . .

*While Adolphus Grigson has been singing, the sound of
a rapidly moving motor is heard, faintly at first, but
growing rapidly louder, till it apparently stops suddenly
somewhere very near the house, bringing Grigson's song
to an abrupt conclusion. They are all startled, and listen
attentively to the throbbing of the engines, which can be
plainly heard. Grigson is considerably sobered, and
anxiously keeps his eyes on the door. Seumas sits up in
bed and listens anxiously. Davoren, with a shaking
hand, lights the candle, and begins to search hurriedly
among the books and papers on the table.*

(*With a tremor in his voice*) There's no need to be afraid,
they couldn't be comin' here.

48

Mrs Grigson God forbid! It ud be terrible if they came at this hour ov the night.

Seumas You never know now, Mrs Grigson; they'd rush in on you when you'd be least expectin' them. What, in the name o' God, is goin' to come out of it all? Nobody now cares a traneen about the orders of the Ten Commandments; the only order that anybody minds now is, 'Put your hands up'. Oh, it's a hopeless country.

Adolphus Grigson Whisht; do you hear them talking outside at the door? You're sure of your life nowhere now; it's just as safe to go everywhere as it is to anywhere. An' they don't give a damn whether you're a loyal man or not. If you're a Republican they make you sing 'God save the King', an' if you're loyal they'll make you sing the 'Soldiers' Song'. The singin' ud be all right if they didn't make you dance afterwards.

Mrs Grigson They'd hardly come here unless they heard something about Mr Davoren.

Davoren About me! What could they hear about me?

Adolphus Grigson You'll never get some people to keep their mouths shut. I was in the Blue Lion this evening, an' who do you think was there, blowin' out av him, but that little blower, Tommy Owens; there he was tellin' everybody that *he* knew where there was bombs; that *he* had a friend that was a General in the IRA; that *he* could tell them what the Staff was thinkin' av doin'; that *he* could lay his hand on tons av revolvers; that they wasn't a mile from where he was livin', but that *he* knew his own know, an' would keep it to himself.

Seumas Well, God blast the little blower, anyway; it's the like ov him that deserves to be plugged! (*To Davoren*) What are you lookin' for among the books, Donal?

Davoren A letter that I got today from Mr Gallogher and Mrs Henderson; I'm blessed if I know where I put it.

Seumas (*peevishly*) Can't you look for it in the mornin'?

Davoren It's addressed to the Irish Republican Army, and, considering the possibility of a raid, it would be safer to get rid of it.

> *Shots again heard out in the lane, followed by loud shouts of 'Halt, halt, halt!'*

Adolphus Grigson I think we had better be gettin' to bed, Debby; it's not right to be keepin' Mr Davoren an' Mr Shields awake.

Seumas An' what made them give you such a letter as that; don't they know the state the country is in? An' you were worse to take it. Have you got it?

Davoren I can't find it anywhere; isn't this terrible!

Adolphus Grigson Goodnight, Mr Davoren; goodnight, Mr Shields.

Mrs Grigson Goodnight, Mr Shields; goodnight, Mr Davoren.

> *They go out. Seumas and Davoren are too much concerned about the letter to respond to their goodnights.*

Seumas What were you thinkin' of when you took such a letter as that? Ye gods, has nobody any brains at all, at all? Oh, this is a hopeless country. Did you try in your pockets?

Davoren (*searching in his pockets*) Oh, thanks be to God, here it is.

Seumas Burn it now, an', for God's sake, don't take any letters like that again . . . There's the motor goin' away;

we can sleep in peace now for the rest of the night. Just to make sure of everything now, have a look in that bag o' Maguire's: not that there can be anything in it.

Davoren If there's nothing in it, what's the good of looking?

Seumas It won't kill you to look, will it?

Davoren goes over to the bag, puts it on the table, opens it, and jumps back, his face pale and his limbs trembling.

Davoren My God, it's full of bombs, Mills bombs!

Seumas Holy Mother of God, you're jokin'!

Davoren If the Tans come you'll find whether I'm jokin' or no.

Seumas Isn't this a nice pickle to be in? St Anthony, look down on us!

Davoren There's no use of blaming St Anthony; why did you let Maguire leave the bag here?

Seumas Why did I let him leave the bag here; why did I let him leave the bag here! How did I know what was in it? Didn't I think there was nothin' in it but spoons an' hairpins? What'll we do now; what'll we do now? Mother o' God, grant there'll be no raid tonight. I knew things ud go wrong when I missed Mass this mornin'.

Davoren Give over your praying and let us try to think of what is best to be done. There's one thing certain: as soon as morning comes I'm on the run out of this house.

Seumas Thinkin' of yourself, like the rest of them. Leavin' me to bear the brunt of it.

Davoren And why shouldn't you bear the brunt of it? Maguire was no friend of mine; besides, it's your fault; you knew the sort of a man he was, and you should have been on your guard.

Seumas Did I know he was a gunman; did I know he was a gunman; did I know he was a gunman? Did . . .

Davoren Do you mean to tell me that . . .

Seumas Just a moment . . .

Davoren You didn't know . . .

Seumas Just a moment . . .

Davoren That Maguire was connected with . . .

Seumas (*loudly*) Just a moment; can't . . .

Davoren The Republican Movement? What's the use of trying to tell damn lies!

Minnie Powell rushes into the room. She is only partly dressed, and has thrown a shawl over her shoulders. She is in a state of intense excitement.

Minnie Mr Davoren, Donal, they're all round the house; they must be goin' to raid the place; I was lookin' out of the window an' I seen them; I do be on the watch every night; have you anything? If you have . . .

There is heard at the street door a violent and continuous knocking, followed by the crash of glass and the beating of the door with rifle butts.

There they are, there they are, there they are!

Davoren reclines almost fainting on the bed; Seumas sits up in an attitude of agonized prayerfulness; Minnie alone retains her presence of mind. When she sees their panic she becomes calm, though her words are rapidly spoken, and her actions are performed with decisive celerity.

What is it; what have you got; where are they?

Davoren Bombs, bombs, bombs; my God! in the bag on the table there; we're done, we're done!

Seumas Hail, Mary, full of grace – pray for us miserable sinners – Holy St Anthony, do you hear them batterin' at the door – now an' at the hour of our death – say an act of contrition, Donal – there's the glass gone!

Minnie I'll take them to my room; maybe they won't search it; if they do aself, they won't harm a girl. Goodbye . . . Donal. (*She glances lovingly at Donal – who is only semi-conscious – as she rushes out with the bag.*)

Seumas If we come through this I'll never miss a Mass again! If it's the Tommies it won't be so bad, but if it's the Tans, we're goin' to have a terrible time.

The street door is broken open and heavy steps are heard in the hall, punctuated with shouts of ' 'Old the light 'ere', 'Put 'em up', etc. An Auxiliary opens the door of the room and enters, revolver in one hand and electric torch in the other. His uniform is black, and he wears a black beret.

The Auxiliary 'Oo's 'ere?

Seumas (*as if he didn't know*) Who – who's that?

The Auxiliary (*peremptorily*) 'Oo's 'ere?

Seumas Only two men, mister; me an' me mate in t'other bed.

The Auxiliary Why didn't you open the door?

Seumas We didn't hear you knockin', sir.

The Auxiliary You must be a little awd of 'earing, ay?

Seumas I had rheumatic fever a few years ago, an' ever since I do be a – I do be a little deaf sometimes.

The Auxiliary (*to Davoren*) 'Ow is it you're not in bed?

Davoren I was in bed; when I heard the knockin' I got up to open the door.

The Auxiliary *You're* a koind blowke, you are. Deloighted, like, to have a visit from us, ay? Ay? (*threatening to strike him*) Why down't you answer?

Davoren Yes, sir.

The Auxiliary What's your name?

Davoren Davoren, Dan Davoren, sir.

The Auxiliary You're not an Irishman, are you?

Davoren I-I-I was born in Ireland.

The Auxiliary Ow, you were, were you; Irish han' proud of it, ay? (*To Seumas*) What's *your* name?

Seumas Seuma . . . Oh no; Jimmie Shields, sir.

The Auxiliary Ow, you're a selt (*he means a Celt*), one of the seltic race that speaks a lingo of its ahn, and that's going to overthrow the British Empire – I don't think! 'Ere, where's your gun?

Seumas I never had a gun in me hand in me life.

The Auxiliary Now; you wouldn't know what a gun is if you sawr one, I suppowse. (*Displaying his revolver in a careless way*) 'Ere, what's that?

Seumas Oh, be careful, please, be careful.

The Auxiliary Why, what 'ave I got to be careful abaht?

Seumas The gun; it-it-it might go off.

The Auxiliary An' what prawse if it did; it can easily be relowded. Any ammunition 'ere? What's in that press? (*He searches and scatters contents of press.*)

Seumas Only a little bit o' grub; you'll get nothin' here, sir; no one in the house has any connection with politics.

The Auxiliary Now? I've never met a man yet that didn't say that, but we're a little bit too ikey now to be kidded with that sort of talk.

Seumas May I go an' get a drink o' water?

The Auxiliary You'll want a barrel of watah before you're done with us. (*The Auxiliary goes about the room examining places.*) 'Ello, what's 'ere? A statue o' Christ! An' a Crucifix! You'd think you was in a bloomin' monastery.

Mrs Grigson enters, dressed disorderly and her hair awry.

Mrs Grigson They're turning the place upside-down. Upstairs an' downstairs they're makin' a litter of everything! I declare to God, it's awful what law-abidin' people have to put up with. An' they found a pint bottle of whiskey under Dolphie's pillow, an' they're drinkin' every drop of it – an' Dolphie 'll be like a devil in the mornin' when he finds he has no curer.

The Auxiliary (*all attention when he hears the word whiskey*) A bottle of whiskey, ay? 'Ere, where do you live – quick, where do you live?

Mrs Grigson Down in the kitchen – an' when you go down will you ask them not to drink – oh, he's gone without listenin' to me.

While Mrs Grigson is speaking the Auxiliary rushes out.

Seumas (*anxiously to Mrs Grigson*) Are they searchin' the whole house, Mrs Grigson?

Mrs Grigson They didn't leave a thing in the kitchen that they didn't flitter about the floor; the things in the cupboard, all the little odds an' ends that I keep in the big box, an . . .

Seumas Oh, they're a terrible gang of blaguards – did they go upstairs? – they'd hardly search Minnie Powell's room – do you think would they, Mrs Grigson?

Mrs Grigson Just to show them the sort of a man he was, before they come in, Dolphie put the big Bible on the table, open at the First Gospel of St Peter, second chapter, an' marked the thirteenth to the seventeenth verse in red ink – you know the passages, Mr Shields – (*quoting*): 'Submit yourselves to every ordinance of man for the Lord's sake; whether it be to the king, as supreme; or unto governors, as unto them that are sent by him for the punishment of evildoers, an' for the praise of them that do well . . . Love the brotherhood. Fear God. Honour the King.'

An' what do you think they did, Mr Shields? They caught a hold of the Bible an' flung it on the floor – imagine that, Mr Shields – flingin' the Bible on the floor! Then one of them says to another – 'Jack,' says he, 'have you seen the light; is your soul saved?' An' then they grabbed hold of poor Dolphie, callin' him Mr Moody an' Mr Sankey, an' wanted him to offer up a prayer for the Irish Republic! An' when they were puttin' me out, there they had the poor man sittin' up in bed, his hands crossed on his breast, his eyes lookin' up at the ceilin', an' he singin' a hymn – 'We shall meet in the Sweet Bye an' Bye' – an' all the time, Mr Shields, there they were drinkin' his whiskey; there's torture for you, an' they all laughin' at poor Dolphie's terrible sufferins.

Davoren In the name of all that's sensible, what did he want to bring whiskey home with him for? They're bad enough sober, what'll they be like when they're drunk?

Mrs Grigson (*plaintively*) He always brings a drop home with him – he calls it his medicine.

Seumas (*still anxious*) They'll hardly search all the house; do you think they will, Mrs Grigson?

Mrs Grigson An' we have a picture over the mantelpiece of King William crossing the Boyne, an' do you know what they wanted to make out, Mr Shields, that it was Robert Emmet, an' the picture of a sacret society!

Seumas She's not listenin' to a word I'm sayin'! Oh, the country is hopeless an' the people is hopeless.

Davoren For God's sake tell her to go to hell out of this – she's worse than the Auxsie.

Seumas (*thoughtfully*) Let her stay where she is; it's safer to have a woman in the room. If they come across the bombs I hope to God Minnie 'll say nothin'.

Davoren We're a pair of pitiable cowards to let poor Minnie suffer when we know that we and not she are to blame.

Seumas What else can we do, man? Do you want us to be done in? If you're anxious to be riddled, I'm not. Besides, they won't harm her, she's only a girl, an' so long as she keeps her mouth shut it'll be all right.

Davoren I wish I could be sure of that.

Seumas D'ye think are they goin', Mrs Grigson? What are they doin' now?

Mrs Grigson (*who is standing at the door, looking out into the hall*) There's not a bit of me that's not shakin' like a jelly!

Seumas Are they gone upstairs, Mrs Grigson? Do you think, Mrs Grigson, will they soon be goin'?

Mrs Grigson When they were makin' poor Dolphie sit up in the bed, I 'clare to God I thought every minute I'd hear their guns goin' off, an' see poor Dolphie stretched out dead in the bed – whisht, God bless us, I think I hear him moanin'!

Seumas You might as well be talking to a stone! They're all hopeless, hopeless, hopeless! She thinks she hears him moanin'! It's bloody near time somebody made him moan!

Davoren (*with a sickly attempt at humour*) He's moaning for the loss of his whiskey.

> *During the foregoing dialogue the various sounds of a raid – orders, the tramping of heavy feet, the pulling about of furniture, etc., are heard. Now a more definite and sustained commotion is apparent. Loud and angry commands of 'Go on', 'Get out and get into the lorry', are heard, mingled with a girl's voice – it is Minnie's – shouting bravely, but a little hysterically, 'Up the Republic'.*

Mrs Grigson (*from the door*) God save us, they're takin' Minnie, they're takin' Minnie Powell! (*Running out*) What in the name of God can have happened?

Seumas Holy Saint Anthony grant that she'll keep her mouth shut.

Davoren (*sitting down on the bed and covering his face with his hands*) We'll never again be able to lift up our heads if anything happens to Minnie.

Seumas For God's sake keep quiet or somebody'll hear you; nothin'll happen to her, nothin' at all – it'll be all right if she only keeps her mouth shut.

Mrs Grigson (*running in*) They're after gettin' a whole lot of stuff in Minnie's room! Enough to blow up the whole street, a Tan says! God tonight, who'd have ever thought that of Minnie Powell!

Seumas Did she say anything, is she sayin' anything, what's she sayin', Mrs Grigson?

Mrs Grigson She's shoutin' 'Up the Republic' at the top of her voice. An' big Mrs Henderson is fightin' with the soldiers – she's after nearly knockin' one of them down, an' they're puttin' her into the lorry too.

Seumas God blast her! Can she not mind her own business? What does she want here – didn't she know there was a raid on? Is the whole damn country goin' mad? They'll open fire in a minute an' innocent people'll be shot!

Davoren What way are they using Minnie, Mrs Grigson; are they rough with her?

Mrs Grigson They couldn't be half rough enough; the little hussy, to be so deceitful; she might as well have had the house blew up! God tonight, who'd think it was in Minnie Powell!

Seumas Oh, grant she won't say anything!

Mrs Grigson There they're goin' away now; ah, then I hope they'll give that Minnie Powell a coolin'.

Seumas God grant she won't say anything! Are they gone, Mrs Grigson?

Mrs Grigson With her fancy stockins, an' her pom-poms, an' her crêpe de chine blouses! I knew she'd come to no good!

Seumas God grant she'll keep her mouth shut! Are they gone, Mrs Grigson?

Mrs Grigson They're gone, Mr Shields, an' here's poor Dolphie an' not a feather astray on him. Oh, Dolphie, dear, you're all right, thanks to God; I thought you'd never see the mornin'.

Adolphus Grigson (*entering without coat or vest*) Of course I'm all right; what ud put a bother on Dolphie Grigson? – not the Tans anyway!

Mrs Grigson When I seen you stretched out on the bed, an' you . . . singin' a hymn . . .

Adolphus Grigson (*fearful of possible humiliation*) Who was singin' a hymn? D'ye hear me talkin' to you – where did you hear me singin' a hymn?

Mrs Grigson I was only jokin', Dolphie, dear; I . . .

Adolphus Grigson Your place is below, an' not gosterin' here to men; down with you quick!

Mrs Grigson hurriedly leaves the room.

(*Nonchalantly taking out his pipe, filling it, lighting it, and beginning to smoke*) Excitin' few moments, Mr Davoren; Mrs G. lost her head completely – panic-stricken. But that's only natural, all women is very nervous. The only thing to do is to show them that they can't put the wind up you; show the least sign of fright an' they'd walk on you, simply walk on you. Two of them come down – 'Put them up', revolvers under your nose – you know, the usual way. 'What's all the bother about?' says I, quite calm. 'No bother at all,' says one of them, 'only this gun might go off an' hit somebody – have you me?' says he. 'What if it does,' says I, 'a man can only die once, an' you'll find Grigson won't squeal.' 'God, you're a cool one,' says the other, 'there's no blottin' it out.'

Seumas That's the best way to take them; it only makes things worse to show that you've got the wind up. 'Any ammunition here?' says the fellow that come in here. 'I don't think so,' says I, 'but you better have a look.' 'No back talk,' says he, 'or you might get plugged.' 'I don't know of any clause,' says I, 'in the British Constitution

that makes it a crime for a man to speak in his own room,'
– with that, he just had a look round, an' off he went.

Adolphus Grigson If a man keeps a stiff upper front –
Merciful God, there's an ambush!

*Explosions of two bursting bombs are heard on the
street outside the house, followed by fierce and rapid
revolver- and rifle-fire. People are heard rushing into the
hall, and there is general clamour and confusion.
Seumas and Davoren cower down in the room;
Grigson, after a few moments' hesitation, frankly rushes
out of the room to what he conceives to be the safer
asylum of the kitchen. A lull follows, punctuated by an
odd rifle-shot; then comes a peculiar and ominous
stillness, broken in a few moments by the sounds of
voices and movement. Questions are heard being asked:
'Who was it was killed?' 'Where was she shot?' which
are answered by: 'Minnie Powell'; 'She went to jump off
the lorry an' she was shot'; 'She's not dead, is she?';
'They say she's dead – shot through the buzzom!'*

Davoren (*in a tone of horror-stricken doubt*) D'ye hear
what they're sayin', Shields, d'ye hear what they're sayin'?
– Minnie Powell is shot.

Seumas For God's sake speak easy, an' don't bring them in
here on top of us again.

Davoren Is that all you're thinking of? Do you realize that
she has been shot to save us?

Seumas Is it my fault; am I to blame?

Davoren It is your fault and mine, both; oh, we're a pair
of dastardly cowards to have let her do what she did.

Seumas She did it off her own bat – we didn't ask her to
do it.

Mrs Grigson enters. She is excited and semi-hysterical, and sincerely affected by the tragic occurrence.

Mrs Grigson (*falling down in a sitting posture on one of the beds*) What's goin' to happen next! Oh, Mr Davoren, isn't it terrible, isn't it terrible! Minnie Powell, poor little Minnie Powell's been shot dead! They were raidin' a house a few doors down, an' had just got up in their lorries to go away, when they was ambushed. You never heard such shootin'! An' in the thick of it, poor Minnie went to jump off the lorry she was on, an' she was shot through the buzzom. Oh, it was horrible to see the blood pourin' out, an' Minnie moanin'. They found some paper in her breast, with 'Minnie' written on it, an' some other name they couldn't make out with the blood; the officer kep' it. The ambulance is bringin' her to the hospital, but what good's that when she's dead! Poor little Minnie, poor little Minnie Powell, to think of you full of life a few minutes ago, an' now she's dead!

Davoren Ah me, alas! Pain, pain, pain ever, for ever! It's terrible to think that little Minnie is dead, but it's still more terrible to think that Davoren and Shields are alive! Oh, Donal Davoren, shame is your portion now till the silver cord is loosened and the golden bowl be broken. Oh, Davoren, Donal Davoren, poet and poltroon, poltroon and poet!

Seumas (*solemnly*) I knew something ud come of the tappin' on the wall!

Curtain.

THE PLOUGH AND THE STARS

A TRAGEDY IN FOUR ACTS

To the gay laugh of my mother
at the gate of the grave

Characters

Jack Clitheroe (a bricklayer), Commandant in the Irish Citizen Army
Nora Clitheroe, his wife
Peter Flynn (a labourer), Nora's uncle
The Young Covey (a fitter), Clitheroe's cousin
Bessie Burgess (a street fruit-vendor)
Mrs Gogan (a charwoman)
Mollser, her consumptive child

Residents in the Tenement

Fluther Good (a carpenter)
Lieut. Langon (a Civil Servant), of the Irish Volunteers
Capt. Brennan (a chicken butcher), of the Irish Citizen Army
Corporal Stoddart, of the Wiltshires
Sergeant Tinley, of the Wiltshires
Rosie Redmond, a daughter of 'the Digs'
A Bartender
A Woman
The Figure in the Window

Act One – The living-room of the Clitheroe flat in a Dublin tenement.
Act Two – A public-house, outside of which a meeting is being held.
Act Three – The street outside the Clitheroe tenement.
Act Four – The room of Bessie Burgess.

Time – Acts One and Two, November 1915; Acts Three and Four, Easter Week, 1916. A few days elapse between Acts Three and Four.

Act One

The home of the Clitheroes. It consists of the front and back drawing-rooms in a fine old Georgian house, struggling for its life against the assaults of time, and the more savage assaults of the tenants. The room shown is the back drawing-room, wide, spacious, and lofty. At back is the entrance to the front drawing-room. The space, originally occupied by folding doors, is now draped with casement cloth of a dark purple, decorated with a design in reddish-purple and cream. One of the curtains is pulled aside, giving a glimpse of front drawing-room, at the end of which can be seen the wide, lofty windows looking out into the street. The room directly in front of the audience is furnished in a way that suggests an attempt towards a finer expression of domestic life. The large fireplace on right is of wood, painted to look like marble (the original has been taken away by the landlord). On the mantelshelf are two candlesticks of dark carved wood. Between them is a small clock. Over the clock is hanging a calendar which displays a picture of The Sleeping Venus. *In the centre of the breast of the chimney hangs a picture of Robert Emmet. On the right of the entrance to the front drawing-room is a copy of* The Gleaners, *on the opposite side a copy of* The Angelus. *Underneath* The Gleaners *is a chest of drawers on which stands a green bowl filled with scarlet dahlias and white chrysanthemums. Near to the fireplace is a settee which at night forms a double bed for Clitheroe and Nora. Underneath* The Angelus *are a number of shelves containing saucepans and a frying-pan. Under these is a table on which are various articles of delftware. Near the end of the room, opposite to the fireplace, is a gate-legged table, covered with a cloth. On top of the table a huge cavalry sword is lying. To the right is a door which leads to a lobby from which the staircase leads to the hall. The floor is covered with a dark green linoleum. The room is dim except where it is illuminated from the glow of the fire. Through the window of the room at back can be seen the flaring of the flame of a gasolene lamp giving light to workmen repairing the street. Occasionally can be heard the clang of crowbars striking the setts. Fluther Good is repairing the lock of door, right. A claw-hammer is on a chair beside him, and he has a screwdriver in his hand. He is a man of forty years of age, rarely surrendering to thoughts of anxiety, fond of his 'oil' but determined to conquer the habit before he dies. He is square-jawed and harshly featured; under the left eye is a scar, and his nose is bent from a smashing blow received in a fistic battle long ago. He is bald, save for a few peeping tufts of reddish hair around his ears; and his upper lip is hidden by a scrubby red moustache, embroidered here and there with a grey hair. He is dressed in a seedy black suit, cotton shirt with a soft collar, and wears a very respectable little black bow. On his head is a faded jerry hat, which, when he is excited, he has a habit of knocking farther back on his head, in a series of taps. In an argument he usually fills with sound and fury generally signifying a row. He is in his shirt-sleeves at present, and wears a soiled white apron, from a pocket in which sticks a carpenter's two-foot rule. He has just finished the job of putting on a new lock, and, filled with satisfaction, he is opening and shutting the door, enjoying the completion of a work well done. Sitting at the fire, airing a white shirt, is Peter Flynn. He is a little, thin bit of a man, with a face shaped like a lozenge; on his cheeks and under his chin is a straggling wiry beard of a dirty-white and lemon hue. His face invariably wears a look of animated anguish, mixed with irritated defiance, as if everybody was at war with*

*him, and he at war with everybody. He is cocking his head
in a way that suggests resentment at the presence of
Fluther, who pays no attention to him, apparently, but is
really furtively watching him. Peter is clad in a singlet,
white whipcord knee-breeches, and is in his stocking-feet.*

*A voice is heard speaking outside of door, left (it is that
of Mrs Gogan).*

Mrs Gogan (*outside*) Who are you lookin' for, sir? Who?
Mrs Clitheroe? . . . Oh, excuse me. Oh ay, up this way.
She's out, I think: I seen her goin'. Oh, you've somethin'
for her; oh, excuse me. You're from Arnott's . . . . I see
. . . . You've a parcel for her. . . . Righto . . . . I'll take it
. . . . I'll give it to her the minute she comes in . . . . It'll be
quite safe . . . . Oh, sign that . . . . Excuse me . . . .
Where? . . . Here? . . . No, there; righto. Am I to put
Maggie or Mrs? What is it? You dunno? Oh, excuse me.

*Mrs Gogan opens the door and comes in. She is a
doleful-looking little woman of forty, insinuating
manner and sallow complexion. She is fidgety and
nervous, terribly talkative, has a habit of taking up
things that may be near her and fiddling with them
while she is speaking. Her heart is aflame with curiosity,
and a fly could not come into nor go out of the house
without her knowing. She has a draper's parcel in her
hand, the knot of the twine tying it is untied. Peter,
more resentful of this intrusion than of Fluther's
presence, gets up from the chair, and without looking
around, his head carried at an angry cock, marches into
the room at back.*

(*Removing the paper and opening the cardboard box it
contains*) I wondher what's that now? A hat! (*She takes
out a hat, black, with decorations in red and gold.*) God,
she's goin' to th' divil lately for style! That hat, now, cost
more than a penny. Such notions of upperosity she's

gettin'. (*Putting the hat on her head*) Oh, swank, what! (*She replaces it in parcel.*)

Fluther She's a pretty little Judy, all the same.

Mrs Gogan Ah, she is, an' she isn't. There's prettiness an' prettiness in it. I'm always sayin' that her skirts are a little too short for a married woman. An' to see her, sometimes of an evenin', in her glad-neck gown would make a body's blood run cold. I do be ashamed of me life before her husband. An' th' way she thries to be polite, with her 'Good mornin', Mrs Gogan,' when she's goin' down, an' her 'Good evenin', Mrs Gogan,' when she's comin' up. But there's politeness an' politeness in it.

Fluther They seem to get on well together, all th' same.

Mrs Gogan Ah, they do, an' they don't. The pair o' them used to be like two turtle doves always billin' an' cooin'. You couldn't come into th' room but you'd feel, instinctive like, that they'd just been afther kissin' an' cuddlin' each other . . . . It often made me shiver, for, afther all, there's kissin' an' cuddlin' in it. But I'm thinkin' he's beginnin' to take things more quietly; the mysthery of havin' a woman's a mysthery no longer . . . . She dhresses herself to keep him with her, but it's no use – afther a month or two, th' wondher of a woman wears off.

Fluther I dunno, I dunno. Not wishin' to say anything derogatory, I think it's all a question of location: when a man finds th' wondher of one woman beginnin' to die, it's usually beginnin' to live in another.

Mrs Gogan She's always grumblin' about havin' to live in a tenement house. 'I wouldn't like to spend me last hour in one, let alone live me life in a tenement,' says she. 'Vaults,' says she, 'that are hidin' th' dead, instead of homes that are sheltherin' th' livin'.' 'Many a good one,' says I, 'was reared in a tenement house.' Oh, you know, she's a well-up

little lassie, too; able to make a shillin' go where another
would have to spend a pound. She's wipin' th' eyes of th'
Covey an' poor oul' Pether – everybody knows that –
screwin' every penny she can out o' them, in ordher to
turn th' place into a babby-house. An' she has th' life
frightened out o' them; washin' their face, combin' their
hair, wipin' their feet, brushin' their clothes, thrimmin'
their nails, cleanin' their teeth – God Almighty, you'd think
th' poor men were undhergoin' penal servitude.

Fluther (*with an exclamation of disgust*) A-a-ah, that's
goin' beyond th' beyonds in a tenement house. That's a
little bit too derogatory.

> *Peter enters from room, back, head elevated and
> resentful fire in his eyes; he is still in his singlet and
> trousers, but is now wearing a pair of unlaced boots –
> possibly to be decent in the presence of Mrs Gogan. He
> places the white shirt, which he has carried in on his
> arm, on the back of a chair near the fire, and, going over
> to the chest of drawers, he opens drawer after drawer,
> looking for something; as he fails to find it he closes
> each drawer with a snap; he pulls out pieces of linen
> neatly folded, and bundles them back again any way.*

Peter (*in accents of anguish*) Well, God Almighty, give me
patience! (*He returns to room, back, giving the shirt a
vicious turn as he passes.*)

Mrs Gogan I wondher what he is foostherin' for now?

Fluther He's adornin' himself for th' meeting tonight.
(*Pulling a handbill from his pocket and reading*) 'Great
Demonstration an' torchlight procession around places in
th' city sacred to th' memory of Irish Patriots, to be
concluded be a meetin', at which will be taken an oath of
fealty to th' Irish Republic. Formation in Parnell Square at
eight o'clock.' Well, they can hold it for Fluther. I'm up th'

pole; no more dhrink for Fluther. It's three days now since I touched a dhrop, an' I feel a new man already.

Mrs Gogan Isn't oul' Peter a funny-lookin' little man? . . . Like somethin' you'd pick off a Christmas Tree . . . . When he's dhressed up in his canonicals, you'd wondher where he'd been got. God forgive me, when I see him in them, I always think he must ha' had a Mormon for a father! He an' th' Covey can't abide each other; th' pair o' them is always at it, thryin' to best each other. There'll be blood dhrawn one o' these days.

Fluther How is it that Clitheroe himself, now, doesn't have anythin' to do with th' Citizen Army? A couple o' months ago, an' you'd hardly ever see him without his gun, an' th' Red Hand o' Liberty Hall in his hat.

Mrs Gogan Just because he wasn't made a Captain of. He wasn't goin' to be in anything where he couldn't be conspishuous. He was so cocksure o' being made one that he bought a Sam Browne belt, an' was always puttin' it on an' standin' in th' door showing it off, till th' man came an' put out th' street lamps on him. God, I think he used to bring it to bed with him! But I'm tellin' you herself was delighted that that cock didn't crow, for she's like a clockin' hen if he leaves her sight for a minute.

> *While she is talking, she takes up book after book from the table, looks into each of them in a near-sighted way, and then leaves them back. She now lifts up the sword, and proceeds to examine it.*

Be th' look of it, this must ha' been a general's sword . . . . All th' gold lace an' th' fine figaries on it . . . . Sure it's twiced too big for him.

Fluther A-ah; it's a baby's rattle he ought to have, an' he as he is with thoughts tossin' in his head of what may happen to him on th' day o' judgement.

*Peter has entered, and seeing Mrs Gogan with the
sword, goes over to her, pulls it resentfully out of her
hands, and marches into the room, back, without
speaking.*

Mrs Gogan (*as Peter whips the sword*) Oh, excuse me!
. . . (*To Fluther*) Isn't he th' surly oul' rascal!

Fluther Take no notice of him . . . You'd think he was
dumb, but when you get his goat, or he has a few jars up,
he's vice versa. (*He coughs.*)

Mrs Gogan (*she has now sidled over as far as the shirt
hanging on the chair*) Oh, you've got a cold on you, Fluther.

Fluther (*carelessly*) Ah, it's only a little one.

Mrs Gogan You'd want to be careful, all th' same. I knew
a woman, a big lump of a woman, red-faced an' round-
bodied, a little awkward on her feet; you'd think, to look
at her, she could put out her two arms an' lift a two-
storeyed house on th' top of her head; got a ticklin' in her
throat, an' a little cough, an' th' next mornin' she had a
little catchin' in her chest, an' they had just time to wet her
lips with a little rum, an' off she went. (*She begins to look
at and handle the shirt.*)

Fluther (*a little nervously*) It's only a little cold I have;
there's nothing derogatory wrong with me.

Mrs Gogan I dunno; there's many a man this minute
lowerin' a pint, thinkin' of a woman, or pickin' out a winner,
or doin' work as you're doin', while th' hearse dhrawn be th'
horses with the black plumes is dhrivin' up to his own hall
door, an' a voice that he doesn't hear is mutterin' in his ear,
'Earth to earth, an' ashes t' ashes, an' dust to dust.'

Fluther (*faintly*) A man in th' pink o' health should have a
holy horror of allowin' thoughts o' death to be festherin'
in his mind, for – (*with a frightened cough*) be God, I

think I'm afther gettin' a little catch in me chest that time –
it's a creepy thing to be thinkin' about.

Mrs Gogan It is, an' it isn't; it's both bad an' good . . . . It
always gives meself a kind o' thresspassin' joy to feel
meself movin' along in a mournin' coach, an me thinkin'
that, maybe, th' next funeral 'll be me own, an' glad, in a
quiet way, that this is somebody else's.

Fluther An' a curious kind of a gaspin' for breath – I hope
there's nothin' derogatory wrong with me.

Mrs Gogan (*examining the shirt*) Frills on it, like a
woman's petticoat.

Fluther Suddenly gettin' hot, an' then, just as suddenly,
gettin' cold.

Mrs Gogan (*holding out the shirt towards Fluther*) How
would you like to be wearin' this Lord Mayor's nightdhress,
Fluther?

Fluther (*vehemently*) Blast you an' your nightshirt! Is a
man fermentin' with fear to stick th' showin' off to him of
a thing that looks like a shinin' shroud?

Mrs Gogan Oh, excuse me!

*Peter has again entered, and he pulls the shirt from the
hands of Mrs Gogan, replacing it on the chair. He
returns to room.*

Peter (*as he goes out*) Well, God Almighty, give me
patience!

Mrs Gogan (*to Peter*) Oh, excuse me!

*There is heard a cheer from the men working outside on
the street, followed by the clang of tools being thrown
down, then silence. The glare of the gasolene light
diminishes and finally goes out.*

(*Running into the back room to look out of the window*)
What's the men repairin' th' streets cheerin' for?

Fluther (*sitting down weakly on a chair*) You can't sneeze
but that oul' one wants to know th' why an' th' wherefore
. . . . I feel as dizzy as bedamned! I hope I didn't give up
th' beer too suddenly.

> *The Covey comes in by door, right. He is about twenty-*
> *five, tall, thin, with lines on his face that form a*
> *perpetual protest against life as he conceives it to be.*
> *Heavy seams fall from each side of nose, down around*
> *his lips, as if they were suspenders keeping his mouth*
> *from falling. He speaks in a slow, wailing drawl; more*
> *rapidly when he is excited. He is dressed in dungarees,*
> *and is wearing a vividly red tie. He flings his cap with a*
> *gesture of disgust on the table, and begins to take off his*
> *overalls.*

Mrs Gogan (*to the Covey, as she runs back into the room*)
What's after happenin', Covey?

The Covey (*with contempt*) Th' job's stopped. They've
been mobilized to march in th' demonstration tonight
undher th' Plough an' th' Stars. Didn't you hear them
cheerin', th' mugs! They have to renew their political
baptismal vows to be faithful *in seculo seculorum.*

Fluther (*forgetting his fear in his indignation*) There's no
reason to bring religion into it. I think we ought to have as
great a regard for religion as we can, so as to keep it out of
as many things as possible.

The Covey (*pausing in the taking off of his dungarees*)
Oh, you're one o' the boys that climb into religion as high
as a short Mass on Sunday mornin's? I suppose you'll be
singin' songs o' Sion an' songs o' Tara at th' meetin', too.

Fluther We're all Irishmen, anyhow; aren't we?

The Covey (*with hand outstretched, and in a professional tone*) Look here, comrade, there's no such thing as an Irishman; or an Englishman, or a German or a Turk; we're all only human bein's. Scientifically speakin', it's all a question of the accidental gatherin' together of mollycewels an' atoms.

> *Peter comes in with a collar in his hand. He goes over to mirror, left, and proceeds to try to put it on.*

Fluther Mollycewels an' atoms! D'ye think I'm goin' to listen to you thryin' to juggle Fluther's mind with complicated cunundhrums of mollycewels an' atoms?

The Covey (*rather loudly*) There's nothin' complicated in it. There's no fear o' th' Church tellin' you that mollycewels is a stickin' together of millions of atoms o' sodium, carbon, potassium o' iodide, etcetera, that, accordin' to th' way they're mixed, make a flower, a fish, a star that you see shinin' in th' sky, or a man with a big brain like me, or a man with a little brain like you!

Fluther (*more loudly still*) There's no necessity to be raisin' your voice; shoutin's no manifestin' forth of a growin' mind.

Peter (*struggling with his collar*) God, give me patience with this thing . . . She makes these collars as stiff with starch as a shinin' band o' solid steel! She does it purposely to thry an' twart me. If I can't get it on th' singlet, how, in th' Name o' God, am I goin' to get it on th' shirt?

The Covey (*loudly*) There's no use o' arguin' with you; it's education you want, comrade.

Fluther The Covey an' God made th' world, I suppose, wha'?

The Covey When I hear some men talkin' I'm inclined to disbelieve that th' world's eight-hundred million years old, for it's not long since th' fathers o' some o' them crawled out o' th' sheltherin' slime o' the sea.

Mrs Gogan (*from room at back*) There, they're afther formin' fours, an' now they're goin' to march away.

Fluther (*scornfully*) Mollycewels! (*He begins to untie his apron.*) What about Adam an' Eve?

The Covey Well, what about them?

Fluther (*fiercely*) What about them, you?

The Covey Adam an' Eve! Is that as far as you've got? Are you still thinkin' there was nobody in th' world before Adam an' Eve? (*Loudly*) Did you ever hear, man, of th' skeleton of th' man o' Java?

Peter (*casting the collar from him*) Blast it, blast it, blast it!

Fluther (*viciously folding his apron*) Ah, you're not goin' to be let tap your rubbidge o' thoughts into th' mind o' Fluther.

The Covey You're afraid to listen to th' thruth!

Fluther Who's afraid?

The Covey You are!

Fluther G'way, you wurum!

The Covey Who's a worum?

Fluther You are, or you wouldn't talk th' way you're talkin'.

The Covey Th' oul', ignorant savage leppin' up in you, when science shows you that th' head of your god is an empty one. Well, I hope you're enjoyin' th' blessin' o' havin' to live be th' sweat of your brow.

Fluther You'll be kickin' an' yellin' for th' priest yet, me boyo. I'm not goin' to stand silent an' simple listenin' to a thick like you makin' a maddenin' mockery o' God Almighty. It 'ud be a nice derogatory thing on me conscience, an' me dyin', to look back in rememberin' shame of talkin' to a word-weavin' little ignorant yahoo of a red flag Socialist!

Mrs Gogan has returned to the front room, and has wandered around looking at things in general, and is now in front of the fireplace looking at the picture hanging over it.

Mrs Gogan For God's sake, Fluther, dhrop it; there's always th' makin's of a row in th' mention of religion . . . (*Looking at picture*) God bless us, it's a naked woman!

Fluther (*coming over to look at it*) What's undher it? (*Reading*) 'Georgina: The Sleepin' Vennis'. Oh, that's a terrible picture; oh, that's a shockin' picture! Oh, th' one that got that taken, she must have been a prime lassie!

Peter (*who also has come over to look, laughing, with his body bent at the waist, and his head slightly tilted back*) Hee, hee, hee, hee, hee!

Fluther (*indignantly, to Peter*) What are you hee, hee-in' for? That's a nice thing to be hee, hee-in' at. Where's your morality, man?

Mrs Gogan God forgive us, it's not right to be lookin' at it.

Fluther It's nearly a derogatory thing to be in th' room where it is.

Mrs Gogan (*giggling hysterically*) I couldn't stop any longer in th' same room with three men, afther lookin' at it!

She goes out. The Covey, who has divested himself of his dungarees, throws them with a contemptuous motion on top of Peter's white shirt.

Peter (*plaintively*) Where are you throwin' them? Are you thryin' to twart an' torment me again?

The Covey Who's thryin' to twart you?

Peter (*flinging the dungarees violently on the floor*) You're not goin' to make me lose me temper, me young Covey.

The Covey (*flinging the white shirt on the floor*) If you're Nora's pet, aself, you're not goin' to get your way in everything.

Peter (*plaintively, with his eyes looking up at the ceiling*) I'll say nothin' . . . . I'll leave you to th' day when th' all-pitiful, all-merciful, all-lovin' God 'll be handin' you to th' angels to be rievin' an' roastin' you, tearin' an' tormentin' you, burnin' an' blastin' you!

The Covey Aren't you th' little malignant oul' bastard, you lemon-whiskered oul' swine!

Peter runs to the sword, draws it, and makes for the Covey, who dodges him around the table; Peter has no intention of striking, but the Covey wants to take no chances.

(*Dodging*) Fluther, hold him, there. It's a nice thing to have a lunatic like this lashin' around with a lethal weapon! (*The Covey darts out of the room, right, slamming the door in the face of Peter.*)

Peter (*battering and pulling at the door*) Lemme out, lemme out; isn't it a poor thing for a man who wouldn't say a word against his greatest enemy to have to listen to that Covey's twartin' animosities, shovin' poor, patient people into a lashin' out of curses that darken his soul with th' shadow of th' wrath of th' last day!

Fluther Why d'ye take notice of him? If he seen you didn't, he'd say nothin' derogatory.

Peter I'll make him stop his laughin' an' leerin', jibin' an' jeerin' an' scarifyin' people with his corner-boy insinuations! . . . He's always thryin' to rouse me: if it's not a song, it's a whistle; if it isn't a whistle, it's a cough. But you can taunt an' taunt – I'm laughin' at you; he, hee, hee, hee, hee, heee!

The Covey (*singing through the keyhole*)
　　Dear harp o' me counthry, in darkness I found thee,
　　The dark chain of silence had hung o'er thee long –

Peter (*frantically*) Jasus, d'ye hear that? D'ye hear him soundin' forth his divil-souled song o' provocation?

The Covey (*singing as before*)
　　When proudly, me own island harp, I unbound thee,
　　An' gave all thy chords to light, freedom an' song!

Peter (*battering the door*) When I get out I'll do for you, I'll do for you, I'll do for you!

The Covey (*through the keyhole*) Cuckoo-oo!

Nora enters by door, right. She is a young woman of twenty-two, alert, swift, full of nervous energy, and a little anxious to get on in the world. The firm lines of her face are considerably opposed by a soft, amorous mouth and gentle eyes. When her firmness fails her, she persuades with her feminine charm. She is dressed in a tailor-made costume, and wears around her neck a silver fox fur.

Nora (*running in and pushing Peter away from the door*) Oh, can I not turn me back but th' two o' yous are at it

78

like a pair o' fightin' cocks! Uncle Peter . . . Uncle Peter . . .
UNCLE PETER!

Peter (*vociferously*) Oh, Uncle Peter, Uncle Peter be
damned! D'ye think I'm goin' to give a free pass to th'
young Covey to turn me whole life into a Holy Manual o'
penances an' martyrdoms?

The Covey (*angrily rushing into the room*) If you won't
exercise some sort o' conthrol over that Uncle Peter o'
yours, there'll be a funeral, an' it won't be me that'll be in
th' hearse!

Nora (*between Peter and the Covey, to the Covey*) Are
yous always goin' to be tearin' down th' little bit of
respectability that a body's thryin' to build up? Am I
always goin' to be havin' to nurse yous into th' hardy
habit o' thryin' to keep up a little bit of appearance?

The Covey Why weren't you here to see th' way he run at
me with th' sword?

Peter What did you call me a lemon-whiskered oul' swine
for?

Nora If th' two o' yous don't thry to make a generous
altheration in your goin's on, an' keep on thryin' t'
inaugurate th' customs o' th' rest o' th' house into this
place, yous can flit into other lodgin's where your bowsey
battlin' 'ill meet, maybe, with an encore.

Peter (*to Nora*) Would you like to be called a lemon-
whiskered oul' swine?

Nora If you attempt to wag that sword of yours at
anybody again, it'll have to be taken off you an' put in a
safe place away from babies that don't know th' danger o'
them things.

Peter (*at entrance to room, Back*) Well, I'm not goin' to let

79

anybody call me a lemon-whiskered oul' swine. (*He goes in.*)

Fluther (*trying the door*) Openin' an' shuttin' now with a well-mannered motion, like a door of a select bar in a high-class pub.

Nora (*to the Covey, as she lays table for tea*) An', once for all, Willie, you'll have to thry to deliver yourself from th' desire of provokin' oul' Pether into a wild forgetfulness of what's proper an' allowable in a respectable home.

The Covey Well, let him mind his own business, then. Yestherday, I caught him hee-hee-in' out of him an' he readin' bits out of Jenersky's *Thesis on th' Origin, Development, an' Consolidation of th' Evolutionary Idea of th' Proletariat.*

Nora Now, let it end at that, for God's sake; Jack'll be in any minute, an' I'm not goin' to have th' quiet of this evenin' tossed about in an everlastin' uproar between you an' Uncle Pether. (*To Fluther*) Well, did you manage to settle th' lock, yet, Mr Good?

Fluther (*opening and shutting door*) It's betther than a new one, now, Mrs Clitheroe; it's almost ready to open and shut of its own accord.

Nora (*giving him a coin*) You're a whole man. How many pints will that get you?

Fluther (*seriously*) Ne'er a one at all, Mrs Clitheroe, for Fluther's on th' wather waggon now. You could stan' where you're stannin' chantin', 'Have a glass o' malt, Fluther; Fluther, have a glass o' malt,' till th' bells would be ringin' th' ould year out an' th' New Year in, an' you'd have as much chance o' movin' Fluther as a tune on a tin whistle would move a deaf man an' he dead.

As Nora is opening and shutting door, Mrs Bessie

Burgess appears at it. She is a woman of forty, vigorously built. Her face is a dogged one, hardened by toil, and a little coarsened by drink. She looks scornfully and viciously at Nora for a few moments before she speaks.

Bessie Puttin' a new lock on her door . . . afraid her poor neighbours ud break through an' steal . . . . (*In a loud tone*) Maybe, now, they're a damn sight more honest than your ladyship . . . checkin' th' children playin' on th' stairs . . . gettin' on th' nerves of your ladyship . . . . Complainin' about Bessie Burgess singin' her hymns at night, when she has a few up . . . . (*She comes in half-way on the threshold, and screams.*) Bessie Burgess 'll sing whenever she damn well likes!

Nora tries to shut door, but Bessie violently shoves it in, and, gripping Nora by the shoulders, shakes her.

You little over-dressed throllope, you, for one pin I'd paste th' white face o' you!

Nora (*frightened*) Fluther, Fluther!

Fluther (*running over and breaking the hold of Bessie from Nora*) Now, now, Bessie, Bessie, leave poor Mrs Clitheroe alone; she'd do no one any harm, an' minds no one's business but her own.

Bessie Why is she always thryin' to speak proud things, an' lookin' like a mighty one in th' congregation o' th' people!

Nora sinks frightened on to the couch as Jack Clitheroe enters. He is a tall, well-made fellow of twenty-five. His face has none of the strength of Nora's. It is a face in which is the desire for authority, without the power to attain it.

Clitheroe (*excitedly*) What's up? what's afther happenin'?

Fluther Nothin', Jack. Nothin'. It's all over now. Come on, Bessie, come on.

Clitheroe (*to Nora*) What's wrong, Nora? Did she say anything to you?

Nora She was bargin' out of her, an' I only told her to g'up ower o' that to her own place; an' before I knew where I was, she flew at me like a tiger, an' thried to guzzle me!

Clitheroe (*going to door and speaking to Bessie*) Get up to your own place, Mrs Burgess, and don't you be interferin' with my wife, or it'll be th' worse for you . . . Go on, go on!

Bessie (*as Clitheroe is pushing her out*) Mind who you're pushin', now . . . . I attend me place o' worship, anyhow . . . not like some o' them that go to neither church, chapel nor meetin'-house . . . . If me son was home from th' threnches he'd see me righted.

Bessie and Fluther depart, and Clitheroe closes the door.

Clitheroe (*going over to Nora, and putting his arm round her*) There, don't mind that old bitch, Nora, darling; I'll soon put a stop to her interferin'.

Nora Some day or another, when I'm here be meself, she'll come in an' do somethin' desperate.

Clitheroe (*kissing her*) Oh, sorra fear of her doin' anythin' desperate. I'll talk to her tomorrow when she's sober. A taste o' me mind that'll shock her into the sensibility of behavin' herself!

Nora gets up and settles the table. She sees the dungarees on the floor and stands looking at them, then she turns to the Covey, who is reading Jenersky's Thesis *at the fire.*

Nora Willie, is that th' place for your dungarees?

The Covey (*getting up and lifting them from the floor*) Ah, they won't do th' floor any harm, will they? (*He carries them into room, Back.*)

Nora (*calling*) Uncle Peter, now, Uncle Peter; tea's ready.

Peter and the Covey come in from room, back; they all sit down to tea. Peter is in full dress of the Foresters: green coat, gold braided; white breeches, top boots, frilled shirt. He carries the slouch hat, with the white ostrich plume, and the sword in his hands. They eat for a few moments in silence, the Covey furtively looking at Peter with scorn in his eyes. Peter knows it and is fidgety.

The Covey (*provokingly*) Another cut o' bread, Uncle Peter?

Peter maintains a dignified silence.

Clitheroe It's sure to be a great meetin' tonight. We ought to go, Nora.

Nora (*decisively*) I won't go, Jack; you can go if you wish.

A pause.

The Covey D'ye want th' sugar, Uncle Peter?

Peter (*explosively*) Now, are you goin' to start your thryin' an' your twartin' again?

Nora Now, Uncle Peter, you musn't be so touchy; Willie has only assed you if you wanted th' sugar.

Peter He doesn't care a damn whether I want th' sugar or no. He's only thryin' to twart me!

Nora (*angrily, to the Covey*) Can't you let him alone, Willie? If he wants the sugar, let him stretch his hand out an' get it himself!

83

The Covey (*to Peter*) Now, if you want the sugar, you can stretch out your hand and get it yourself!

Clitheroe Tonight is th' first chance that Brennan has got of showing himself off since they made a Captain of him – why, God only knows. It'll be a treat to see him swankin' it at th' head of the Citizen Army carryin' th' flag of the Plough an' th' Stars . . . . (*Looking roguishly at Nora*) He was sweet on you, once, Nora?

Nora He may have been . . . I never liked him. I always thought he was a bit of a thick.

The Covey They're bringin' nice disgrace on that banner now.

Clitheroe (*remonstratively*) How are they bringin' disgrace on it?

The Covey (*snappily*) Because it's a Labour flag, an' was never meant for politics . . . . What does th' design of th' field plough, bearin' on it th' stars of th' heavenly plough, mean, if it's not Communism? It's a flag that should only be used when we're buildin' th' barricades to fight for a Workers' Republic!

Peter (*with a puff of derision*) P-phuh.

The Covey (*angrily*) What are you phuhin' out o' you for? Your mind is th' mind of a mummy. (*Rising*) I betther go an' get a good place to have a look at Ireland's warriors passin' by. (*He goes into room, Left, and returns with his cap.*)

Nora (*to the Covey*) Oh, Willie, brush your clothes before you go.

The Covey Oh, they'll do well enough.

Nora Go an' brush them; th' brush is in th' drawer there.

*The Covey goes to the drawer, muttering, gets the
brush, and starts to brush his clothes.*

The Covey (*singing at Peter, as he does so*)
Oh, where's th' slave so lowly,
Condemn'd to chains unholy,
Who, could he burst his bonds at first,
Would pine beneath them slowly?

We tread th' land that . . . bore us,
Th' green flag glitters . . . o'er us,
Th' friends we've tried are by our side,
An' th' foe we hate . . . before us!

Peter (*leaping to his feet in a whirl of rage*) Now, I'm
tellin' you, me young Covey, once for all, that I'll not stick
any longer these tittherin' taunts of yours, rovin' around to
sing your slights an' slandhers, reddenin' th' mind of a
man to th' thinkin' an' sayin' of things that sicken his soul
with sin! (*Hysterically; lifting up a cup to fling at the
Covey*) Be God, I'll –

Clitheroe (*catching his arm*) Now then, none o' that, none
o' that!

Nora Uncle Pether, Uncle Pether, UNCLE PETHER!

The Covey (*at the door, about to go out*) Isn't that th'
malignant oul' varmint! Lookin' like th' illegitimate son of
an illegitimate child of a corporal in th' Mexican army!
(*He goes out.*)

Peter (*plaintively*) He's afther leavin' me now in such a
state of agitation that I won't be able to do meself justice
when I'm marchin' to th' meetin'.

Nora (*jumping up*) Oh, for God's sake, here, buckle your
sword on, and go to your meetin', so that we'll have at
least one hour of peace! (*She proceeds to belt on the
sword.*)

Clitheroe (*irritably*) For God's sake hurry him up ou' o' this, Nora.

Peter Are yous all goin' to thry to start to twart me now?

Nora (*putting on his plumed hat*) S-s-sh. Now, your hat's on, your house is thatched; off you pop! (*She gently pushes him from her.*)

Peter (*going, and turning as he reaches the door*) Now, if that young Covey –

Nora Go on, go on.

> *Peter goes. Clitheroe sits down in the lounge, lights a cigarette, and looks thoughtfully into the fire. Nora takes the things from the table, placing them on the chest of drawers. There is a pause, then she swiftly comes over to him and sits beside him.*

(*Softly*) A penny for them, Jack!

Clitheroe Me? Oh, I was thinkin' of nothing.

Nora You were thinkin' of th' . . . meetin' . . . Jack. When we were courtin' an' I wanted you to go, you'd say, 'Oh, to hell with meetin's,' an' that you felt lonely in cheerin' crowds when I was absent. An' we weren't a month married when you began that you couldn't keep away from them.

Clitheroe Oh, that's enough about th' meetin'. It looks as if you wanted me to go, th' way you're talkin'. You were always at me to give up th' Citizen Army, an' I gave it up; surely that ought to satisfy you.

Nora Ay, you gave it up – because you got th' sulks when they didn't make a Captain of you. It wasn't for my sake, Jack.

Clitheroe For your sake or no, you're benefitin' by it,

aren't you? I didn't forget this was your birthday, did I? (*He puts his arms around her.*) And you liked your new hat; didn't you, didn't you? (*He kisses her rapidly several times.*)

Nora (*panting*) Jack, Jack; please, Jack! I thought you were tired of that sort of thing long ago.

Clitheroe Well, you're finding out now that I amn't tired of it yet, anyhow. Mrs Clitheroe doesn't want to be kissed, sure she doesn't? (*He kisses her again.*) Little, little red-lipped Nora!

Nora (*coquettishly removing his arm from around her*) Oh, yes, your little, little red-lipped Nora's a sweet little girl when th' fit seizes you; but your little, little red-lipped Nora has to clean your boots every mornin', all the same.

Clitheroe (*with a movement of irritation*) Oh, well, if we're goin' to be snotty!

A pause.

Nora It's lookin' like as if it was you that was goin' to be . . . snotty! Bridlin' up with bittherness, th' minute a body attempts t'open her mouth.

Clitheroe Is it any wondher, turnin' a tendher sayin' into a meanin' o' malice an' spite!

Nora It's hard for a body to be always keepin' her mind bent on makin' thoughts that'll be no longer than th' length of your own satisfaction. (*A pause. Standing up*) If we're goin' to dhribble th' time away sittin' here like a pair o' cranky mummies, I'd be as well sewin' or doin' something about th' place.

She looks appealingly at him for a few moments; he doesn't speak. She swiftly sits down beside him, and puts her arm around his neck.

87

(*Imploringly*) Ah, Jack, don't be so cross!

Clitheroe (*doggedly*) Cross? I'm not cross; I'm not a bit cross. It was yourself started it.

Nora (*coaxingly*) I didn't mean to say anything out o' the way. You take a body up too quickly, Jack. (*In an ordinary tone as if nothing of an angry nature had been said*) You didn't offer me me evenin' allowance yet.

> *Clitheroe silently takes out a cigarette for her and himself and lights both.*

(*Trying to make conversation*) How quiet th' house is now; they must be all out.

Clitheroe (*rather shortly*) I suppose so.

Nora (*rising from the seat*) I'm longin' to show you me new hat, to see what you think of it. Would you like to see it?

Clitheroe Ah, I don't mind.

> *Nora suppresses a sharp reply, hesitates for a moment, then gets the hat, puts it on, and stands before Clitheroe.*

Nora Well, how does Mr Clitheroe like me new hat?

Clitheroe It suits you, Nora, it does right enough.

> *He stands up, puts his hand beneath her chin, and tilts her head up. She looks at him roguishly. He bends down and kisses her.*

Nora Here, sit down, an' don't let me hear another cross word out of you for th' rest o' the night.

> *They sit down.*

Clitheroe (*with his arms around her*) Little, little, red-lipped Nora!

Nora (*with a coaxing movement of her body towards him*) Jack!

Clitheroe (*tightening his arms around her*) Well?

Nora You haven't sung me a song since our honeymoon. Sing me one now, do . . . please, Jack!

Clitheroe What song? 'Since Maggie Went Away'?

Nora Ah, no, Jack, not that; it's too sad. 'When You Said You Loved Me.'

Clearing his throat, Clitheroe thinks for a moment, and then begins to sing. Nora, putting an arm around him, nestles her head on his breast and listens delightedly.

Clitheroe (*singing verses following to the air of 'When You and I Were Young, Maggie'*)
Th' violets were scenting th' woods, Nora,
    Displaying their charm to th' bee,
When I first said I lov'd only you, Nora,
    An' you said you lov'd only me!

Th' chestnut blooms gleam'd through th' glade, Nora,
    A robin sang loud from a tree,
When I first said I lov'd only you, Nora,
    An' you said you lov'd only me!

Th' golden-rob'd daffodils shone, Nora,
    An' danc'd in th' breeze on th' lea,
When I first said I lov'd only you, Nora,
    An' you said you lov'd only me!

Th' trees, birds, an' bees sang a song, Nora,
    Of happier transports to be,
When I first said I lov'd only you, Nora,
    An' you said you lov'd only me!

Nora kisses him. A knock is heard at the door, right; a pause as they listen. Nora clings closely to Clitheroe.

Another knock, more imperative than the first.

I wonder who can that be, now?

Nora (*a little nervous*) Take no notice of it, Jack; they'll go away in a minute.

Another knock, followed by a voice.

Voice Commandant Clitheroe, Commandant Clitheroe, are you there? A message from General Jim Connolly.

Clitheroe Damn it, it's Captain Brennan.

Nora (*anxiously*) Don't mind him, don't mind, Jack. Don't break our happiness . . . Pretend we're not in. Let us forget everything tonight but our two selves!

Clitheroe (*reassuringly*) Don't be alarmed, darling; I'll just see what he wants, an' send him about his business.

Nora (*tremulously*) No, no. Please, Jack; don't open it. Please, for your own little Nora's sake!

Clitheroe (*rising to open the door*) Now don't be silly, Nora.

Clitheroe opens door, and admits a young man in the full uniform of the Irish Citizen Army – green suit; slouch green hat caught up at one side by a small Red Hand badge; Sam Browne belt, with a revolver in the holster. He carries a letter in his hand. When he comes in he smartly salutes Clitheroe. The young man is Captain Brennan.

Capt. Brennan (*giving the letter to Clitheroe*) A dispatch from General Connolly.

While Clitheroe reads out the letter Brennan's eyes are fixed on Nora, who droops as she sits on the lounge.

Clitheroe (*reading*) 'Commandant Clitheroe is to take command of the eighth battalion of the ICA which will assemble to proceed to the meeting at nine o'clock. He is to see that all units are provided with full equipment; two days' rations and fifty rounds of ammunition. At two o'clock a.m. the army will leave Liberty Hall for a reconnaissance attack on Dublin Castle. – Com.-Gen. Connolly.' I don't understand this. Why does General Connolly call me Commandant?

Capt. Brennan Th' Staff appointed you Commandant, and th' General agreed with their selection.

Clitheroe When did this happen?

Capt. Brennan A fortnight ago.

Clitheroe How is it word was never sent to me?

Capt. Brennan Word was sent to you . . . I meself brought it.

Clitheroe Who did you give it to, then?

Capt. Brennan (*after a pause*) I think I gave it to Mrs Clitheroe, there.

Clitheroe Nora, d'ye hear that?

Nora makes no answer.

(*There is a note of hardness in his voice.*) Nora . . . Captain Brennan says he brought a letter to me from General Connolly, and that he gave it to you . . . Where is it? What did you do with it?

Nora (*running over to him, and pleadingly putting her arms around him*) Jack, please, Jack, don't go out tonight an' I'll tell you; I'll explain everything . . . Send him away, an' stay with your own little red-lipp'd Nora.

Clitheroe (*removing her arms from around him*) None o' this nonsense, now; I want to know what you did with th' letter.

Nora goes slowly to the lounge and sits down.

(*Angrily*) Why didn't you give me th' letter? What did you do with it? . . . (*He shakes her by the shoulder.*) What did you do with th' letter?

Nora (*flaming up*) I burned it, I burned it! That's what I did with it! Is General Connolly an' th' Citizen Army goin' to be your only care? Is your home goin' to be only a place to rest in? Am I goin' to be only somethin' to provide merry-makin' at night for you? Your vanity'll be th' ruin of you an' me yet . . . That's what's movin' you: because they've made an officer of you, you'll make a glorious cause of what you're doin', while your little red-lipp'd Nora can go on sittin' here, makin' a companion of th' loneliness of th' night!

Clitheroe (*fiercely*) You burned it, did you? (*He grips her arm.*) Well, me good lady –

Nora Let go – you're hurtin' me!

Clitheroe You deserve to be hurt . . . Any letter that comes to me for th' future, take care that I get it . . . D'ye hear – take care that I get it!

He goes to the chest of drawers and takes out a Sam Browne belt, which he puts on, and then puts a revolver in the holster. He puts on his hat, and looks towards Nora. While this dialogue is proceeding, and while Clitheroe prepares himself, Brennan softly whistles 'The Soldiers' Song'.

(*At door, about to go out*) You needn't wait up for me; if I'm in at all, it won't be before six in th' morning.

Nora (*bitterly*) I don't care if you never come back!

Clitheroe (*to Capt. Brennan*) Come along, Ned.

They go out. There is a pause. Nora pulls the new hat

from her head and with a bitter movement flings it to the other end of the room. There is a gentle knock at door, right, which opens, and Mollser comes into the room. She is about fifteen, but looks to be only about ten, for the ravages of consumption have shrivelled her up. She is pitifully worn, walks feebly, and frequently coughs. She goes over to Nora.

Mollser (*to Nora*) Mother's gone to th' meetin', an' I was feelin' terrible lonely, so I come down to see if you'd let me sit with you, thinkin' you mightn't be goin' yourself . . . . I do be terrible afraid I'll die sometime when I'm be meself . . . . I often envy you, Mrs Clitheroe, seein' th' health you have, an' th' lovely place you have here, an' wondherin' if I'll ever be sthrong enough to be keepin' a home together for a man. Oh, this must be some more o' the Dublin Fusiliers flyin' off to the front.

Just before Mollser ceases to speak, there is heard in the distance the music of a brass band playing a regiment to the boat on the way to the front. The tune that is being played is 'It's a Long Way to Tipperary'; as the band comes to the chorus, the regiment is swinging into the street by Nora's house, and the voices of the soldiers can be heard lustily singing the chorus of the song.

Soldiers (*off*)
It's a long way to Tipperary, it's a long way to go;
It's a long way to Tipperary, to th' sweetest girl I know!
Goodbye Piccadilly, farewell Leicester Square.
It's a long, long way to Tipperary, but my heart's right
    there!

Nora and Mollser remain silently listening. As the chorus ends and the music is faint in the distance again, Bessie Burgess appears at door, right, which Mollser has left open.

Bessie (*speaking in towards the room*) There's th' men marchin' out into th' dhread dimness o' danger, while th' lice is crawlin' about feedin' on th' fatness o' the land! But yous'll not escape from th' arrow that flieth be night, or th' sickness that wasteth be day . . . . An' ladyship an' all, as some o' them may be, they'll be scattered abroad, like th' dust in th' darkness!

Bessie goes away; Nora steals over and quietly shuts the door. She comes back to the lounge and wearily throws herself on it beside Mollser.

Mollser (*after a pause and a cough*) Is there anybody goin', Mrs Clitheroe, with a titther o' sense?

Curtain.

Act Two

A commodious public-house at the corner of the street in which the meeting is being addressed from Platform No. 1. It is the south corner of the public-house that is visible to the audience. The counter, beginning at Back about one-fourth of the width of the space shown, comes across two-thirds of the length of the stage, and, taking a circular sweep, passes out of sight to left. On the counter are beer-pulls, glasses, and a carafe. The other three-fourths of the back is occupied by a tall, wide, two-paned window. Beside this window at the right is a small, box-like, panelled snug. Next to the snug is a double swing door, the entrance to that particular end of the house. Farther on is a shelf on which customers may rest their drinks. Underneath the windows is a cushioned seat. Behind the counter at Back can be seen the shelves running the whole length of the counter. On these shelves can be seen the end (or the beginning) of rows of bottles. The Barman is seen wiping the part of the counter which is in view. Rosie is standing at the counter toying with what remains of a half of whiskey in a wineglass. She is a sturdy, well-shaped girl of twenty; pretty, and pert in manner. She is wearing a cream blouse, with an obviously suggestive glad neck; a grey tweed dress, brown stockings and shoes. The blouse and most of the dress are hidden by a black shawl. She has no hat, and in her hair is jauntily set a cheap, glittering, jewelled ornament. It is an hour later.

Barman (*wiping counter*) Nothin' much doin' in your line tonight, Rosie?

Rosie Curse o' God on th' haporth, hardly, Tom. There isn't much notice taken of a pretty petticoat of a night like this . . . . They're all in a holy mood. Th' solemn-lookin' dials on th' whole o' them an' they marchin' to th' meetin'. You'd think they were th' glorious company of th' saints, an' th' noble army of martyrs thrampin' through th' sthreets of paradise. They're all thinkin' of higher things than a girl's garthers . . . . It's a tremendous meetin'; four platforms they have – there's one o' them just outside opposite th' window.

Barman Oh, ay; sure when th' speaker comes (*motioning with his hand*) to th' near end, here, you can see him plain, an' hear nearly everythin' he's spoutin' out of him.

Rosie It's no joke thryin' to make up fifty-five shillin's a week for your keep an' laundhry, an' then taxin' you a quid for your own room if you bring home a friend for th' night . . . . If I could only put by a couple of quid for a swankier outfit, everythin' in th' garden ud look lovely –

Barman Whisht, till we hear what he's sayin'.

Through the window is silhouetted the figure of a tall man who is speaking to the crowd. The Barman and Rosie look out of the window and listen.

Voice of the Man It is a glorious thing to see arms in the hands of Irishmen. We must accustom ourselves to the thought of arms, we must accustom ourselves to the sight of arms, we must accustom ourselves to the use of arms . . . . Bloodshed is a cleansing and sanctifying thing, and the nation that regards it as the final horror has lost its manhood . . . . There are many things more horrible than bloodshed, and slavery is one of them!

The figure moves away towards the right, and is lost to sight and hearing.

Rosie It's th' sacred thruth, mind you, what that man's afther sayin'.

Barman If I was only a little younger, I'd be plungin' mad into th' middle of it!

Rosie (*who is still looking out of the window*) Oh, here's the two gems runnin' over again for their oil!

> *Peter and Fluther enter tumultuously. They are hot, and full and hasty with the things they have seen and heard. Emotion is bubbling up in them, so that when they drink, and when they speak, they drink and speak with the fullness of emotional passion. Peter leads the way to the counter.*

Peter (*splutteringly to the Barman*) Two halves . . . (*To Fluther*) A meetin' like this always makes me feel as if I could dhrink Loch Erinn dhry!

Fluther You couldn't feel any way else at a time like this when th' spirit of a man is pulsin' to be out fightin' for th' thruth with his feet thremblin' on th' way, maybe to th' gallows, an' his ears tinglin' with th' faint, far-away sound of burstin' rifle-shots that'll maybe whip th' last little shock o' life out of him that's left lingerin' in his body!

Peter I felt a burnin' lump in me throat when I heard th' band playin' 'The Soldiers' Song', rememberin' last hearin' it marchin' in military formation, with th' people starin' on both sides at us, carryin' with us th' pride an' resolution o' Dublin to th' grave of Wolfe Tone.

Fluther Get th' Dublin men goin' an' they'll go on full force for anything that's thryin' to bar them away from what they're wantin', where th' slim thinkin' counthry boyo ud limp away from th' first faintest touch of compromization!

Peter (*hurriedly to the Barman*) Two more, Tom! . . . (*To*

Fluther) Th' memory of all th' things that was done, an' all th' things that was suffered be th' people, was boomin' in me brain . . . . Every nerve in me body was quiverin' to do somethin' desperate!

Fluther Jammed as I was in th' crowd, I listened to th' speeches pattherin' on th' people's head, like rain fallin' on th' corn; every derogatory thought went out o' me mind, an' I said to meself, 'You can die now, Fluther, for you've seen th' shadow-dhreams of th' past leppin' to life in th' bodies of livin' men that show, if we were without a titther o' courage for centuries, we're vice versa now!' Looka here. (*He stretches out his arm under Peter's face and rolls up his sleeve.*) The blood was BOILIN' in me veins!

    The silhouette of the tall figure again moves into the
    frame of the window speaking to the people.

Peter (*unaware, in his enthusiasm, of the speaker's appearance, to Fluther*) I was burnin' to dhraw me sword, an' wave an' wave it over me –

Fluther (*overwhelming Peter*) Will you stop your blatherin' for a minute, man, an' let us hear what he's sayin'!

Voice of the Man Comrade soldiers of the Irish Volunteers and of the Citizen Army, we rejoice in this terrible war. The old heart of the earth needed to be warmed with the red wine of the battlefields . . . . Such august homage was never offered to God as this: the homage of millions of lives given gladly for love of country. And we must be ready to pour out the same red wine in the same glorious sacrifice, for without shedding of blood there is no redemption!

    The figure moves out of sight and hearing.

Fluther (*gulping down the drink that remains in his glass,* *and rushing out*) Come on, man; this is too good to be missed!

Peter finishes his drink less rapidly, and as he is going out wiping his mouth with the back of his hand he runs into the Covey coming in. He immediately erects his body like a young cock, and with his chin thrust forward, and a look of venomous dignity on his face, he marches out.

The Covey (*at counter*) Give us a glass o' malt, for God's sake, till I stimulate meself from th' shock o' seein' th' sight that's afther goin' out!

Rosie (*all business, coming over to the counter, and standing near the Covey*) Another one for me, Tommy; (*to the Barman*) th' young gentleman's ordherin' it in th' corner of his eye.

The Barman brings the drink for the Covey, and leaves it on the counter. Rosie whips it up.

Barman Ay, houl' on there, houl' on there, Rosie!

Rosie (*to the Barman*) What are you houldin' on out o' you for? Didn't you hear th' young gentleman say that he couldn't refuse anything to a nice little bird? (*To the Covey*) Isn't that right, Jiggs? (*The Covey says nothing.*) Didn't I know, Tommy, it would be all right? It takes Rosie to size a young man up, an' tell th' thoughts that are thremblin' in his mind. Isn't that right, Jiggs?

The Covey stirs uneasily, moves a little farther away, and pulls his cap over his eyes.

(*Moving after him*) Great meetin' that's gettin' held outside. Well, it's up to us all, anyway, to fight for our freedom.

The Covey (*to Barman*) Two more, please. (*To Rosie*)

Freedom! What's th' use o' freedom, if it's not economic freedom?

Rosie (*emphasizing with extended arm and moving finger*) I used them very words just before you come in. 'A lot o' thricksters,' says I, 'that wouldn't know what freedom was if they got it from their mother.' . . . (*To Barman*) Didn't I, Tommy?

Barman I disremember.

Rosie No, you don't disremember. Remember you said, yourself, it was all 'only a flash in th' pan'. Well, 'flash in th' pan, or no flash in th' pan,' says I, 'they're not goin' to get Rosie Redmond,' says I, 'to fight for freedom that wouldn't be worth winnin' in a raffle!'

The Covey There's only one freedom for th' workin' man: conthrol o' th' means o' production, rates of exchange, an' th' means of disthribution. (*Tapping Rosie on the shoulder*) Look here, comrade, I'll leave here tomorrow night for you a copy of Jenersky's *Thesis on the Origin, Development, an' Consolidation of the Evolutionary Idea of the Proletariat.*

Rosie (*throwing off her shawl on to the counter, and showing an exemplified glad neck, which reveals a good deal of a white bosom*) If y'ass Rosie, it's heartbreakin' to see a young fella thinkin' of anything, or admirin' anything, but silk thransparent stockin's showin' off the shape of a little lassie's legs!

The Covey, frightened, moves a little away.

(*Following on*) Out in th' park in th' shade of a warm summery evenin', with your little darlin' bridie to be, kissin' an' cuddlin' (*she tries to put her arm around his neck*), kissin' an' cuddlin', ay?

The Covey (*frightened*) Ay, what are you doin'? None o'

that, now; none o' that. I've something else to do besides
shinannickin' afther Judies!

*He turns away, but Rosie follows, keeping face to face
with him.*

Rosie Oh, little duckey, oh, shy little duckey! Never held a
mot's hand, an' wouldn't know how to tittle a little Judy!
(*She clips him under the chin.*) Tittle him undher th' chin,
tittle him undher th' chin!

The Covey (*breaking away and running out*) Ay, go on,
now; I don't want to have any meddlin' with a lassie like
you!

Rosie (*enraged*) Jasus, it's in a monasthery some of us
ought to be, spendin' our holidays kneelin' on our adorers,
tellin' our beads, an' knockin' hell out of our buzzums!

The Covey (*outside*) Cuckoo-oo!

*Peter and Fluther come in again, followed by Mrs Gogan,
carrying a baby in her arms. They go over to the counter.*

Peter (*with plaintive anger*) It's terrible that young Covey
can't let me pass without proddin' at me! Did you hear
him murmurin' 'cuckoo' when we were passin'?

Fluther (*irritably*) I wouldn't be everlastin' cockin' me ear
to every little whisper that was floatin' around about me!
It's my rule never to lose me temper till it would be
dethrimental to keep it. There's nothin' derogatory in
th' use o' th' word 'cuckoo', is there?

Peter (*tearfully*) It's not th' word; it's th' way he says it:
he never says it straight out, but murmurs it with curious
quiverin' ripples, like variations on a flute!

Fluther Ah, what odds if he gave it with variations on a
thrombone! (*To Mrs Gogan*) What's yours goin' to be,
ma'am?

Mrs Gogan Ah, a half o' malt, Fluther.

Fluther (*to Barman*) Three halves, Tommy.

The Barman brings the drinks.

Mrs Gogan (*drinking*) The Foresthers' is a gorgeous dhress! I don't think I've seen nicer, mind you, in a pantomime . . . . Th' loveliest part of th' dhress, I think, is th' osthrichess plume . . . . When yous are goin' along, an' I see them wavin' an' noddin' an' waggin', I seem to be lookin' at each of yous hangin' at th' end of a rope, your eyes bulgin' an' your legs twistin' an' jerkin', gaspin' an' gaspin' for breath while yous are thryin' to die for Ireland!

Fluther If any o' them is hangin' at the end of a rope, it won't be for Ireland!

Peter Are you goin' to start th' young Covey's game o' proddin' an' twartin' a man? There's not many that's talkin' can say that for twenty-five years he never missed a pilgrimage to Bodenstown!

Fluther You're always blowin' about goin' to Bodenstown. D'ye think no one but yourself ever went to Bodenstown?

Peter (*plaintively*) I'm not blowin' about it; but there's not a year that I go there but I pluck a leaf off Tone's grave, an' this very day me prayer-book is nearly full of them.

Fluther (*scornfully*) Then Fluther has a vice versa opinion of them that put ivy leaves into their prayer-books, scabbin' it on th' clergy, an' thryin' to out-do th' haloes o' th' saints be lookin' as if he was wearin' around his head a glittherin' aroree boree allis! (*Fiercely*) Sure, I don't care a damn if you slep' in Bodenstown! You can take your breakfast, dinner, an' tea on th' grave in Bodenstown, if you like, for Fluther!

Mrs Gogan Oh, don't start a fight, boys, for God's sake; I was only sayin' what a nice costume it is – nicer than th' kilts, for, God forgive me, I always think th' kilts is hardly decent.

Fluther Ah, sure, when you'd look at him, you'd wondher whether th' man was makin' fun o' th' costume, or th' costume was makin' fun o' th' man!

Barman Now, then, thry to speak asy, will yous? We don't want no shoutin' here.

The Covey, followed by Bessie Burgess, comes in. They go over to the opposite end of the counter, and direct their gaze on the other group.

The Covey (*to Barman*) Two glasses o' malt.

Peter There he is, now; I knew he wouldn't be long till he folleyed me in.

Bessie (*speaking to the Covey, but really at the other party*) I can't for th' life o' me undherstand how they can call themselves Catholics, when they won't lift a finger to help poor little Catholic Belgium.

Mrs Gogan (*raising her voice*) What about poor little Catholic Ireland?

Bessie (*over to Mrs Gogan*) You mind your own business, ma'am, an' stupefy your foolishness be gettin' dhrunk.

Peter (*anxiously*) Take no notice of her; pay no attention to her. She's just tormentin' herself towards havin' a row with somebody.

Bessie There's a storm of anger tossin' in me heart, thinkin' of all th' poor Tommies, an' with them me own son, dhrenched in water an' soaked in blood, gropin' their way to a shattherin' death, in a shower o' shells! Young men with th' sunny lust o' life beamin' in them, layin' down their white bodies, shredded into torn an' bloody pieces, on th' althar that God Himself has built for th' sacrifice of heroes!

Mrs Gogan Isn't it a nice thing to have to be listenin' to a lassie an' hangin' our heads in a dead silence, knowin' that some persons think more of a ball of malt than they do of th' blessed saints.

Fluther Whisht; she's always dangerous an' derogatory when she's well oiled. Th' safest way to hindher her from havin' any enjoyment out of her spite, is to dip our thoughts into the fact of her bein' a female person that has moved out of th' sight of ordinary sensible people.

Bessie To look at some o' th' women that's knockin' about, now, is a thing to make a body sigh . . . . A woman on her own, dhrinkin' with a bevy o' men, is hardly an example to her sex . . . . A woman dhrinkin' with a woman is one thing, an' a woman dhrinkin' with herself is still a woman – flappers may be put in another category altogether – but a middle-aged married woman makin' herself th' centre of a circle of men is as a woman that is loud an' stubborn, whose feet abideth not in her own house.

The Covey (*to Bessie*) When I think of all th' problems in front o' th' workers, it makes me sick to be lookin' at oul' codgers goin' about dhressed up like green-accoutred figures gone asthray out of a toyshop!

Peter Gracious God, give me patience to be listenin' to that blasted young Covey proddin' at me from over at th' other end of th' shop!

Mrs Gogan (*dipping her finger in the whiskey, and moistening with it the lips of her baby*) Cissie Gogan's a woman livin' for nigh on twenty-five years in her own room, an' beyond biddin' th' time o' day to her neighbours, never yet as much as nodded her head in th' direction of other people's business, while she knows some as are never content unless they're standin' senthry over other people's doin's!

Bessie is about to reply, when the tall, dark figure is again silhouetted against the window, and the voice of the Speaker is heard speaking passionately.

Voice of Speaker The last sixteen months have been the most glorious in the history of Europe. Heroism has come back to the earth. War is a terrible thing, but war is not an evil thing. People in Ireland dread war because they do not know it. Ireland has not known the exhilaration of war for over a hundred years. When war comes to Ireland she must welcome it as she would welcome the Angel of God! (*The figure passes out of sight and hearing.*)

The Covey (*towards all present*) Dope, dope. There's only one war worth havin': th' war for th' economic emancipation of th' proletariat.

Bessie They may crow away out o' them; but it ud be fitther for some o' them to mend their ways, an' cease from havin' scouts out watchin' for th' comin' of th' Saint Vincent de Paul man, for fear they'd be nailed lowerin' a pint of beer, mockin' th' man with an angel face, shinin' with th' glamour of deceit an' lies!

Mrs Gogan An' a certain lassie standin' stiff behind her own door with her ears cocked listenin' to what's being said, stuffed till she's sthrained with envy of a neighbour thryin' for a few little things that may be got be hard sthrivin' to keep up to th' letther an' th' law, an' th' practices of th' Church!

Peter (*to Mrs Gogan*) If I was you, Mrs Gogan, I'd parry her jabbin' remarks be a powerful silence that'll keep her tantalizin' words from penethratin' into your feelin's. It's always betther to leave these people to th' vengeance o' God!

Bessie Bessie Burgess doesn't put up to know much, never havin' a swaggerin' mind, thanks be to God, but goin' on packin' up knowledge accordin' to her conscience: precept upon precept, line upon line; here a little, an' there a little. But (*with a passionate swing of her shawl*), thanks be to Christ, she knows when she was got, where she was got, an' how she was got; while there's some she knows, decoratin' their finger with a well-polished weddin' ring, would be hard put to it if they were assed to show their weddin' lines!

Mrs Gogan (*plunging out into the centre of the floor in a wild tempest of hysterical rage*) Y' oul' rip of a blasted liar, me weddin' ring's been well earned be twenty years be th' side o' me husband, now takin' his rest in heaven, married to me be Father Dempsey, in th' Chapel o' Saint Jude's, in th' Christmas Week of eighteen hundhred an' ninety-five; an' any kid, livin' or dead, that Jinnie Gogan's had since, was got between th' bordhers of th' Ten Commandments! . . . An' that's more than some o' you can say that are kep' from th' dhread o' desthruction be a few drowsy virtues, that th' first whisper of temptation lulls into a sleep, that'll know one sin from another only on th' day of their last anointin', an' that use th' innocent light o' th' shinin' stars to dip into th' sins of a night's diversion!

Bessie (*jumping out to face Mrs Gogan, and bringing the palms of her hands together in sharp claps to emphasize her remarks*) Liar to you, too, ma'am, y' oul' hardened thresspasser on other people's good nature, wizenin' up your soul in th' arts o' dodgeries, till every dhrop of respectability in a female is dhried up in her, lookin' at your ready-made manoeuverin' with th' menkind!

Barman Here, there; here, there; speak asy there. No rowin' here, no rowin' here, now.

Fluther (*trying to calm Mrs Gogan*) Now Jinnie, Jinnie, it's a derogatory thing to be smirchin' a night like this with a row; it's rompin' with th' feelin's of hope we ought to be, instead o' bein' vice versa!

Peter (*trying to quiet Bessie*) I'm terrible dawny, Mrs Burgess, an' a fight leaves me weak for a long time aftherwards . . . . Please, Mrs Burgess, before there's damage done, thry to have a little respect for yourself.

Bessie (*with a push of her hand that sends Peter tottering to the end of the shop*) G'way, you little sermonizing, little yella-faced, little consequential, little pudgy, little bum, you!

Mrs Gogan (*screaming*) Fluther, leggo! I'm not goin' to keep an unresistin' silence, an' her scattherin' her festherin' words in me face, stirrin' up every dhrop of decency in a respectable female, with her restless rally o' lies that would make a saint say his prayer backwards!

Bessie (*shouting*) Ah, everybody knows well that th' best charity that can be shown to you is to hide th' thruth as much as our thrue worship of God Almighty will allow us!

Mrs Gogan (*frantically*) Here, houl' th' kid, one o' yous; houl' th' kid for a minute! There's nothin' for it but to show this lassie a lesson or two . . . . (*To Peter*) Here, houl' th' kid, you. (*Before Peter is aware of it, she places the infant in his arms. To Bessie, standing before her in a fighting attitude*) Come on, now, me loyal lassie, dyin' with grief for little Catholic Belgium! When Jinnie Gogan's done with you, you'll have a little leisure lyin' down to think an' pray for your king an' counthry!

Barman (*coming from behind the counter, getting between the women, and proceeding to push them towards the door*) Here, now, since yous can't have a little friendly argument quietly, you'll get out o' this place in quick time.

Go on, an' settle your differences somewhere else – I don't want to have another endorsement on me licence.

Peter (*anxiously, over to Mrs Gogan*) Here, take your kid back, ower this. How nicely I was picked, now, for it to be plumped into me arms!

The Covey She knew who she was givin' it to, maybe.

Peter (*hotly to the Covey*) Now, I'm givin' you fair warnin', me young Covey, to quit firin' your jibes an' jeers at me . . . . For one o' these days, I'll run out in front o' God Almighty an' take your sacred life!

Barman (*pushing Bessie out after Mrs Gogan*) Go on, now; out you go.

Bessie (*as she goes out*) If you think, me lassie, that Bessie Burgess has an untidy conscience, she'll soon show you to th' differ!

Peter (*leaving the baby down on the floor*) Ay, be Jasus, wait there, till I give her back her youngster! (*He runs to the door.*) Ay, there, ay! (*He comes back.*) There, she's afther goin' without her kid. What are we goin' to do with it, now?

The Covey What are we goin' to do with it? Bring it outside an' show everybody what you're afther findin'!

Peter (*in a panic to Fluther*) Pick it up, you, Fluther, an' run afther her with it, will you?

Fluther What d'ye take Fluther for? You must think Fluther's a right gom. D'ye think Fluther's like yourself, destitute of a titther of undherstandin'?

Barman (*imperatively to Peter*) Take it up, man, an' run out afther her with it, before she's gone too far. You're not goin' to leave th' bloody thing here, are you?

Peter (*plaintively, as he lifts up the baby*) Well, God Almighty, give me patience with all th' scorners, tormentors, an' twarters that are always an' ever thryin' to goad me into prayin' for their blindin' an' blastin' an' burnin' in th' world to come! (*He goes out.*)

Fluther God, it's a relief to get rid o' that crowd. Women is terrible when they start to fight. There's no holdin' them back. (*To the Covey*) Are you goin' to have anything?

The Covey Ah, I don't mind if I have another half.

Fluther (*to Barman*) Two more, Tommy, me son.

   The Barman gets the drinks.

You know, there's no conthrollin' a woman when she loses her head.

   Rosie enters and goes over to the counter on the side nearest to Fluther.

Rosie (*to Barman*) Divil a use o' havin' a thrim little leg on a night like this; things was never worse . . . . Give us a half till tomorrow, Tom, duckey.

Barman (*coldly*) No more tonight, Rosie; you owe me for three already.

Rosie (*combatively*) You'll be paid, won't you?

Barman I hope so.

Rosie You hope so! Is that th' way with you, now?

Fluther (*to Barman*) Give her one; it'll be all right.

Rosie (*clapping Fluther on the back*) Oul' sport!

Fluther Th' meetin' should be soon over, now.

The Covey Th' sooner th' betther. It's all a lot o' blasted nonsense, comrade.

Fluther Oh, I wouldn't say it was all nonsense. Afther all, Fluther can remember th' time, an' him only a dawny chiselur, bein' taught at his mother's knee to be faithful to th' Shan Van Vok!

The Covey That's all dope, comrade; th' sort o' thing that workers are fed on be th' Boorzwawzee.

Fluther (*a little sharply*) What's all dope? Though I'm sayin' it that shouldn't: (*catching his cheek with his hand, and pulling down the flesh from the eye*) d'ye see that mark there, undher me eye? . . . A sabre slice from a dragoon in O'Connell Street! (*Thrusting his head forward towards Rosie*) Feel that dint in th' middle o' me nut!

Rosie (*rubbing Fluther's head, and winking at the* Covey) My God, there's a holla!

Fluther (*putting on his hat with quiet pride*) A skelp from a bobby's baton at a Labour meetin' in th' Phoenix Park!

The Covey He must ha' hitten you in mistake. I don't know what you ever done for th' Labour Movement.

Fluther (*loudly*) D'ye not? Maybe, then, I done as much, an' know as much about th' Labour Movement as th' chancers that are blowin' about it!

Barman Speak easy, Fluther, thry to speak easy.

The Covey There's no necessity to get excited about it, comrade.

Fluther (*more loudly*) Excited? Who's gettin' excited? There's no one gettin' excited! It would take something more than a thing like you to flutther a feather o' Fluther. Blatherin', an', when all is said, you know as much as th' rest in th' wind up!

The Covey Well, let us put it to th' test, then, an' see what

you know about th' Labour Movement: what's the
mechanism of exchange?

Fluther (*roaring, because he feels he is beaten*) How th'
hell do I know what it is? There's nothin' about that in th'
rules of our Thrades Union!

Barman For God's sake, thry to speak easy, Fluther.

The Covey What does Karl Marx say about th' Relation
of Value to th' Cost o' Production?

Fluther (*angrily*) What th' hell do I care what he says?
I'm Irishman enough not to lose me head be follyin'
foreigners!

Barman Speak easy, Fluther.

The Covey It's only waste o' time talkin' to you, comrade.

Fluther Don't be comradin' me, mate. I'd be on me last
legs if I wanted you for a comrade.

Rosey (*to the Covey*) It seems a highly rediculous thing to
hear a thing that's only an inch or two away from a kid,
swingin' heavy words about he doesn't know th' meanin'
of, an' uppishly thryin' to down a man like Misther
Fluther here, that's well flavoured in th' knowledge of th'
world he's livin' in.

The Covey (*savagely to Rosie*) Nobody's askin' you to be
buttin' in with your prate . . . . I have you well taped, me
lassie . . . . Just you keep your opinions for your own
place . . . . It'll be a long time before th' Covey takes any
insthructions or reprimandin' from a prostitute!

Rosie (*wild with humiliation*) You louse, you louse, you!
. . . You're no man . . . . You're no man . . . I'm a
woman, anyhow, an' if I'm a prostitute aself, I have me
feelin's . . . . Thryin' to put his arm around me a minute
ago, an' givin' me th' glad eye, th' little wrigglin' lump o'

desolation turns on me now, because he saw there was
nothin' doin' . . . . You louse, you! If I was a man, or you
were a woman, I'd bate th' puss o' you!

Barman Ay, Rosie, ay! You'll have to shut your mouth
altogether, if you can't learn to speak easy!

Fluther (*to Rosie*) Houl' on there, Rosie; houl' on there.
There's no necessity to flutther yourself when you're with
Fluther . . . . Any lady that's in th' company of Fluther is
goin' to get a fair hunt . . . . This is outside your province
. . . . I'm not goin' to let you demean yourself be talkin' to
a tittherin' chancer . . . . Leave this to Fluther – this is a
man's job. (*To the* Covey) Now, if you've anything to say,
say it to Fluther, an', let me tell you, you're not goin' to be
pass-remarkable to any lady in my company.

The Covey Sure I don't care if you were runnin' all night
afther your Mary o' th' Curlin' Hair, but, when you start
tellin' luscious lies about what you done for th' Labour
Movement, it's nearly time to show y'up!

Fluther (*fiercely*) Is it you show Fluther up? G'way, man,
I'd beat two o' you before me breakfast!

The Covey (*contemptuously*) Tell us where you bury your
dead, will you?

Fluther (*with his face stuck into the face of the* Covey)
Sing a little less on th' high note, or, when I'm done with
you, you'll put a Christianable consthruction on things,
I'm tellin' you!

The Covey You're a big fella, you are.

Fluther (*tapping the* Covey *threateningly on the shoulder*)
Now, you're temptin' Providence when you're temptin'
Fluther!

The Covey (*losing his temper, and bawling*) Easy with

them hands, there, easy with them hands! You're startin'
to take a little risk when you commence to paw the Covey!

*Fluther suddenly springs into the middle of the shop,
flings his hat into the corner, whips off his coat, and
begins to paw the air.*

Fluther (*roaring at the top of his voice*) Come on, come
on, you lowser; put your mits up now, if there's a man's
blood in you! Be God, in a few minutes you'll see some
snots flyin' around, I'm tellin' you . . . . When Fluther's
done with you, you'll have a vice versa opinion of him!
Come on, now, come on!

Barman (*running from behind the counter and catching
hold of the Covey*) Here, out you go, me little bowsey.
Because you got a couple o' halves you think you can act
as you like. (*He pushes the Covey to the door.*) Fluther's a
friend o' mine, an' I'll not have him insulted.

The Covey (*struggling with the Barman*) Ay, leggo, leggo
there; fair hunt, give a man a fair hunt! One minute with
him is all I ask; one minute alone with him, while you're
runnin' for th' priest an' th' doctor.

Fluther (*to the Barman*) Let him go, let him go, Tom: let
him open th' door to sudden death if he wants to!

Barman (*to the Covey*) Go on, out you go an' do th'
bowsey somewhere else. (*He pushes the Covey out and
comes back.*)

Rosie (*getting Fluther's hat as he is putting on his coat*) Be
God, you put th' fear o' God in his heart that time! I
thought you'd have to be dug out of him . . . . Th' way
you lepped out without any of your fancy side-steppin'!
'Men like Fluther', say I to meself, 'is gettin' scarce
nowadays.'

Fluther (*with proud complacency*) I wasn't goin' to let meself be malignified by a chancer. . . . He got a little bit too derogatory for Fluther. . . . Be God, to think of a cur like that comin' to talk to a man like me!

Rosie (*fixing on his hat*) Did j'ever!

Fluther He's lucky he got off safe. I hit a man last week, Rosie, an' he's fallin' yet!

Rosie Sure, you'd ha' broken him in two if you'd ha' hitten him one clatther!

Fluther (*amorously, putting his arm around Rosie*) Come on into th' snug, me little darlin', an' we'll have a few dhrinks before I see you home.

Rosie Oh, Fluther, I'm afraid you're a terrible man for th' women.

> *They go into the snug as Clitheroe, Captain Brennan, and Lieut. Langon of the Irish Volunteers enter hurriedly. Captain Brennan carries the banner of The Plough and the Stars, and Lieut. Langon a green, white and orange Tricolour. They are in a state of emotional excitement. Their faces are flushed and their eyes sparkle; they speak rapidly, as if unaware of the meaning of what they said. They have been mesmerized by the fervency of the speeches.*

Clitheroe (*almost pantingly*) Three glasses o' port!

> *The Barman brings the drinks.*

Capt. Brennan We won't have long to wait now.

Lieut. Langon Th' time is rotten ripe for revolution.

Clitheroe You have a mother, Langon.

Lieut. Langon Ireland is greater than a mother.

Capt. Brennan You have a wife, Clitheroe.

Clitheroe Ireland is greater than a wife.

Lieut. Langon Th' time for Ireland's battle is now – th' place for Ireland's battle is here.

The tall, dark figure again is silhouetted against the window. The three men pause and listen.

Voice of the Man Our foes are strong, but strong as they are, they cannot undo the miracles of God, who ripens in the heart of young men the seeds sown by the young men of a former generation. They think they have pacified Ireland; think they have foreseen everything; think they have provided against everything; but the fools, the fools, the fools! – they have left us our Fenian dead, and, while Ireland holds these graves, Ireland, unfree, shall never be at peace!

Capt. Brennan (*catching up The Plough and the Stars*) Imprisonment for th' Independence of Ireland!

Lieut. Langon (*catching up the Tricolour*) Wounds for th' Independence of Ireland!

Clitheroe Death for th' Independence of Ireland!

The Three (*together*) So help us God!

They drink. A bugle blows the Assembly. They hurry out. A pause. Fluther and Rosie come out of the snug; Rosie is linking Fluther, who is a little drunk. Both are in a merry mood.

Rosie Come on home, ower o' that, man. Are you afraid or what? Are you goin' to come home, or are you not?

Fluther Of course I'm goin' home. What ud ail me that I wouldn't go?

Rosie (*lovingly*) Come on, then, oul' sport.

Officer's Voice (*giving command outside*) Irish Volunteers, by th' right, quick march!

Rosie (*putting her arm round Fluther and singing*)
  I once had a lover, a tailor, but he could do nothin' for
    me,
  An' then I fell in with a sailor as strong an' as wild as th'
    sea.
  We cuddled an' kissed with devotion, till th' night from
    th' mornin' had fled;
  An' there, to our joy, a bright bouncin' boy
  Was dancin' a jig in th' bed!

  Dancin' a jig in th' bed, an' bawlin' for butther an'
    bread.
  An' there, to our joy, a bright bouncin' boy
  Was dancin' a jig in th' bed!

  They go out with their arms round each other.

Clitheroe's Voice (*in command outside*) Dublin Battalion
of the Irish Citizen Army, by th' right, quick march!

  Curtain.

Act Three

*The corner house in a street of tenements: it is the home
of the Clitheroes. The house is a long, gaunt, five-storey
tenement; its brick front is chipped and scarred with age
and neglect. The wide and heavy hall door, flanked by
two pillars, has a look of having been charred by a fire in
the distant past. The door lurches a little to one side,
disjointed by the continual and reckless banging when it is
being closed by most of the residents. The diamond-paned
fanlight is destitute of a single pane, the framework alone
remaining. The windows, except the two looking into the
front parlour (Clitheroe's room), are grimy, and are
draped with fluttering and soiled fragments of lace
curtains. The front parlour windows are hung with rich,
comparatively, casement cloth. Five stone steps lead from
the door to the path on the street. Branching on each side
are railings to prevent people from falling into the area. At
the left corner of the house runs a narrow lane, bisecting
the street, and connecting it with another of the same kind.
At the corner of the lane is a street lamp.*

*As the house is revealed, Mrs Gogan is seen helping
Mollser to a chair, which stands on the path beside the
railings, at the left side of the steps. She then wraps a
shawl around Mollser's shoulders. It is some months later.*

Mrs Gogan (*arranging shawl around Mollser*) Th' sun'll
do you all th' good in th' world. A few more weeks o' this
weather, an' there's no knowin' how well you'll be . . . .
Are you comfy, now?

Mollser (*weakly and wearily*) Yis, ma; I'm all right.

Mrs Gogan How are you feelin'?

Mollser Betther, ma, betther. If th' horrible sinkin' feelin' ud go, I'd be all right.

Mrs Gogan Ah, I wouldn't put much pass on that. Your stomach maybe's out of ordher . . . . Is th' poor breathin' any betther, d'ye think?

Mollser Yis, yis, ma; a lot betther.

Mrs Gogan Well, that's somethin' anyhow . . . . With th' help o' God, you'll be on th' mend from this out . . . . D'your legs feel any sthronger undher you, d'ye think?

Mollser (*irritably*) I can't tell, ma. I think so . . . . A little.

Mrs Gogan Well, a little aself is somethin' . . . . I thought I heard you coughin' a little more than usual last night . . . . D'ye think you were?

Mollser I wasn't, ma, I wasn't.

Mrs Gogan I thought I heard you, for I was kep' awake all night with th' shootin'. An' thinkin' o' that madman, Fluther, runnin' about through th' night lookin' for Nora Clitheroe to bring her back when he heard she'd gone to folly her husband, an' in dhread any minute he might come staggerin' in covered with bandages, splashed all over with th' red of his own blood, an' givin' us barely time to bring th' priest to hear th' last whisper of his final confession, as his soul was passin' through th' dark doorway o' death into th' way o' th' wondherin' dead . . . . You don't feel cold, do you?

Mollser No, ma; I'm all right.

Mrs Gogan Keep your chest well covered, for that's th' delicate spot in you . . . . if there's any danger, I'll whip you in again . . . . (*Looking up the street*) Oh, here's th' Covey an' oul' Pether hurryin' along. God Almighty,

sthrange things is happenin' when them two is pullin'
together.

The Covey and Peter come in, breathless and excited.

(*To the two men*) Were yous far up th' town? Did yous see
any sign o' Fluther or Nora? How is things lookin'? I hear
they're blazin' away out o' th' GPO. That th' Tommies is
sthretched in heaps around Nelson's Pillar an' th' Parnell
Statue, an' that th' pavin' sets in O'Connell Street is nearly
covered be pools o' blood.

Peter We seen no sign o' Nora or Fluther anywhere.

Mrs Gogan We should ha' held her back be main force
from goin' to look for her husband . . . . God knows
what's happened to her – I'm always seein' her sthretched
on her back in some hospital, moanin' with th' pain of a
bullet in her vitals, an' nuns thryin' to get her to take a last
look at th' crucifix!

The Covey We can do nothin'. You can't stick your nose
into O'Connell Street, an' Tyler's is on fire.

Peter An' we seen th' Lancers –

The Covey (*interrupting*) Throttin' along, heads in th' air;
spurs an' sabres jinglin', an' lances quiverin', an' lookin' as
if they were assin' themselves, 'Where's these blighters, till
we get a prod at them?' when there was a volley from th'
Post Office that stretched half o' them, an' sent th' rest
gallopin' away wondherin' how far they'd have to go
before they'd feel safe.

Peter (*rubbing his hands*) 'Damn it,' says I to meself, 'this
looks like business!'

The Covey An' then out comes General Pearse an' his
staff, an', standin' in th' middle o' th' street, he reads th'
Proclamation.

Mrs Gogan What proclamation?

Peter Declarin' an Irish Republic.

Mrs Gogan Go to God!

Peter The gunboat *Helga*'s shellin' Liberty Hall, an' I hear the people livin' on th' quays had to crawl on their bellies to Mass with th' bullets that were flyin' around from Boland's Mills.

Mrs Gogan God bless us, what's goin' to be th' end of it all!

Bessie (*looking out of the top window*) Maybe yous are satisfied now; maybe yous are satisfied now. Go on an' get guns if yous are men – Johnny get your gun, get your gun, get your gun! Yous are all nicely shanghaied now; th' boyo hasn't a sword on his thigh now! Oh, yous are all nicely shanghaied now!

Mrs Gogan (*warningly to Peter and the Covey*) S-s-sh, don't answer her. She's th' right oul' Orange bitch! She's been chantin' 'Rule, Britannia' all th' mornin'.

Peter I hope Fluther hasn't met with any accident, he's such a wild card.

Mrs Gogan God grant it; but last night I dreamt I seen gettin' carried into th' house a sthretcher with a figure lyin' on it, stiff an' still, dhressed in th' habit of Saint Francis. An, then, I heard th' murmurs of a crowd no one could see sayin' th' litany for th' dead; an' then it got so dark that nothin' was seen but th' white face of th' corpse, gleamin' like a white wather-lily floatin' on th' top of a dark lake. Then a tiny whisper thrickled into me ear, sayin', 'Isn't the face very like th' face o' Fluther?' an' then, with a thremblin' flutther, th' dead lips opened, an', although I couldn't hear, I knew they were sayin', 'Poor oul' Fluther, afther havin' handed in his gun at last, his shakin' soul moored in th' place where th' wicked are at rest an' th' weary cease from throublin'.'

Peter (*who has put on a pair of spectacles, and has been looking down the street*) Here they are, be God, here they are; just afther turnin' th' corner – Nora an' Fluther!

The Covey She must be wounded or something – he seems to be carryin' her.

Fluther and Nora enter. Fluther has his arm around her and is half leading, half carrying her in. Her eyes are dim and hollow, her face pale and strained-looking; her hair is tossed, and her clothes are dusty.

Mrs Gogan (*running over to them*) God bless us, is it wounded y'are, Mrs Clitheroe, or what?

Fluther Ah, she's all right, Mrs Gogan; only worn out from thravellin' an' want o' sleep. A night's rest, now, an' she'll be as fit as a fiddle. Bring her in, an' make her lie down.

Mrs Gogan (*to Nora*) Did you hear e'er a whisper o' Mr Clitheroe?

Nora (*wearily*) I could find him nowhere, Mrs Gogan. None o' them would tell me where he was. They told me I shamed my husband an' th' women of Ireland be carryin' on as I was . . . . They said th' women must learn to be brave an' cease to be cowardly . . . . Me who risked more for love than they would risk for hate . . . . (*Raising her voice in hysterical protest*) My Jack will be killed, my Jack will be killed! . . . He is to be butchered as a sacrifice to th' dead!

Bessie (*from upper window*) Yous are all nicely shanghaied now! Sorra mend th' lasses that have been kissin' an' cuddlin' their boys into th' sheddin' of blood! . . . Fillin' their minds with fairy tales that had no

beginnin', but, please God, 'll have a bloody quick endin'!
. . . Turnin' bitther into sweet, an' sweet into bitther . . . .
Stabbin' in th' back th' men that are dyin' in th' threnches
for them! It's a bad thing for anyone that thries to jilt th'
Ten Commandments, for judgements are prepared for
scorners an' sthripes for th' back o' fools! (*Going away
from window as she sings*)

> Rule, Britannia, Brittania rules th' waves,
> Britons never, never, never shall be slaves!

Fluther (*with a roar up at the window*) Y'ignorant oul'
throllope, you!

Mrs Gogan (*to Nora*) He'll come home safe enough to
you, you'll find, Mrs Clitheroe; afther all, there's a power
o' women that's handed over sons an' husbands to take a
runnin' risk in th' fight they're wagin'.

Nora I can't help thinkin' every shot fired 'll be fired at
Jack, an' every shot fired at Jack 'll be fired at me. What
do I care for th' others? I can think only of me own self
. . . . An' there's no woman gives a son or a husband to be
killed – if they say it, they're lyin', lyin', against God,
Nature, an' against themselves! . . . One blasted hussy
at a barricade told me to go home an' not be thryin' to
dishearten th' men . . . . That I wasn't worthy to bear a
son to a man that was out fightin' for freedom I
clawed at her, an' smashed her in th' face till we were
separated . . . . I was pushed down th' street, an' I cursed
them – cursed the rebel ruffians an' Volunteers that had
dhragged me ravin' mad into th' sthreets to seek me
husband!

Peter You'll have to have patience, Nora. We all have to
put up with twarthers an' tormentors in this world.

The Covey If they were fightin' for anything worth while,
I wouldn't mind.

Fluther (*to Nora*) Nothin' derogatory 'll happen to Mr Clitheroe. You'll find, now, in th' finish up it'll be vice versa.

Nora Oh, I know that wherever he is, he's thinkin' of wantin' to be with me. I know he's longin' to be passin' his hand through me hair, to be caressin' me neck, to fondle me hand an' to feel me kisses clingin' to his mouth . . . An' he stands wherever he is because he's brave? (*Vehemently*) No, but because he's a coward, a coward, a coward!

Mrs Gogan Oh, they're not cowards anyway.

Nora (*with denunciatory anger*) I tell you they're afraid to say they're afraid! . . . Oh, I saw it, I saw it, Mrs Gogan . . . . At th' barricade in North King Street I saw fear glowin' in all their eyes . . . . An' in th' middle o' th' sthreet was somethin' huddled up in a horrible, tangled heap . . . . His face was jammed again th' stones, an' his arm was twisted round his back . . . . An' every twist of his body was a cry against th' terrible thing that had happened to him . . . . An' I saw they were afraid to look at it . . . . An' some o' them laughed at me, but th' laugh was a frightened one . . . . An' some o' them shouted at me, but th' shout had in it th' shiver o' fear . . . . I tell you they were afraid, afraid, afraid!

Mrs Gogan (*leading her towards the house*) Come on in, dear. If you'd been a little longer together, th' wrench asundher wouldn't have been so sharp.

Nora Th' agony I'm in since he left me has thrust away every rough thing he done, an' every unkind word he spoke; only th' blossoms that grew out of our lives are before me now; shakin' their colours before me face, an' breathin' their sweet scent on every thought springin' up in me mind, till, sometimes, Mrs Gogan, sometimes I think I'm goin' mad!

Mrs Gogan You'll be a lot betther when you have a little lie down.

Nora (*turning towards Fluther as she is going in*) I don't know what I'd have done, only for Fluther. I'd have been lyin' in th' streets, only for him . . . . (*As she goes in*) They have dhriven away th' little happiness life had to spare for me. He has gone from me for ever, for ever . . . . Oh, Jack, Jack, Jack!

> *She is led in by Mrs Gogan as Bessie comes out with a shawl around her shoulders. She passes by them with her head in the air. When they have gone in, she gives a mug of milk to Mollser silently.*

Fluther Which of yous has th' tossers?

The Covey I have.

Bessie (*as she is passing them to go down the street*) You an' your Leadhers an' their sham-battle soldiers has landed a body in a nice way, havin' to go an' ferret out a bit o' bread God knows where . . . . Why aren't yous in th' GPO if yous are men? It's paler an' paler yous are gettin' . . . . A lot o' vipers, that's what th' Irish people is! (*She goes out.*)

Fluther Never mind her . . . . (*To the Covey*) Make a start an' keep us from th' sin o' idleness. (*To Mollser*) Well, how are you today, Mollser, oul' son? What are you dhrinkin', milk?

Mollser Grand, Fluther, grand, thanks. Yis, milk.

Fluther You couldn't get a betther thing down you . . . . This turn-up has done one good thing, anyhow; you can't get dhrink anywhere, an' if it lasts a week, I'll be so used to it that I won't think of a pint.

The Covey (*who has taken from his pocket two worn*

coins and a thin strip of wood about four inches long)
What's th' bettin'?

Peter Heads, a juice.

Fluther Harps, a tanner.

*The Covey places the coins on the strip of wood, and
flips them up into the air. As they jingle on the ground
the distant boom of a big gun is heard. They stand for a
moment listening.*

What th' hell's that?

The Covey It's like th' boom of a big gun!

Fluther Surely to God they're not goin' to use artillery on us?

The Covey (*scornfully*) Not goin'! (*Vehemently*) Wouldn't
they use anything on us, man?

Fluther Aw, holy Christ, that's not playin' th' game!

Peter (*plaintively*) What would happen if a shell landed
here now?

The Covey (*ironically*) You'd be off to heaven in a fiery
chariot.

Peter In spite of all th' warnin's that's ringin' around us,
are you goin' to start your pickin' at me again?

Fluther Go on, toss them again, toss them again . . . .
Harps, a tanner.

Peter Heads, a juice.

The Covey tosses the coins.

Fluther (*as the coins fall*) Let them roll, let them roll.
Heads, be God!

*Bessie runs in excitedly. She has a new hat on her head,
a fox fur round her neck over her shawl, three umbrellas*

under her right arm, and a box of biscuits under her left.
She speaks rapidly and breathlessly.

Bessie They're breakin' into th' shops, they're breakin'
into th' shops! Smashin' th' windows, battherin' in th'
doors, an' whippin' away everything! An' th' Volunteers is
firin' on them. I seen two men an' a lassie pushin' a piano
down th' sthreet, an' th' sweat rollin' off them thryin' to
get it up on th' pavement; an' an oul' wan that must ha'
been seventy lookin' as if she'd dhrop every minute with
th' dint o' heart beatin', thryin' to pull a big double bed
out of a broken shop-window! I was goin' to wait till I
dhressed meself from th' skin out.

Mollser (*to Bessie, as she is going in*) Help me in, Bessie;
I'm feelin' curious.

Bessie leaves the looted things in the house, and, rapidly
returning, helps Mollser in.

The Covey Th' selfishness of that one – she waited till she
got all she could carry before she'd come to tell anyone!

Fluther (*running over to the door of the house and*
shouting in to Bessie) Ay, Bessie, did you hear of e'er a pub
gettin' a shake up?

Bessie (*inside*) I didn't hear o' none.

Fluther (*in a burst of enthusiasm*) Well, you're goin' to
hear of one soon!

The Covey Come on, man, an' don't be wastin' time.

Peter (*to them as they are about to run off*) Ay, ay, are you
goin' to leave me here?

Fluther Are you goin' to leave yourself here?

Peter (*anxiously*) Didn't yous hear her sayin' they were
firin' on them?

The Covey and Fluther (*together*) Well?

Peter Supposin' I happened to be potted?

Fluther We'd give you a Christian burial, anyhow.

The Covey (*ironically*) Dhressed up in your regimentals.

Peter (*to the Covey, passionately*) May th' all-lovin' God give you a hot knock one o' these days, me young Covey, tuthorin' Fluther up now to be tiltin' at me, an' crossin' me with his mockeries an' jibin'!

A fashionably dressed, middle-aged, stout woman comes hurriedly in, and makes for the group. She is almost fainting with fear.

Woman For Gawd's sake, will one of you kind men show any safe way for me to get to Wrathmines? . . . I was foolish enough to visit a friend, thinking the howl thing was a joke, and now I cawn't get a car or a tram to take me home – isn't it awful?

Fluther I'm afraid, ma'am, one way is as safe as another.

Woman And what am I gowing to do? Oh, isn't this awful? . . . I'm so different from others . . . . The mowment I hear a shot, my legs give way under me – I cawn't stir, I'm paralysed – isn't it awful?

Fluther (*moving away*) It's a derogatory way to be, right enough, ma'am.

Woman (*catching Fluther's coat*) Creeping along the street there, with my head down and my eyes half shut, a bullet whizzed past within an inch of my nowse. . . . I had to lean against the wall for a long time, gasping for breath – I nearly passed away – it was awful! . . . I wonder, would you kind men come some of the way and see me safe?

Fluther I have to go away, ma'am, to thry an' save a few things from th' burnin' buildin's.

The Covey Come on, then, or there won't be anything left to save.

The Covey and Fluther hurry away.

Woman (*to Peter*) Wasn't it an awful thing for me to leave my friend's house? Wasn't it an idiotic thing to do? . . . I haven't the slightest idea where I am . . . . You have a kind face, sir. Could you possibly come and pilot me in the direction of Wrathmines?

Peter (*indignantly*) D'ye think I'm goin' to risk me life throttin' in front of you? An' maybe get a bullet that would gimme a game leg or something that would leave me a jibe an' a jeer to Fluther an' th' young Covey for th' rest o' me days! (*With an indignant toss of his head he walks into the house.*)

Woman (*going out*) I know I'll fall down in a dead faint if I hear another shot go off anyway near me – isn't it awful!

Mrs Gogan comes out of the house pushing a pram before her. As she enters the street, Bessie rushes out, follows Mrs Gogan, and catches hold of the pram, stopping Mrs Gogan's progress.

Bessie Here, where are you goin' with that? How quick you were, me lady, to clap your eyes on th' pram . . . . Maybe you don't know that Mrs Sullivan, before she went to spend Easther with her people in Dunboyne, gave me sthrict injunctions to give an accasional look to see if it was still standin' where it was left in th' corner of th' lobby.

Mrs Gogan That remark of yours, Mrs Bessie Burgess, requires a little considheration, seein' that th' pram was left on our lobby, an' not on yours; a foot or two a little to th' left of th' jamb of me own room door; nor is it needful to mention th' name of th' person that gave a squint to see if it was there th' first thing in th' mornin', an' th' last thing in th' stillness o' th' night; never failin' to realize that her eyes couldn't be goin' wrong, be sthretchin' out her arm an' runnin' her hand over th' pram, to make sure that th' sight was no deception! Moreover, somethin's tellin' me that th' runnin' hurry of an inthrest you're takin' in it now is a sudden ambition to use th' pram for a purpose that a loyal woman of law an' ordher would stagger away from! (*She gives the pram a sudden push that pulls Bessie forward.*)

Bessie (*still holding the pram*) There's not as much as one body in th' house that doesn't know that it wasn't Bessie Burgess that was always shakin' her voice complainin' about people leavin' bassinettes in th' way of them that, week in an' week out, had to pay their rent, an' always had to find a regular accommodation for her own furniture in her own room . . . . An' as for law an' ordher, puttin' aside th' harp an' shamrock, Bessie Burgess 'll have as much respect as she wants for th' lion an' unicorn!

Peter (*appearing at the door*) I think I'll go with th' pair of yous an' see th' fun. A fella might as well chance it, anyhow.

Mrs Gogan (*taking no notice of Peter, and pushing the pram on another step*) Take your rovin' lumps o' hands from pattin' th' bassinette, if you please, ma'am; an', steppin' from th' threshold of good manners, let me tell you, Mrs Burgess, that's it's a fat wondher to Jennie Gogan that a lady-like singer o' hymns like yourself would lower her thoughts from sky-thinkin' to sthretch out her arm in a sly-seekin' way to pinch anything dhriven asthray in th' confusion of th' battle our boys is makin' for th' freedom of their counthry!

Peter (*laughing and rubbing his hands together*) Hee, hee, hee, hee, hee! I'll go with th' pair o' yous an' give yous a hand.

Mrs Gogan (*with a rapid turn of her head as she shoves the pram forward*) Get up in th' prambulator an' we'll wheel you down.

Bessie (*to Mrs Gogan*) Poverty an' hardship has sent Bessie Burgess to abide with sthrange company, but she always knew them she had to live with from backside to breakfast time; an' she can tell them, always havin' had a Christian kinch on her conscience, that a passion for thievin' an' pinchin' would find her soul a foreign place to live in, an' that her present intention is quite th' lofty-hearted one of pickin' up anything shaken up an' scatthered about in th' loose confusion of a general plundher!

> *By this time they have disappeared from view. Peter is following, when the boom of a big gun in the distance brings him to a quick halt.*

Peter God Almighty, that's th' big gun again! God forbid any harm would happen to them, but sorra mind I'd mind if they met with a dhrop in their mad endeyvours to plundher an' desthroy.

> *He looks down the street for a moment, then runs to the hall door of the house, which is open, and shuts it with a vicious pull; he then goes to the chair in which Mollser had sat, sits down, takes out his pipe, lights it and begins to smoke with his head carried at a haughty angle. The Covey comes staggering in with a ten-stone sack of flour on his back. On the top of the sack is a ham. He goes over to the door, pushes it with his head, and finds he can't open it; he turns slightly in the direction of Peter.*

The Covey (*to Peter*) Who shut th' door? . . . (*He kicks at it.*) Here, come on an' open it, will you? This isn't a mot's hand-bag I've got on me back.

Peter Now, me young Covey, d'ye think I'm goin' to be your lackey?

The Covey (*angrily*) Will you open th' door, y'oul' –

Peter (*shouting*) Don't be assin' me to open any door, don't be assin' me to open any door for you . . . . Makin' a shame an' a sin o' th' cause that good men are fightin' for . . . . Oh, God forgive th' people that, instead o' burnishin' th' work th' boys is doin' today with quiet honesty an' patience, is revilin' their sacrifices with a riot of lootin' an' roguery!

The Covey Isn't your own eyes leppin' out o' your head with envy that you haven't th' guts to ketch a few o' th' things that God is givin' to His chosen people? . . . Y'oul' hypocrite, if everyone was blind you'd steal a cross off an ass's back!

Peter (*very calmly*) You're not going to make me lose me temper; you can go on with your proddin' as long as you like; goad an' goad an' goad away; hee, hee, heee! I'll not lose me temper.

Somebody opens door and the Covey goes in.

The Covey (*inside, mockingly*) Cuckoo-oo!

Peter (*running to the door and shouting in a blaze of passion as he follows the Covey in*) You lean, long, lanky lath of a lowsey bastard . . . . (*Following him in*) Lowsey bastard, lowsey bastard!

Bessie and Mrs Gogan enter, the pride of a great joy illuminating their faces. Bessie is pushing the pram, which is filled with clothes and boots; on the top of the boots and clothes is a fancy table, which Mrs Gogan is holding on with her left hand, while with her right hand she holds a chair on the top of her head. They are heard talking to each other before they enter.

Mrs Gogan (*outside*) I don't remember ever havin' seen such lovely pairs as them, (*they appear*) with th' pointed toes an' th' cuban heels.

Bessie They'll go grand with th' dhresses we're afther liftin', when we've stitched a sthray bit o' silk to lift th' bodices up a little bit higher, so as to shake th' shame out o' them, an' make them fit for women that hasn't lost themselves in th' nakedness o' th' times.

They fussily carry in the chair, the table, and some of the other goods. They return to bring in the rest.

Peter (*at door, sourly to Mrs Gogan*) Ay, you. Mollser looks as if she was goin' to faint, an' your youngster is roarin' in convulsions in her lap.

Mrs Gogan (*snappily*) She's never any other way but faintin'!

She goes to go in with some things in her arms, when a shot from a rifle rings out. She and Bessie make a bolt for the door, which Peter, in a panic, tries to shut before they have got inside.

Ay, ay, ay, you cowardly oul' fool, what are you thryin' to shut th' door on us for?

They retreat tumultuously inside. A pause; then Captain Brennan comes in supporting Lieutenant Langon, whose arm is around Brennan's neck. Langon's face, which is ghastly white, is momentarily convulsed with spasms of agony. He is in a state of collapse, and Brennan is almost carrying him. After a few moments Clitheroe, pale, and in a state of calm nervousness, follows, looking back in the direction from which he came, a rifle, held at the ready, in his hands.

Capt. Brennan (*savagely to Clitheroe*) Why did you fire over their heads? Why didn't you fire to kill?

Clitheroe No, no, Bill; bad as they are they're Irish men an' women.

Capt. Brennan (*savagely*) Irish be damned! Attackin' an' mobbin' th' men that are riskin' their lives for them. If these slum lice gather at our heels again, plug one o' them, or I'll soon shock them with a shot or two meself!

Lieut. Langon (*moaningly*) My God, is there ne'er an ambulance knockin' around anywhere? . . . Th' stomach is ripped out o' me; I feel it – o-o-oh, Christ!

Capt. Brennan Keep th' heart up, Jim; we'll soon get help, now.

> *Nora rushes wildly out of the house and flings her arms round the neck of Clitheroe with a fierce and joyous insistence. Her hair is down, her face is haggard, but her eyes are agleam with the light of happy relief.*

Nora Jack, Jack, Jack; God be thanked . . . be thanked . . . . He has been kind and merciful to His poor handmaiden . . . . My Jack, my own Jack, that I thought was lost is found, that I thought was dead is alive again! . . . Oh, God be praised for ever, evermore! . . . My poor Jack . . . . Kiss me, kiss me, Jack, kiss your own Nora!

Clitheroe (*kissing her, and speaking brokenly*) My Nora; my little, beautiful Nora, I wish to God I'd never left you.

Nora It doesn' t matter – not now, not now, Jack. It will make us dearer than ever to each other . . . . Kiss me, kiss me again.

Clitheroe Now, for God's sake, Nora, don't make a scene.

Nora I won't, I won't; I promise, I promise, Jack; honest to God. I'll be silent an' brave to bear th' joy of feelin' you safe in my arms again . . . . It's hard to force away th' tears of happiness at th' end of an awful agony.

Bessie (*from the upper window*) Th' Minsthrel Boys aren't feelin' very comfortable now. Th' big guns has knocked all th' harps out of their hands. General Clitheroe'd rather be unlacin' his wife's bodice than standin' at a barricade . . . . An' th' professor of chicken-butcherin' there, finds he's up against somethin' a little tougher even than his own chickens, an' that's sayin' a lot!

Capt. Brennan (*up to Bessie*) Shut up, y'oul' hag!

Bessie (*down to Brennan*) Choke th' chicken, choke th' chicken, choke th' chicken!

Lieut. Langon For God's sake, Bill, bring me some place where me wound 'll be looked afther . . . . Am I to die before anything is done to save me?

Capt. Brennan (*to Clitheroe*) Come on, Jack. We've got to get help for Jim, here – have you no thought for his pain an' danger?

Bessie Choke th' chicken, choke th' chicken, choke th' chicken!

Clitheroe (*to Nora*) Loosen me, darling, let me go.

Nora (*clinging to him*) No, no, no, I'll not let you go! Come on, come up to our home, Jack, my sweetheart, my lover, my husband, an' we'll forget th' last few terrible days! . . . I look tired now, but a few hours of happy rest in your arms will bring back th' bloom of freshness again, an' you will be glad, you will be glad, glad . . . glad!

Lieut. Langon Oh, if I'd kep' down only a little longer, I mightn't ha' been hit! Everyone else escapin', an' me gettin' me belly ripped asundher! . . . I couldn't scream, couldn't even scream . . . . D'ye think I'm really badly wounded, Bill? Me clothes seem to be all soakin' wet . . . . It's blood . . . My God, it must be me own blood!

Capt. Brennan (*to Clitheroe*) Go on, Jack, bid her goodbye with another kiss, an' be done with it! D'ye want Langon to die in me arms while you're dallyin' with your Nora?

Clitheroe (*to Nora*) I must go, I must go, Nora. I'm sorry we met at all . . . . It couldn't be helped – all other ways were blocked be th' British . . . . Let me go, can't you, Nora? D'ye want me to be unthrue to me comrades?

Nora No, I won't let you go . . . . I want you to be thrue to me, Jack . . . . I'm your dearest comrade; I'm your thruest comrade . . . . They only want th' comfort of havin' you in th' same danger as themselves . . . . Oh, Jack, I can't let you go!

Clitheroe You must, Nora, you must.

Nora All last night at th' barricades I sought you, Jack . . . . I didn't think of th' danger – I could only think of you . . . . I asked for you everywhere . . . . Some o' them laughed . . . . I was pushed away, but I shoved back . . . . Some o' them even sthruck me, . . . an' I screamed an' screamed your name!

Clitheroe (*in fear her action would give him future shame*) What possessed you to make a show of yourself, like that? . . . What way d'ye think I'll feel when I'm told my wife was bawlin' for me at th' barricades? What are you more than any other woman?

Nora No more, maybe; but you are more to me than any other man, Jack . . . . I didn't mean any harm, honestly, Jack . . . . I couldn't help it . . . . I shouldn't have told you . . . . My love for you made me mad with terror.

Clitheroe (*angrily*) They'll say now that I sent you out th' way I'd have an excuse to bring you home . . . . Are you goin' to turn all th' risks I'm takin' into a laugh?

Lieut. Langon Let me lie down, let me lie down, Bill; th'
pain would be easier, maybe, lyin' down . . . . Oh, God,
have mercy on me!

Capt. Brennan (*to Langon*) A few steps more, Jim, a few
steps more; thry to stick it for a few steps more.

Lieut. Langon Oh, I can't, I can't, I can't!

Capt. Brennan (*to Clitheroe*) Are you comin', man, or are
you goin' to make an arrangement for another
honeymoon? . . . If you want to act th' renegade, say so,
an' we'll be off!

Bessie (*from above*) Runnin' from th' Tommies – choke
th' chicken. Runnin' from th' Tommies – choke th'
chicken!

Clitheroe (*savagely to Brennan*) Damn you, man, who
wants to act th' renegade? (*to Nora*) Here, let go your
hold; let go, I say!

Nora (*clinging to Clitheroe, and indicating Brennan*)
Look, Jack, look at th' anger in his face; look at th' fear
glintin' in his eyes . . . . He himself's afraid, afraid, afraid!
. . . He wants you to go th' way he'll have th' chance of
death sthrikin' you an' missin' him! . . . Turn round an'
look at him, Jack, look at him, look at him! . . . His very
soul is cold . . . shiverin' with th' thought of what may
happen to him . . . . It is his fear that is thryin' to frighten
you from recognizin' th' same fear that is in your own
heart!

Clitheroe (*struggling to release himself from Nora*) Damn
you, woman, will you let me go!

Capt. Brennan (*fiercely, to Clitheroe*) Why are you
beggin' her to let you go? Are you afraid of her, or what?
Break her hold on you, man, or go up, an' sit on her lap!

Clitheroe tries roughly to break Nora's hold.

Nora (*imploringly*) Oh, Jack . . . . Jack . . . . Jack!

Lieut. Langon (*agonizingly*) Brennan, a priest; I'm dyin', I think, I'm dyin'!

Clitheroe (*to Nora*) If you won't do it quietly, I'll have to make you! (*To Brennan*) Here, hold this gun, you, for a minute. (*He hands the gun to Brennan.*)

Nora (*pitifully*) Please, Jack . . . . You're hurting me, Jack . . . . Honestly . . . . Oh, you're hurting . . . me! . . . I won't, I won't, I won't! . . . Oh, Jack, I gave you everything you asked of me . . . . Don't fling me from you, now!

> *Clitheroe roughly loosens her grip, and pushes her away from him. Nora sinks to the ground and lies there.*

(*Weakly*) Ah, Jack . . . . Jack . . . . Jack!

Clitheroe (*taking the gun back from Brennan*) Come on, come on.

> *They go out. Bessie looks at Nora lying on the street, for a few moments, then, leaving the window, she comes out, runs over to Nora, lifts her up in her arms, and carries her swiftly into the house. A short pause, then down the street is heard a wild, drunken yell; it comes nearer, and Fluther enters, frenzied, wild-eyed, mad, roaring drunk. In his arms is an earthen half-gallon jar of whiskey; streaming from one of the pockets of his coat is the arm of a new tunic shirt; on his head is a woman's vivid blue hat with gold lacing, all of which he has looted.*

Fluther (*singing in a frenzy*)
Fluther's a jolly good fella! . . . Fluther's a jolly good
    fella!

Up th' rebels! . . . That nobody can deny!

(*He beats on the door.*) Get us a mug or a jug, or somethin', some o' yous, one o' yous, will yous, before I lay one o' yous out! . . . (*Looking down the street*) Bang an' fire away for all Fluther cares . . . . (*Banging at door*) Come down an' open th' door, some of yous, one o' yous, will yous, before I lay some o' yous out! . . . Th' whole city can topple home to hell, for Fluther!

> *Inside the house is heard a scream from Nora, followed by a moan.*

Fluther (*singing furiously*)
   That nobody can deny, that nobody can deny,
   For Fluther's a jolly good fella, Fluther's a jolly good
      fella,
   Fluther's a jolly good fella . . . Up th' rebels! That
      nobody can deny!

(*His frantic movements cause him to spill some of the whiskey out of the jar.*) Blast you, Fluther, don't be spillin' th' precious liquor! (*He kicks at the door.*) Ay, give us a mug or a jug or somethin', one o' yous, some o' yous, will yous, before I lay one o' yous out!

> *The door suddenly opens, and Bessie, coming out, grips him by the collar.*

Bessie (*indignantly*) You bowsey, come in ower o' that . . . . I'll thrim your thricks o' dhrunken dancin' for you, an' none of us knowin' how soon we'll bump into a world we were never in before!

Fluther (*as she is pulling him in*) Ay, th' jar, th' jar, th' jar!

> *A short pause, then again is heard a scream of pain from Nora. The door opens and Mrs Gogan and Bessie are seen standing at it.*

Bessie Fluther would go, only he's too dhrunk . . . . Oh, God, isn't it a pity he's so dhrunk! We'll have to thry to get a docthor somewhere.

Mrs Gogan I'd be afraid to go . . . . Besides, Mollser's terrible bad. I don't think you'll get a docthor to come. It's hardly any use goin'.

Bessie (*determinedly*) I'll risk it . . . . Give her a little of Fluther's whiskey . . . . It's th' fright that's brought it on her so soon . . . . Go on back to her, you.

Mrs Gogan goes in, and Bessie softly closes the door. She is moving forward, when the sound of some rifle shots, and the tok, tok, tok of a distant machine-gun bring her to a sudden halt. She hesitates for a moment, then she tightens her shawl round her, as if it were a shield, then she firmly and swiftly goes out.

(*As she goes out*) Oh, God, be Thou my help in time o' throuble. An' shelter me safely in th' shadow of Thy wings!

Curtain.

Act Four

The living-room of Bessie Burgess. It is one of two small attic rooms (the other, used as a bedroom, is to the left), the ceiling slopes up towards the back, giving to the apartment a look of compressed confinement. In the centre of the ceiling is a small skylight. There is an unmistakable air of poverty bordering on destitution. The paper on the walls is torn and soiled, particularly near the fire where the cooking is done, and near the washstand where the washing is done. The fireplace is to the left. A small armchair near fire. One small window at back. A pane of this window is starred by the entrance of a bullet. Under the window to the right is an oak coffin standing on two kitchen chairs. Near the coffin is a home-manufactured stool, on which are two lighted candles. Beside the window is a worn-out dresser on which is a small quantity of delft. Tattered remains of cheap lace curtains drape the window. Standing near the window on left is a brass standard-lamp with a fancy shade; hanging on the wall near the same window is a vividly crimson silk dress, both of which have been looted. A door on left leading to the bedroom. Another opposite giving a way to the rest of the house. To the left of this door a common washstand. A tin kettle, very black, and an old saucepan inside the fender. There is no light in the room but that given from the two candles and the fire. The dusk has well fallen, and the glare of the burning buildings in the town can be seen through the window, in the distant sky. The Covey and Fluther have been playing cards, sitting on the floor by the light of the candles on the stool near the coffin. When the curtain rises the Covey is shuffling the cards, Peter is sitting in a stiff,

140

dignified way beside him, and Fluther is kneeling beside the
window, cautiously looking out. It is a few days later.

Fluther (*furtively peeping out of the window*) Give them a
good shuffling . . . . Th' sky's gettin' reddher an' reddher
. . . . You'd think it was afire . . . . Half o' th' city must be
burnin'.

The Covey If I was you, Fluther, I'd keep away from that
window . . . . It's dangerous, an' besides, if they see you,
you'll only bring a nose on th' house.

Peter Yes; an' he knows we had to leave our own place th'
way they were riddlin' it with machine-gun fire . . . . He'll
keep on pimpin' and pimpin' there, till we have to fly out
o' this place too.

Fluther (*ironically*) If they make any attack here, we'll
send you out in your green an' glory uniform, shakin' your
sword over your head, an' they'll fly before you as th'
Danes flew before Brian Boru!

The Covey (*placing the cards on the floor, after shuffling
them*) Come on, an' cut.

Fluther comes over, sits on floor, and cuts the cards.

(*Having dealt the cards*) Spuds up again.

Nora moans feebly in room on left.

Fluther There, she's at it again. She's been quiet for a long
time, all th' same.

The Covey She was quiet before, sure, an' she broke out
again worse than ever . . . . What was led that time?

Peter Thray o' Hearts, Thray o' Hearts, Thray o' Hearts.

Fluther It's damned hard lines to think of her dead-born
kiddie lyin' there in th' arms o' poor little Mollser. Mollser
snuffed it sudden too, afther all.

The Covey Sure she never got any care. How could she get it, an' th' mother out day an' night lookin' for work, an' her consumptive husband leavin' her with a baby to be born before he died!

Voices (*in a lilting chant to the left in a distant street*) Red Cr . . . oss, Red Cr . . . oss! . . . Ambu . . . lance, Ambu . . . lance!

The Covey (*to Fluther*) Your deal, Fluther.

Fluther (*shuffling and dealing the cards*) It'll take a lot out o' Nora – if she'll ever be th' same.

The Covey The docthor thinks she'll never be th' same; thinks she'll be a little touched here. (*He touches his forehead.*) She's ramblin' a lot; thinkin' she's out in th' counthry with Jack; or gettin' his dinner ready for him before he comes home; or yellin' for her kiddie. All that, though, might be th' chloroform she got . . . . I don't know what we'd have done only for oul' Bessie; up with her for th' past three nights, hand runnin'.

Fluther I always knew there was never anything really derogatory wrong with poor oul' Bessie. (*To Peter, who is taking a trick*) Ay, houl' on, there, don't be so damn quick – that's my thrick.

Peter What's your thrick? It's my thrick, man.

Fluther (*loudly*) How is it your thrick?

Peter (*answering as loudly*) Didn't I lead th' deuce!

Fluther You must be gettin' blind, man; don't you see th' ace?

Bessie (*appearing at door of room, left; in a tense whisper*) D'ye want to waken her again on me, when she's just gone asleep? If she wakes will yous come an' mind

142

her? If I hear a whisper out o' one o' yous again, I'll . . . gut yous!

The Covey (*in a whisper*) S-s-s-h. She can hear anything above a whisper.

Peter (*looking up at the ceiling*) Th' gentle an' merciful God 'll give th' pair o' yous a scawldin' an' a scarifyin' one o' these days!

Fluther takes a bottle of whiskey from his pocket, and takes a drink.

The Covey (*to Fluther*) Why don't you spread that out, man, an' thry to keep a sup for tomorrow?

Fluther Spread it out? Keep a sup for tomorrow? How th' hell does a fella know there'll be any tomorrow? If I'm goin' to be whipped away, let me be whipped away when it's empty, an' not when it's half full! (*To Bessie, who has seated herself in an armchair at the fire*) How is she, now, Bessie?

Bessie I left her sleeping quietly. When I'm listenin' to her babblin', I think she'll never be much betther than she is. Her eyes have a hauntin' way of lookin' in instead of lookin' out, as if her mind had been lost alive in madly minglin' memories of th' past . . . . (*Sleepily*) Crushin' her thoughts . . . together . . . in a fierce . . . an' fanciful . . . (*she nods her head and starts wakefully*) idea that dead things are livin', an' livin' things are dead . . . . (*with a start*) Was that a scream I heard her give? (*Reassured*) Blessed God, I think I hear her screamin' every minute! An' it's only there with me that I'm able to keep awake.

The Covey She'll sleep, maybe, for a long time, now. Ten there.

Fluther Ten here. If she gets a long sleep, she might be all right. Peter's th' lone five.

The Covey Whisht! I think I hear somebody movin'
below. Whoever it is, he's comin' up.

*A pause. Then the door opens and Captain Brennan
comes into the room. He has changed his uniform for a
suit of civvies. His eyes droop with the heaviness of
exhaustion; his face is pallid and drawn. His clothes are
dusty and stained here and there with mud. He leans
heavily on the back of a chair as he stands.*

Capt. Brennan Mrs Clitheroe; where's Mrs Clitheroe? I
was told I'd find her here.

Bessie What d'ye want with Mrs Clitheroe?

Capt. Brennan I've a message, a last message for her from
her husband.

Bessie Killed! He's not killed, is he!

Capt. Brennan (*sinking stiffly and painfully on to a chair*)
In th' Imperial Hotel; we fought till th' place was in
flames. He was shot through th' arm, an' then through th'
lung . . . . I could do nothin' for him – only watch his
breath comin' an' goin' in quick, jerky gasps, an' a tiny
sthream o' blood thricklin' out of his mouth, down over
his lower lip . . . . I said a prayer for th' dyin', an' twined
his Rosary beads around his fingers . . . . Then I had to
leave him to save meself . . . . (*He shows some holes in his
coat.*) Look at th' way a machine-gun tore at me coat, as I
belted out o' th' buildin' an' darted across th' sthreet for
shelter . . . . An' then, I seen The Plough an' th' Stars fallin'
like a shot as th' roof crashed in, an' where I'd left poor
Jack was nothin' but a leppin' spout o' flame!

Bessie (*with partly repressed vehemence*) Ay, you left him!
You twined his Rosary beads round his fingers, an' then
you run like a hare to get out o' danger!

Capt. Brennan I took me chance as well as him . . . . He

144

took it like a man. His last whisper was to 'Tell Nora to be brave; that I'm ready to meet my God, an' that I'm proud to die for Ireland.' An' when our General heard it he said that 'Commandant Clitheroe's end was a gleam of glory.' Mrs Clitheroe's grief will be a joy when she realizes that she has had a hero for a husband.

Bessie If you only seen her, you'd know to th' differ.

Nora appears at door, left. She is clad only in her nightdress; her hair, uncared for some days, is hanging in disorder over her shoulders. Her pale face looks paler still because of a vivid red spot on the tip of each cheek. Her eyes are glimmering with the light of incipient insanity; her hands are nervously fiddling with her nightgown. She halts at the door for a moment, looks vacantly around the room, and then comes slowly in. The rest do not notice her till she speaks.

Nora (*in a quiet and monotonous tone*) No . . . Not there, Jack . . . . I can feel comfortable only in our own familiar place beneath th' bramble tree . . . . We must be walking for a long time; I feel very, very tired . . . . Have we to go farther, or have we passed it by? (*Passing her hand across her eye*) Curious mist on my eyes . . . . Why don't you hold my hand, Jack . . . . (*Excitedly*) No, no, Jack, it's not. Can't you see it's a goldfinch. Look at th' black-satiny wings with th' gold bars, an' th' splash of crimson on its head . . . . (*Wearily*) Something ails me, something ails me . . . . Don't kiss me like that; you take my breath away, Jack . . . . Why do you frown at me? . . . You're going away, and (*frightened*) I can't follow you. Something's keeping me from moving . . . . (*Crying out*) Jack, Jack, Jack!

Bessie (*who has gone over and caught Nora's arm*) Now, Mrs Clitheroe, you're a terrible woman to get up out of bed . . . . You'll get cold if you stay here in them clothes.

Nora Cold? I'm feelin' very cold; it's chilly out here in th' counthry . . . . (*Looking around frightened*) What place is this? Where am I?

Bessie (*coaxingly*) You're all right, Nora; you're with friends, an' in a safe place. Don't you know your uncle an' your cousin, an poor oul' Fluther?

Peter (*about to go over to Nora*) Nora, darlin', now –

Fluther (*pulling him back*) Now, leave her to Bessie, man. A crowd 'll only make her worse.

Nora (*thoughtfully*) There is something I want to remember, an' I can't. (*With agony*) I can't, I can't, I can't! My head, my head! (*Suddenly breaking from Bessie, and running over to the men, and gripping Fluther by the shoulders*) Where is it? Where's my baby? Tell me where you've put it, where've you hidden it? My baby, my baby; I want my baby! My head, my poor head . . . . Oh, I can't tell what is wrong with me. (*Screaming*) Give him to me, give me my husband!

Bessie Blessin' o' God on us, isn't this pitiful!

Nora (*struggling with Bessie*) I won't go away for you; I won't. Not till you give me back my husband. (*Screaming*) Murderers, that's what yous are; murderers, murderers!

Bessie S-s-sh. We'll bring Mr Clitheroe back to you, if you'll only lie down an' stop quiet . . . . (*Trying to lead her in*) Come on, now, Nora, an' I'll sing something to you.

Nora I feel as if my life was thryin' to force its way out of my body . . . . I can hardly breathe . . . . I'm frightened, I'm frightened, I'm frightened! For God's sake, don't leave me, Bessie. Hold my hand, put your arms around me!

Fluther (*to Brennan*) Now you can see th' way she is, man.

Peter An' what way would she be if she heard Jack had gone west?

The Covey (*to Peter*) Shut up, you, man!

Bessie (*to Nora*) We'll have to be brave, an' let patience clip away th' heaviness of th' slow-movin' hours, rememberin' that sorrow may endure for th' night, but joy cometh in th' mornin' . . . . Come on in, an' I'll sing to you, an' you'll rest quietly.

Nora (*stopping suddenly on her way to the room*) Jack an' me are goin' out somewhere this evenin'. Where I can't tell. Isn't it curious I can't remember. . . . Maura, Maura, Jack, if th' baby's a girl; any name you like, if th' baby's a boy! . . . He's there. (*Screaming*) He's there, an' they won't give him back to me!

Bessie S-ss-s-h, darlin', s-ssh. I won't sing to you, if you're not quiet.

Nora (*nervously holding Bessie*) Hold my hand, hold my hand, an' sing to me, sing to me!

Bessie Come in an' lie down, an' I'll sing to you.

Nora (*vehemently*) Sing to me, sing to me; sing, sing!

Bessie (*singing as she leads Nora into room*)
Lead, kindly light, amid th' encircling gloom,
    Lead Thou me on.
Th' night is dark an' I am far from home,
    Lead Thou me on.
Keep Thou my feet, I do not ask to see
Th' distant scene – one step enough for me.

So long that Thou hast blessed me, sure Thou still
    Wilt lead me on;

They go in.

(*Singing in room*)
> O'er moor an' fen, o'er crag an' torrent, till
>> Th' night is gone.
> An' in th' morn those angel faces smile
> That I have lov'd long since, an' lost awhile!

The Covey (*to Brennan*) Now that you've seen how bad she is, an' that we daren't tell her what has happened till she's betther, you'd best be slippin' back to where you come from.

Capt. Brennan There's no chance o' slippin' back now, for th' military are everywhere: a fly couldn't get through. I'd never have got here, only I managed to change me uniform for what I'm wearin' . . . . I'll have to take me chance, an' thry to lie low here for a while.

The Covey (*frightened*) There's no place here to lie low. Th' Tommies 'll be hoppin' in here, any minute!

Peter (*aghast*) An' then we'd all be shanghaied!

The Covey Be God, there's enough afther happenin' to us!

Fluther (*warningly, as he listens*) Whisht, whisht, th' whole o' yous. I think I heard th' clang of a rifle butt on th' floor of th' hall below. (*All alertness*) Here, come on with th' cards again. I'll deal. (*He shuffles and deals the cards to all.*) Clubs up. (*To Brennan*) Thry to keep your hands from shakin', man. You lead, Peter.

As Peter throws out a card.

Four o' Hearts led.

The door opens and Corporal Stoddart of the Wiltshires enters in full war kit; steel helmet, rifle and bayonet, and trench tool. He looks round the room. A pause and a palpable silence.

(*Breaking the silence*) Two tens an' a five.

Corporal Stoddart 'Ello. (*Indicating the coffin*) This the stiff?

The Covey Yis.

Corporal Stoddart Who's gowing with it? Ownly one allowed to gow with it, you know.

The Covey I dunno.

Corporal Stoddart You dunnow?

The Covey I dunno.

Bessie (*coming into the room*) She's afther slippin' off to sleep again, thanks be to God. I'm hardly able to keep me own eyes open. (*To the soldier*) Oh, are yous goin' to take away poor little Mollser?

Corporal Stoddart Ay; 'oo's agowing with 'er?

Bessie Oh, th' poor mother, o' course. God help her, it's a terrible blow to her!

Fluther A terrible blow? Sure, she's in her element now, woman, mixin' earth to earth, an' ashes t'ashes an' dust to dust, an' revellin' in plumes an' hearses, last days an' judgements!

Bessie (*falling into chair by the fire*) God bless us! I'm jaded!

Corporal Stoddart Was she plugged?

The Covey Ah, no; died o' consumption.

Corporal Stoddart Ow, is that all? Thought she moight 'ave been plugged.

The Covey Is that all? Isn't it enough? D'ye know, comrade, that more die o' consumption than are killed in th' wars? An' it's all because of th' system we're livin' undher?

Corporal Stoddart Ow, I know. I'm a Sowcialist moiself, but I 'as to do my dooty.

The Covey (*ironically*) Dooty! Th' only dooty of a Socialist is th' emancipation of th' workers.

Corporal Stoddart Ow, a man's a man, an 'e 'as to foight for 'is country, 'asn't 'e?

Fluther (*aggressively*) You're not fightin' for your counthry here, are you?

Peter (*anxiously to Fluther*) Ay, ay, Fluther, none o' that, none o' that!

The Covey Fight for your counthry! Did y'ever read, comrade, Jenersky's *Thesis on the Origin, Development, an' Consolidation of th' Evolutionary Idea of the Proletariat*?

Corporal Stoddart Ow, cheese it, Paddy, cheese it!

Bessie (*sleepily*) How is things in th' town, Tommy?

Corporal Stoddart Ow, I fink it's nearly hover. We've got 'em surrounded, and we're clowsing in on the bloighters. Ow, it was only a little bit of a dawg-foight.

The sharp ping of the sniper's rifle is heard, followed by a squeal of pain.

Voices (*to the left in a chant*) Red Cr . . . oss, Red Cr . . . oss! Ambu . . . lance, Ambu . . . lance!

Corporal Stoddart (*excitedly*) Christ, that's another of our men 'it by that blawsted sniper! 'E's knocking abaht 'ere, somewheres. Gawd, when we gets th' bloighter, we'll give 'im the cold steel, we will. We'll jab the belly aht of 'im, we will!

Mrs Gogan comes in tearfully, and a little proud of the importance of being directly connected with death.

Mrs Gogan (*to Fluther*) I'll never forget what you done
for me, Fluther, goin' around at th' risk of your life settlin'
everything with th' undhertaker an' th' cemetery people.
When all me own were afraid to put their noses out, you
plunged like a good one through hummin' bullets, an' they
knockin' fire out o' th' road, tinklin' through th' frightened
windows, an' splashin' themselves to pieces on th' walls!
An' you'll find that Mollser, in th' happy place she's gone
to, won't forget to whisper, now an' again, th' name o'
Fluther.

Corporal Stoddart Git it aht, mother, git it aht.

Bessie (*from the chair*) It's excusin' me you'll be, Mrs
Gogan, for not stannin' up, seein' I'm shaky on me feet for
want of a little sleep, an' not desirin' to show any
disrespect to poor little Mollser.

Fluther Sure, we all know, Bessie, that it's vice versa with
you.

Mrs Gogan (*to Bessie*) Indeed, it's meself that has well
chronicled, Mrs Burgess, all your gentle hurryin's to me
little Mollser, when she was alive, bringin' her somethin'
to dhrink, or somethin' t'eat, an' never passin' her
without liftin' up her heart with a delicate word o'
kindness.

Corporal Stoddart (*impatiently, but kindly*) Git it aht, git
it aht, mother.

*The Covey, Fluther, Brennan, and Peter carry out the
coffin, followed by Mrs Gogan.*

(*To Bessie, who is almost asleep*) 'Ow many men is in this
'ere 'ouse?

No answer.

(*Loudly*) 'Ow many men is in this 'ere 'ouse?

Bessie (*waking with a start*) God, I was nearly asleep! . . .
How many men? Didn't you see them?

Corporal Stoddart Are they all that are in the 'ouse?

Bessie Oh, there's none higher up, but there may be more
lower down. Why?

Corporal Stoddart All men in the district 'as to be
rounded up. Somebody's giving 'elp to the snipers, and we
'as to take precautions. If I 'ad my woy, I'd make 'em all
join hup, and do their bit! But I suppowse they and you
are all Shinners.

Bessie (*who has been sinking into sleep, waking up to a
sleepy vehemence*) Bessie Burgess is no Shinner, an' never
had no thruck with anything spotted be th' fingers o' th'
Fenians; but always made it her business to harness herself
for Church whenever she knew that God Save the King
was goin' to be sung at t'end of th' service; whose only son
went to th' front in th' first contingent of the Dublin
Fusiliers, an' that's on his way home carryin' a shatthered
arm that he got fightin' for his King an' counthry!

> *Her head sinks slowly forward again. Peter comes into
> the room; his body is stiffened and his face is wearing a
> comically indignant look. He walks to and fro at the
> back of the room, evidently repressing a violent desire to
> speak angrily. He is followed in by Fluther, the Covey,
> and Brennan, who slinks into an obscure corner of the
> room, nervous of notice.*

Fluther (*after an embarrassing pause*) Th' air in th' sthreet
outside's shakin' with the firin' o' rifles an' machine-guns.
It must be a hot shop in th' middle o' th' scrap.

Corporal Stoddart We're pumping lead in on 'em from
every side, now; they'll soon be shoving up th' white flag.

Peter (*with a shout*) I'm tellin' you either o' yous two lowsers 'ud make a betther hearse-man than Peter; proddin' an' pokin' at me an' I helpin' to carry out a corpse!

Fluther It wasn't a very derogatory thing for th' Covey to say that you'd make a fancy hearse-man, was it?

Peter (*furiously*) A pair o' redjesthered bowseys pondherin' from mornin' till night on how they'll get a chance to break a gap through th' quiet nature of a man that's always endeavourin' to chase out of him any sthray thought of venom against his fella-man!

The Covey Oh, shut it, shut it, shut it!

Peter As long as I'm a livin' man, responsible for me thoughts, words, an' deeds to th' Man above. I'll feel meself instituted to fight again' th' sliddherin' ways of a pair o' picaroons, whisperin', concurrin', concoctin', an' conspirin' together to rendher me unconscious of th' life I'm thryin' to live!

Corporal Stoddart (*dumbfounded*) What's wrong, Daddy; wot 'ave they done to you?

Peter (*savagely to the Corporal*) You mind your own business! What's it got to do with you, what's wrong with me?

Bessie (*in a sleepy murmur*) Will yous thry to conthrol yourselves into quietness? Yous'll waken her . . . up . . . on . . . me . . . again. (*She sleeps.*)

Fluther Come on, boys, to th' cards again, an' never mind him.

Corporal Stoddart No use of you gowing to start cawds; you'll be gowing out of 'ere, soon as Sergeant comes.

Fluther Goin' out o' here? An' why're we goin' out o' here?

Corporal Stoddart All men in district to be rounded up, and 'eld in till the scrap is hover.

Fluther An' where're we goin' to be held in?

Corporal Stoddart They're puttin 'em in a church.

The Covey A church?

Fluther What sort of a church? Is it a Protestan' Church?

Corporal Stoddart I dunnow; I suppowse so.

Fluther (*dismayed*) Be God, it'll be a nice thing to be stuck all night in a Protestan' Church!

Corporal Stoddart Bring the cawds; you moight get a chance of a goime.

Fluther Ah, no, that wouldn't do . . . . I wondher? (*After a moment's thought*) Ah, I don't think we'd be doin' anything derogatory be playin' cards in a Protestan' Church.

Corporal Stoddart If I was you I'd bring a little snack with me; you moight be glad of it before the mawning. (*Sings.*)

I do loike a snoice mince poy,
I do loike a snoice mince poy!

The snap of the sniper's rifle rings out again, followed simultaneously by a scream of pain. Corporal Stoddart goes pale, and brings his rifle to the ready, listening.

Voices (*chanting to the right*) Red Cro . . . ss, Red Cro . . . ss! Ambu . . . lance, Ambu . . . lance!

Sergeant Tinley comes in rapidly, pale, agitated, and fiercely angry.

Corporal Stoddart (*to Sergeant*) One of hour men 'it, Sergeant?

Sergeant Tinley Private Taylor; got 'it roight through the chest, 'e did; an 'ole in front of 'im as 'ow you could put your fist through, and 'arf 'is back blown awoy! Dum-dum bullets they're using. Gang of Hassassins potting at us from behind roofs. That's not playing the goime: why down't they come into the owpen and foight fair!

Fluther (*unable to stand the slight*) Fight fair! A few hundhred scrawls o' chaps with a couple o' guns an' Rosary beads, again' a hundhred thousand thrained men with horse, fut, an' artillery . . . an' he wants us to fight fair! (*To Sergeant*) D'ye want us to come out in our skins an' throw stones!

Sergeant Tinley (*to Corporal*) Are these four all that are 'ere?

Corporal Stoddart Four; that's all, Sergeant.

Sergeant Tinley (*vindictively*) Come on, then; get the blighters aht. (*To the men*) 'Ere, 'op it aht! Aht into the streets with you, and if a snoiper sends another of our men west, you gow with 'im! (*He catches Fluther by the shoulder.*) Gow on, git aht!

Fluther Eh, who are you chuckin', eh?

Sergeant Tinley (*roughly*) Gow on, git aht, you blighter.

Fluther Who are you callin' a blighter to, eh? I'm a Dublin man, born an' bred in th' city, see?

Sergeant Tinley I down't care if you were Broin Buroo; git aht, git aht.

Fluther (*halting as he is going out*) Jasus, you an' your guns! Leave them down, an' I'd beat th' two o' yous without sweatin'!

> *Peter, Brennan, the Covey, and Fluther, followed by the soldiers, go out. Bessie is sleeping heavily on the chair*

*by the fire. After a pause, Nora appears at door, left, in
her nightdress. Remaining at door for a few moments
she looks vaguely around the room. She then comes in
quietly, goes over to the fire, pokes it, and puts the kettle
on. She thinks for a few moments, pressing her hand to
her forehead. She looks questioningly at the fire, and
then at the press at back. She goes to the press, opens it,
takes out a soiled cloth and spreads it on the table. She
then places things for tea on the table.*

Nora I imagine th' room looks very odd somehow I
was nearly forgetting Jack's tea . . . . Ah, I think I'll have
everything done before he gets in . . . . (*She lilts gently, as
she arranges the table.*)

> Th' violets were scenting th' woods, Nora,
>> Displaying their charms to th' bee,
> When I first said I lov'd only you, Nora,
>> An' you said you lov'd only me.

> Th' chestnut blooms gleam'd through th' glade, Nora,
>> A robin sang loud from a tree,
> When I first said I lov'd only you, Nora,
>> An' you said you lov'd only me.

> *She pauses suddenly, and glances round the room.*

(*Doubtfully*) I can't help feelin' this room very strange
. . . . What is it? . . . . What is it? . . . . I must think I
must thry to remember . . .

Voices (*chanting in a distant street*) Ambu . . . lance,
Ambu . . . lance! Red Cro . . . ss, Red Cro . . . ss!

Nora (*startled and listening for a moment, then resuming
the arrangement of the table*)
> Trees, birds, an' bees sang a song, Nora,
>> Of happier transports to be,
> When I first said I lov'd only you, Nora,

An' you said you lov'd only me.

A burst of rifle fire is heard in a street near by, followed by the rapid rok, tok, tok of a machine-gun.

(*Staring in front of her and screaming*) Jack, Jack, Jack! My baby, my baby, my baby!

Bessie (*waking with a start*) You divil, are you afther gettin' out o' bed again!

She rises and runs towards Nora, who rushes to the window, which she frantically opens.

Nora (*at window, screaming*) Jack, Jack, for God's sake, come to me!

Soldiers (*outside, shouting*) Git away, git away from that window, there!

Bessie (*seizing hold of Nora*) Come away, come away, woman, from that window!

Nora (*struggling with Bessie*) Where is it; where have you hidden it? Oh, Jack, Jack, where are you?

Bessie (*imploringly*) Mrs Clitheroe, for God's sake, come away!

Nora (*fiercely*) I won't; he's below. Let . . . me . . . go! You're thryin' to keep me from me husband. I'll follow him. Jack, Jack, come to your Nora!

Bessie Hus-s-sh, Nora, Nora! He'll be here in a minute. I'll bring him to you, if you'll only be quiet – honest to God, I will.

With a great effort Bessie pushes Nora away from the window, the force used causing her to stagger against it herself. Two rifle shots ring out in quick succession. Bessie jerks her body convulsively; stands stiffly for a moment, a look of agonized astonishment on her face,

157

*then she staggers forward, leaning heavily on the table
with her hands.*

(*With an arrested scream of fear and pain*) Merciful
God, I'm shot, I'm shot, I'm shot! . . . Th' life's pourin'
out o' me! (*To Nora*) I've got this through . . . through
you . . . through you, you bitch, you! . . . O God, have
mercy on me! . . . (*To Nora*) You wouldn't stop quiet,
no, you wouldn't, you wouldn't, blast you! Look at
what I'm afther gettin', look at what I'm afther gettin'
. . . I'm bleedin' to death, an' no one's here to stop th'
flowin' blood! (*Calling*) Mrs Gogan, Mrs Gogan!
Fluther, Fluther, for God's sake, somebody, a doctor, a
doctor!

> *She staggers frightened towards the door, to seek for
> aid, but, weakening half-way across the room, she sinks
> to her knees, and bending forward, supports herself
> with her hands resting on the floor. Nora is standing
> rigidly with her back to the wall opposite, her trembling
> hands held out a little from the sides of her body, her
> lips quivering, her breast heaving, staring wildly at the
> figure of Bessie.*

Nora (*in a breathless whisper*) Jack, I'm frightened . . . .
I'm frightened, Jack . . . . Oh, Jack, where are you?

Bessie (*moaningly*) This is what's afther comin' on me for
nursin' you day an' night . . . . I was a fool, a fool, a fool!
Get me a dhrink o' wather, you jade, will you? There's a
fire burnin' in me blood! (*Pleadingly*) Nora, Nora, dear,
for God's sake, run out an' get Mrs Gogan, or Fluther, or
somebody to bring a doctor, quick, quick, quick!

> *Nora does not stir.*

Blast you, stir yourself, before I'm gone!

Nora Oh, Jack, Jack, where are you?

Bessie (*in a whispered moan*) Jesus Christ, me sight's goin'! It's all dark, dark! Nora, hold me hand! (*Bessie's body lists over and she sinks into a prostrate position on the floor.*) I'm dyin', I'm dyin' . . . I feel it . . . . Oh God, oh God! (*She feebly sings.*)

> I do believe, I will believe
> > That Jesus died for me;
> That on th' cross He shed His blood,
> > From sin to set me free . . . .

> I do believe . . . I will believe
> > . . . Jesus died . . . me;
> . . . th' cross He shed . . . blood,
> > From sin . . . free.

She ceases singing, and lies stretched out, still and very rigid. A pause. Then Mrs Gogan runs in hastily.

Mrs Gogan (*quivering with fright*) Blessed be God, what's afther happenin'? (*To Nora*) What's wrong, child, what's wrong? (*She sees Bessie, runs to her and bends over the body.*) Bessie, Bessie! (*She shakes the body.*) Mrs Burgess, Mrs Burgess! (*She feels Bessie's forehead.*) My God, she's as cold as death. They're afther murdherin' th' poor inoffensive woman!

Sergeant Tinley and Corporal Stoddart enter agitatedly, their rifles at the ready.

Sergeant Tinley (*excitedly*) This is the 'ouse. That's the window!

Nora (*pressing back against the wall*) Hide it, hide it; cover it up, cover it up!

Sergeant Tinley (*going over to the body*) 'Ere, what's this? Who's this? (*Looking at Bessie*) Oh Gawd, we've plugged one of the women of the 'ouse.

Corporal Stoddart Whoy the 'ell did she gow to the window? Is she dead?

Sergeant Tinley Oh, dead as bedamned. Well, we couldn't afford to toike any chawnces.

Nora (*screaming*) Hide it, hide it; don't let me see it! Take me away, take me away, Mrs Gogan!

> *Mrs Gogan runs into room, left, and runs out again with a sheet which she spreads over the body of Bessie.*

Mrs Gogan (*as she spreads the sheet*) Oh, God help her, th' poor woman, she's stiffenin' out as hard as she can! Her face has written on it th' shock o' sudden agony, an' her hands is whitenin' into th' smooth shininess of wax.

Nora (*whimperingly*) Take me away, take me away; don't leave me here to be lookin' an' lookin' at it!

Mrs Gogan (*going over to Nora and putting her arm around her*) Come on with me, dear, an' you can doss in poor Mollser's bed, till we gather some neighbours to come an' give th' last friendly touches to Bessie in th' lonely layin' of her out.

> *Mrs Gogan and Nora go out slowly.*

Corporal Stoddart (*who has been looking around, to Sergeant Tinley*) Tea here, Sergeant. Wot abaht a cup of scald?

Sergeant Tinley Pour it aht, Stoddart, pour it aht. I could scoff hanything just now.

> *Corporal Stoddart pours out two cups of tea, and the two soldiers begin to drink. In the distance is heard a bitter burst of rifle and machine-gun fire, interspersed with the boom, boom of artillery. The glare in the sky seen through the window flares into a fuller and a deeper red.*

There gows the general attack on the Powst Office.

Voices (*in a distant street*) Ambu . . . lance, Ambu . . . lance! Red Cro. . . . ss, Red Cro . . . ss!

Voices of Soldiers (*at a barricade outside the house; singing*)
> They were summoned from the 'illside,
> They were called in from the glen,
> And the country found 'em ready
> At the stirring call for men.
> Let not tears add to their 'ardship,
> As the soldiers pass along,
> And although our 'eart is breaking,
> Make it sing this cheery song.

Sergeant Tinley and Corporal Stoddart (*joining in the chorus, as they sip the tea*)
> Keep the 'owme fires burning,
> While your 'earts are yearning;
> Though your lads are far away
> They dream of 'owme;
> There's a silver loining
> Through the dark cloud shoining,
> Turn the dark cloud inside out,
> Till the boys come 'owme!

Curtain.

THE SILVER TASSIE

A TRAGI-COMEDY IN FOUR ACTS

To Eileen with the yellow daffodils
in the green vase

Characters
(as they appear)

Sylvester Heegan
Mrs Heegan, his wife
Simon Norton
Susie Monican
Mrs Foran
Teddy Foran, her husband
Harry Heegan, DCM, Heegan's son
Jessie Taite
Barney Bagnal
The Croucher
1st Soldier
2nd Soldier
3rd Soldier
4th Soldier
The Corporal
The Visitor
The Staff Wallah
1st Stretcher-bearer
2nd Stretcher-bearer
3rd Stretcher-bearer
4th Stretcher-bearer
1st Casualty
2nd Casualty
Surgeon Forby Maxwell
The Sister of the Ward

Act One – Room in Heegan's home
Act Two – Somewhere in France (later on).
Act Three – Ward in a hospital (a little later on).
Act Four – Room in premises of Avondale Football Club.

Notes

The Croucher's make-up should come as close as possible to a death's head, a skull; and his hands should show like those of a skeleton's. He should sit somewhere *above* the group of Soldiers; preferably to one side, on the left, from view-point of audience, so as to overlook the Soldiers. He should look languid, as if very tired of life.

The group of Soldiers – Act Two – should enter in a close mass, as if each was keeping the other from falling, utterly weary and tired out. They should appear as if they were almost locked together.

The Soldiers' last response to the Staff Wallah's declaration, namely, 'To the Guns!' should have in these three words the last high notes of 'The Last Post'.

The song sung at the end of the play should be given to the best two (or one) singers in the cast. If, on the other hand, there be no passable singer among the players, the song should be omitted.

Perhaps a more suitable Spiritual than 'Sweet Chariot' would be chosen for Harry to sing. For instance, 'Keep Inchin' Along', or 'Keep Me from Sinkin' Down'.

The Chants in the play are simple Plain Song. The first chant is given in full as an example of the way in which they are sung. In the others, the dots . . . indicate that the note preceding them should be sustained till the music indicates a change. There are three parts in each chant: the Intonation; the Meditation; and the Ending. After a little practice, they will be found to be easy to sing. The Soldiers having the better voices should be selected to intone the chants, irrespective of the numbers allotted to them as characters in the book of the play.

Act One

The eating, sitting, and part sleeping room of the Heegan
family. A large window at back looks on to a quay, from
which can be seen the centre mast of a steamer, at the top
of which gleams a white light. Another window at right
looks down on a side street. Under the window at back,
plumb in the centre, is a stand, the legs gilded silver and
the top gilded gold; on the stand is a purple velvet shield
on which are pinned a number of silver medals
surrounding a few gold ones. On each side of the shield is
a small vase holding a bunch of artificial flowers. The
shield is draped with red and yellow ribbons. To the left of
the stand is a bed covered with a bedspread of black
striped with vivid green. To the right of the stand is a
dresser and chest of drawers combined. The fireplace is to
the left. Beside the fireplace is a door leading to a
bedroom, another door which gives access to the rest of
the house and the street, on the right. At the corner left is a
red-coloured stand resembling an easel, having on it a
silver-gilt framed picture photograph of Harry Heegan in
football dress, crimson jersey with yellow collar and cuffs
and a broad yellow belt, black stockings, and yellow
football boots. A table on which are a half-pint bottle of
whiskey, a large parcel of bread and meat sandwiches, and
some copies of English illustrated magazines.

Sylvester Heegan and Simon Norton are sitting by the
fire. Sylvester Heegan is a stockily built man of sixty-five;
he has been a docker all his life since first the muscles of
his arms could safely grip a truck, and even at sixty-five
the steel in them is only beginning to stiffen.

Simon Norton is a tall man, originally a docker too, but

by a little additional steadiness, a minor effort towards
self-education, a natural, but very slight superior
nimbleness of mind, has risen in the Company's estimation
and has been given the position of checker, a job entailing
as many hours of work as a docker, almost as much
danger, twice as much responsibility, and a corresponding
reduction in his earning powers. He is not so warmly, but
a little more circumspectly dressed than Sylvester, and in
his manner of conduct and speech there is a hesitant
suggestion of greater refinement than in those of Sylvester,
and a still more vague indication that he is aware of it.
This timid semi-conscious sense of superiority, which
Simon sometimes forgets, is shown frequently by a
complacent stroking of a dark beard which years are
beginning to humiliate. The night is cold, and Simon and
Sylvester occasionally stretch longingly towards the fire.
They are fully dressed and each has his topcoat and hat
beside him, as if ready to go out at a moment's notice.
Susie Monican is standing at the table polishing a Lee-
Enfield rifle with a chamois cloth; the butt of the rifle is
resting on the table. She is a girl of twenty-two, well-
shaped limbs, challenging breasts, all of which are
defiantly hidden by a rather long dark blue skirt and
bodice buttoning up to the throat, relieved by a crimson
scarf around her neck, knotted in front and falling down
her bosom like a man's tie. She is undeniably pretty, but
her charms are almost completely hidden by her sombre,
ill-fitting dress, and the rigid manner in which she has
made her hair up declares her unflinching and
uncompromising modesty. Just now she is standing
motionless, listening intently, looking towards the door on
right.

Mrs Heegan is standing at the window at right, listening
too, one hand pulling back the curtain, but her attention,
taken from the window, is attracted to the door. She is
older than Sylvester, stiffened with age and rheumatism;

*the end of her life is unknowingly lumbering towards a
rest: the impetus necessity has given to continual toil and
striving is beginning to slow down, and everything she has
to do is done with a quiet mechanical persistence. Her
inner ear cannot hear even a faint echo of a younger day.
Neither Sylvester nor Simon has noticed the attentive
attitude of Mrs Heegan or Susie, for Sylvester, with one
arm outstretched crooked at the elbow, is talking with
subdued intensity to Simon.*

Sylvester I seen him do it, mind you. I seen him do it.

Simon I quite believe you, Sylvester.

Sylvester Break a chain across his bisseps! (*With
pantomime action*) Fixes it over his arm . . . bends it up
. . . a little strain . . . snaps in two . . . right across his
bisseps!

Susie Shush you, there!

> *Mrs Heegan goes out with troubled steps by door. The
> rest remain still for a few moments.*

Sylvester A false alarm.

Simon No cause for undue anxiety; there's plenty of time
yet.

Susie (*chanting as she resumes the polishing of gun*)
  Man walketh in a vain shadow, and disquieteth himself
     in vain:
  He heapeth up riches, and cannot tell who shall gather
     them.

(*She sends the chant in the direction of Sylvester and
Simon, coming close to the two men and sticking an angry
face in between them.*) When the two of yous stand
quiverin' together on the dhread day of the Last
Judgement, how will the two of yous feel if yous have

169

nothin' to say but 'he broke a chain across his bisseps'?
Then the two of you'll know that the wicked go down into
hell, an' all the people who forget God!

*She listens a moment, and leaving down the rifle, goes
out by door left.*

Sylvester It's persecutin', that tambourine theology of
Susie's. I always get a curious, sickenin' feelin', Simon,
when I hear the Name of the Supreme Bein' tossed into the
quietness of a sensible conversation.

Simon The day he won the Cross Country Championship
of County Dublin, Syl, was a day to be chronicled.

Sylvester In a minor way, yes, Simon. But the day that
caps the chronicle was the one when he punched the fear
of God into the heart of Police Constable 63 C under the
stars of a frosty night on the way home from Terenure.

Simon Without any exaggeration, without any
exaggeration, mind you, Sylvester, that could be called a
memorable experience.

Sylvester I can see him yet (*he gets up, slides from side to
side, dodging and parrying imaginary blows*) glidin' round
the dazzled Bobby, cross-ey'd tryin' to watch him.

Simon (*tapping his pipe resolutely on the hob*)
Unperturbed, mind you, all the time.

Sylvester An' the hedges by the road-side standin' stiff in
the silent cold of the air, the frost beads on the branches
glistenin' like toss'd-down diamonds from the breasts of
the stars, the quietness of the night stimulated to a fuller
stillness by the mockin' breathin' of Harry, an' the heavy,
ragin' pantin' of the Bobby, an' the quickenin' beats of
our own hearts afraid, of hopin' too little or hopin' too
much.

*During the last speech by Sylvester, Susie has come in
with a bayonet, and has commenced to polish it.*

Susie We don't go down on our knees often enough; that's
why we're not able to stand up to the Evil One: we don't
go down on our knees enough . . . . I can hear some
persons fallin' with a splash of sparks into the lake of
everlastin' fire . . . . An account of every idle word shall be
given at the last day. (*She goes out again with rifle.
Bending towards Simon and Sylvester as she goes*) God is
listenin' to yous; God is listenin' to yous!

Sylvester Dtch, dtch, dtch. People ought to be forcibly
restrained from constantly cannonadin' you with the name
of the Deity.

Simon Dubiety never brush'd a thought into my mind,
Syl, while I was waitin' for the moment when Harry
would stretch the Bobby hors dee combaa on the ground.

Sylvester (*resuming his pantomime actions*) There he was
staggerin', beatin' out blindly, every spark of energy panted
out of him, while Harry feinted, dodg'd, side-stepp'd, then
suddenly sail'd in an' put him asleep with . . .

Simon } (*together*) A right-handed hook to the jaw!
Sylvester   A left-handed hook to the jaw!

Sylvester (*after a pause*) A left-handed hook to the jaw,
Simon.

Simon No, no, Syl, a right-handed hook to the jaw.

*Mrs Foran runs quickly in by the door with a frying-pan
in her hand, on which is a steak. She comes to the fire,
pushing, so as to disturb the two men. She is one of the
many gay, careworn women of the working class.*

Mrs Foran (*rapidly*) A pot of clothes is boilin' on the fire
above, an' I knew yous wouldn't mind me slappin' a bit of

steak on here for a second to show him, when he comes in
before he goes away, that we're mindful of his needs, an'
I'm hopeful of a dream tonight that the sea's between us,
not lookin' very haggard in the mornin' to find the dream
a true one. (*With satisfied anticipation*)

> For I'll be single again, yes, I'll be single again;
> An' I eats what I likes, . . . an' I drinks what I likes,
> An' I likes what I likes, when I'm –

(*Stopping suddenly*) What's the silence for?

Sylvester (*slowly and decidedly*) I was at the fight, Simon,
an' I seen him givin' a left-handed hook to the jaw.

Mrs Foran What fight?

Simon (*slowly and decidedly*) I was there too, an' I saw
him down the Bobby with a right-handed hook to the jaw.

Mrs Foran What Bobby?

> *A pause.*

Sylvester It was a close up, an' I don't know who'd know
better if it wasn't the boy's own father.

Mrs Foran What boy . . . what father?

Sylvester Oh, shut up, woman, an' don't be smotherin' us
with a shower of questions.

Susie (*who has entered on the last speech, and has started
to polish a soldier's steel helmet*) Oh, the miserableness of
them that don't know the things that belong unto their
peace. They try one thing after another, they try
everything, but they never think of trying God. (*Coming
nearer to them*) Oh, the happiness of knowing that God's
hand has pick'd you out for heaven. (*To Mrs Foran*)
What's the honey-pot kiss of a lover to the kiss of
righteousness and peace?

Mrs Foran, embarrassed, goes over to window.

(*Turning to Simon*) Simon, will you not close the dandy door of the public-house and let the angels open the pearly gates of heaven for you?

Sylvester We feel very comfortable where we are, Susie.

Susie Don't mock, Sylvester, don't mock. You'd run before a great wind, tremble in an earthquake, and flee from a fire; so don't treat lightly the still, small voice calling you to repentance and faith.

Sylvester (*with appeal and irritation*) Oh, do give over worryin' a man, Susie.

Susie God shows His love by worrying, and worrying, and worrying the sinner. The day will come when you will call on the mountains to cover you, and then you'll weep and gnash your teeth that you did not hearken to Susie's warning. (*Putting her hands appealingly on his shoulders*) Sylvester, if you pray long enough, and hard enough, and deep enough, you'll get the power to fight and conquer Beelzebub.

Mrs Foran I'll be in a doxological mood tonight, not because the kingdom of heaven 'll be near me, but because my husband 'll be far away, and tomorrow (*singing*)

I'll be single again, yes, single again;
An' I goes where I likes, an' I does what I likes,
An' I likes what I likes now I'm single again!

Simon Go on getting Harry's things ready, Susie, and defer the dosing of your friends with canticles till the time is ripe with rest for them to listen quietly.

Simon and Sylvester are very self-conscious during Susie's talk to them. Simon empties his pipe by tapping the head on the hob of the grate. He then blows through it. As he is blowing through it, Sylvester is emptying his

by tapping it on the hob; as he is blowing it Simon taps
his again; as Simon taps Sylvester taps with him, and then
they look into the heads of the pipes and blow together.

Susie It must be mercy or it must be judgement: if not
mercy today it may be judgement tomorrow. He is never
tired of waiting and waiting and waiting; and watching
and watching and watching; and knocking and knocking
and knocking for the sinner – you, Sylvester, and you,
Simon – to turn from his wickedness and live. Oh, if the
two of you only knew what it was to live! Not to live leg-
staggering an' belly-creeping among the pain-spotted and
sin-splashed desires of the flesh; but to live, oh, to live
swift-flying from a holy peace to a holy strength, and from
holy strength to a holy joy, like the flashing flights of a
swallow in the deep beauty of a summer sky.

Simon and Sylvester shift about, self-conscious and
uneasy.

(*Placing her hand first on Simon's shoulder and then on*
Sylvester's) The two of you God's elegant swallows; a
saved pair; a loving pair strong-wing'd, freed from the gin
of the snarer, tip of wing to tip of wing, flying fast or
darting swift together to the kingdom of heaven.

Simon (*expressing a protecting thought to Sylvester*) One of
the two of us should go out and hunt back the old woman
from the perishing cold of watching for the return of Harry.

Sylvester She'll be as cold as a naked corpse, an' unstinted
watchin' won't bring Harry back a minute sooner. I'll go
an' drive her back. (*He rises to go.*) I'll be back in a
minute, Susie.

Simon (*hurriedly*) Don't bother, Syl, I'll go; she won't be
farther than the corner of the street; you go on toasting
yourself where you are. (*He rises.*) I'll be back in a minute,
Susie.

Mrs Foran (*running to the door*) Rest easy the two of you, an' I'll go, so as to give Susie full time to take the sin out of your bones an' put you both in first-class form for the kingdom of heaven. (*She goes out.*)

Susie Sinners that jeer often add to the glory of God: going out, she gives you, Sylvester, and you, Simon, another few moments, precious moments – oh, how precious, for once gone, they are gone for ever – to listen to the warning from heaven.

Simon (*suddenly*) Whisht, here's somebody coming, I think?

Sylvester I'll back this is Harry comin' at last.

A pause as the three listen.

No, it's nobody.

Simon Whoever it was 's gone by.

Susie Oh, Syl, oh, Simon, don't try to veil the face of God with an evasion. You can't, you can't cod God. This may be your last chance before the pains of hell encompass the two of you. Hope is passing by; salvation is passing by, and glory arm-in-arm with her. In the quietness left to you go down on your knees and pray that they come into your hearts and abide with you for ever . . . (*With fervour, placing her left hand on Simon's shoulder and her right hand on Sylvester's, and shaking them*) Get down on your knees, get down on your knees, get down on your knees and pray for conviction of sin, lest your portion in David become as the portion of the Canaanites, the Amorites, the Perizzites and the Jebusites!

Sylvester Eh, eh, Susie; cautious now – you seem to be forgettin' yourself.

Simon Desist, Susie, desist. Violence won't gather people

to God. It only ingenders hostility to what you're trying to
do.

Sylvester You can't batter religion into a man like that.

Simon Religion is love, but that sort of thing is simply a
nullification of religion.

Susie Bitterness and wrath in exhortation is the only hope
of rousing the pair of yous into a sense of coming and
everlasting penalties.

Sylvester Well, give it a miss, give it a miss to me now.
Don't try to claw me into the kingdom of heaven. An' you
only succeed in distempering piety when you try to mangle
it into a man's emotions.

Simon Heaven is all the better, Susie, for being a long way
off.

Sylvester If I want to pray I do it voluntarily, but I'm not
going to be goaded an' goaded into it.

Susie I go away in a few days to help to nurse the
wounded, an' God's merciful warnings may depart along
with me, then sin 'll usher the two of you into Gehenna for
all eternity. Oh, if the two of you could only grasp the
meaning of the word eternity! (*Bending down and looking
up into their faces*) Time that had no beginning and never
can have an end – an' there you'll be – two cockatrices
creeping together, a desolation, an astonishment, a curse
and a hissing from everlasting to everlasting. (*She goes
into room.*)

Sylvester Cheerful, what! Cockatrices – be-God, that's a
good one, Simon.

Simon Always a trying thing to have to listen to one that's
trying to push the kingdom of God into a reservation of a
few yards.

Sylvester A cockatrice! Now where did she manage to pick up that term of approbation, I wonder?

Simon From the Bible. An animal somewhere mentioned in the Bible, I think, that a serpent hatched out of a cock's egg.

Sylvester A cock's egg! It couldn't have been the egg of an ordinary cock. Not the male of what we call a hen?

Simon I think so.

Sylvester Well, be-God, that's a good one! You know Susie'll have to be told to disintensify her soul-huntin', for religion even isn't an excuse for saying that a man 'll become a cockatrice.

Simon In a church, somehow or other, it seems natural enough, and even in the street it's alright, for one thing is as good as another in the wide-open ear of the air, but in the delicate quietness of your own home it, it –

Sylvester Jars on you!

Simon Exactly!

Sylvester If she'd only confine her glory-to-God business to the festivals, Christmas, now, or even Easter, Simon, it would be recommendable; for a few days before Christmas, like the quiet raisin' of a curtain, an' a few days after, like the gentle lowerin' of one, there's nothing more . . . more –

Simon Appropriate . . . .

Sylvester Exhilaratin' than the singin' of the Adestay Fidellis.

Simon She's damned pretty, an' if she dressed herself justly, she'd lift some man's heart up, an' toss down many another. It's a mystery now, what affliction causes the disablement, for most women of that kind are plain, an' when a woman's born plain she's born good. I wonder what caused the peculiar bend in Susie's nature? Narrow your imagination to the limit and you couldn't call it an avocation.

Sylvester (*giving the head of his pipe a sharp, quick blow on the palm of his hand to clear it*) Adoration.

Simon What?

Sylvester Adoration, Simon, accordin' to the flesh . . . She fancied Harry and Harry fancied Jessie, so she hides her rage an' loss in the love of a scorchin' Gospel.

Simon Strange, strange.

Sylvester Oh, very curious, Simon.

Simon It's a problem, I suppose.

Sylvester An inconsolable problem, Simon.

Mrs Foran enters by door, helping in Mrs Heegan, who is pale and shivering with cold.

Mrs Heegan (*shivering and shuddering*) U-u-uh, I feel the stream of blood that's still trickling through me old veins icifyin' fast; u-uh.

Mrs Foran Madwoman, dear, to be waitin' out there on the quay an' a wind risin' as cold as a stepmother's breath, piercin' through your old bones, mockin' any effort a body would make to keep warm, an' (*suddenly rushing over to the fireplace in an agony of dismay, scattering Simon and Sylvester, and whipping the frying-pan off the fire*) – The steak, the steak; I forgot the blasted steak an' onions fryin' on the fire! God Almighty, there's not as much as a bead of juice left in either of them. The scent of the burnin' would penetrate to the street, an' not one of you'd stir a hand to lift them out of danger. Oh, look at the condition they're in. Even the gospel-gunner couldn't do a little target practice by helpin' the necessity of a neighbour. (*As she goes out.*) I can hear the love for your neighbours almost fizzlin' in your hearts.

Mrs Heegan (*pushing in to the fire, to Simon and Sylvester*) Push to the right and push to the left till I get to the fosterin' fire. Time eatin' his heart out, an' no sign of him yet. The two of them, the two of my legs is numb . . . an' the wind's risin' that'll make the sea heave an' sink under the boat tonight, under shaded lights an' the submarines about.

Susie comes in, goes over to window, and looks out.

Hours ago the football match must have been over, an' no word of him yet, an' all drinkin' if they won, an' all drinkin' if they lost; with Jessie hitchin' on after him, an' no one thinkin' of me an' the maintenance money.

Sylvester He'll come back in time; he'll have to come back; he must come back.

Simon He got the goals, Mrs Heegan, that won the last two finals, and it's only fair he'd want to win this, which'll mean that the Cup won before two –

Sylvester (*butting in*) Times hand runnin'.

Simon Two times consecutively before, makin' the Cup the property of the Club.

Sylvester Exactly!

Mrs Heegan The chill's residin' in my bones, an' feelin's left me just the strength to shiver. He's overstayed his leave a lot, an' if he misses now the tide that's waitin', he skulks behind desertion from the colours.

Susie On Active Service that means death at dawn.

Mrs Heegan An' my governmental money grant would stop at once.

Susie That would gratify Miss Jessie Taite, because you put her weddin' off with Harry till after the duration of the war, an' cut her out of the allowance.

Sylvester (*with a sickened look at Simon*) Dtch, dtch, dtch, the way the women wag the worst things out of happenings! (*To the women*) My God Almighty, he'll be back in time an' fill yous all with disappointment.

Mrs Heegan She's coinin' money workin' at munitions, an' doesn't need to eye the little that we get from Harry; for one evening hurryin' with him to the pictures she left her bag behind, an' goin' through it what would you think I found?

Susie A saucy book, now, or a naughty picture?

Mrs Heegan Lion and Unicorn standin' on their Jew ay mon draw. With all the rings an' dates, an' rules an' regulations.

Simon What was it, Mrs Heegan?

Mrs Heegan Spaced an' lined; signed an' signatured; nestlin' in a blue envelope to keep it warm.

Sylvester (*testily*) Oh, sing it out, woman, an' don't be takin' the value out of what you're goin' to tell us.

Mrs Heegan A Post Office Savings Bank Book.

Sylvester Oh, hairy enough, eh?

Simon How much, Mrs Heegan?

Mrs Heegan Pounds an' shillings with the pence missin'; backed by secrecy, an' security guaranteed by Act of Parliament.

Sylvester (*impatiently*) Dtch, dtch. Yes, yes, woman, but how much was it?

Mrs Heegan Two hundred an' nineteen pounds, sixteen shillings, an' no pence.

Sylvester Be God, a nice little nest egg, right enough!

Susie I hope in my heart that she came by it honestly, and that she remembers that it's as true now as when it was first spoken that it's harder for a camel to go through the eye of a needle than for a rich person to enter the kingdom of heaven.

Simon And she hidin' it all under a veil of silence, when there wasn't the slightest fear of any of us bein' jealous of her.

A tumult is heard on the floor over their heads, followed by a crash of breaking delft. They are startled, and listen attentively.

Mrs Heegan (*breaking the silence*) Oh, there he's at it again. An' she sayin' that he was a pattern husband since he came home on leave, merry-making with her an' singin' dolorously the first thing every mornin'. I was thinkin' there'd be a rough house sometime over her lookin' so well after his long absence . . . you'd imagine now, the trenches would have given him some idea of the sacredness of life!

Another crash of breaking delftware.

An' the last week of his leave she was too fond of breakin' into song in front of him.

Sylvester Well, she's gettin' it now for goin' round heavin' her happiness in the poor man's face.

A crash, followed by screams from Mrs Foran.

Susie I hope he won't be running down here as he often does.

Simon (*a little agitated*) I couldn't stay here an' listen to that; I'll go up and stop him: he might be killing the poor woman.

Mrs Heegan Don't do anything of the kind, Simon; he might down you with a hatchet or something.

Simon Phuh, I'll keep him off with the left and hook him with the right. (*Putting on his hat and coat as he goes to the door*) Looking prim and careless 'll astonish him. Monstrous to stay here, while he may be killing the woman.

Mrs Heegan (*to Simon as he goes out*) For God's sake mind yourself, Simon.

Sylvester (*standing beside closed door on right with his ear close to one of the panels, listening intently*) Simon's a tidy little man with his fists, an' would make Teddy Foran feel giddy if he got home with his left hook.

   Crash.

I wonder is that Simon knockin' down Foran, or Foran knockin' down Simon?

Mrs Heegan If he came down an' we had the light low, an' kept quiet, he might think we were all out.

Sylvester Shush. I can hear nothin' now. Simon must have awed him. Quiet little man, but when Simon gets goin'. Shush? No, nothin' . . . Something unusual has happened. O, oh, be-God!

The door against which Sylvester is leaning bursts in suddenly. Sylvester is flung headlong to the floor, and Mrs Foran, her hair falling wildly over her shoulders, a cut over her eye, frantic with fear, rushes in and

scrambles in a frenzy of haste under the bed. Mrs
Heegan, quickened by fear, runs like a good one,
followed by Susie, into the room, the door of which they
bang after them. Sylvester hurriedly fights his way under
the bed with Mrs Foran.

Mrs Foran (*speaking excitedly and jerkily as she climbs*
under the bed) Flung his dinner into the fire – and started
to smash the little things in the room. Tryin' to save the
dresser, I got a box in the eye. I locked the door on him as
I rushed out, an' before I was half-way down, he had one
of the panels flyin' out with – a hatchet!

Sylvester (*under the bed – out of breath*) Whythehell
didn'tyou sing out beforeyousent thedoor flyin' inontop o'
me!

Mrs Foran How could I an' I flyin' before danger to me –
life?

Sylvester Yes, an'you'vegot meinto a nice extremity now!

Mrs Foran An' I yelled to Simon Norton when he had me
– down, but the boyo only ran the faster out of the –
house!

Sylvester Oh, an' the regal like way he went out to fight!
Oh, I'm findin' out that everyone who wears a cocked hat
isn't a Napoleon!

Teddy Foran, Mrs Foran's husband, enters by door,
with a large, fancy, vividly yellow-coloured bowl,
ornamented with crimson roses, in one hand and a
hatchet in the other. He is big and powerful, rough and
hardy. A man who would be dominant in a public-
house, and whose opinions would be listened to with
great respect. He is dressed in khaki uniform of a soldier
home on leave.

Teddy Under the bed, eh! Right place for a guilty

conscience. I should have thrown you out of the window with the dinner you put before me. Out with you from under there, an' come up with your husband.

Susie (*opening suddenly door right, putting in her head, pulling it back and shutting door again*) God is looking at you, God is looking at you!

Mrs Foran I'll not budge an inch from where I am.

Teddy (*looking under the bed and seeing Sylvester*) What are you doin' there encouragin' her against her husband?

Sylvester You've no right to be rippin' open the poor woman's life of peace with violence.

Teddy (*with indignation*) She's my wife, isn't she?

Mrs Foran Nice thing if I lose the sight of my eye with the cut you gave me!

Teddy She's my wife, isn't she? An' you've no legal right to be harbourin' her here, keepin' her from her household duties. Stunned I was when I seen her lookin' so well after me long absence. Blowin' her sighin' in me face all day, an' she sufferin' the tortures of hell for fear I'd miss the boat!

Sylvester Go on up to your own home; you've no right to be violatin' this place.

Teddy You'd like to make her your cheery amee, would you? It's napoo, there, napoo, you little pip-squeak. I seen you an' her goin' down the street arm-in-arm.

Sylvester Did you expect to see me goin' down the street leg-in-leg with her?

Teddy Thinkin' of her Ring-papers instead of her husband. (*To Mrs Foran*) I'll teach you to be rippling with joy an' your husband goin' away! (*He shows the bowl.*)

Your weddin' bowl, look at it; pretty, isn't it? Take your last eyeful of it now, for it's goin' west quick!

Susie (*popping her head in again*) God is watching you, God is watching you!

Mrs Foran (*appealingly*) Teddy, Teddy, don't smash the poor weddin' bowl.

Teddy (*smashing the bowl with a blow of the hatchet*) It would be a pity, wouldn't it? Damn it, an' damn you. I'm off now to smash anything I missed, so that you'll have a gay time fittin' up the little home again by the time your loving husband comes back. You can come an' have a look, an' bring your mon amee if you like.

> *He goes out, and there is a pause as Mrs Foran and Sylvester peep anxiously towards the door.*

Sylvester Cautious, now cautious; he might be lurking outside that door there, ready to spring on you the minute you show'd your nose!

Mrs Foran Me lovely little weddin' bowl, me lovely little weddin' bowl!

> *Teddy is heard breaking things in the room above.*

Sylvester (*creeping out from under the bed*) Oh, he is gone up. He was a little cow'd, I think, when he saw me.

Mrs Foran Me little weddin' bowl, wrapp'd in tissue paper, an' only taken out for a few hours every Christmas – me poor little weddin' bowl.

Susie (*popping her head in*) God is watching – oh, he's gone!

Sylvester (*jubilant*) Vanished! He was a little cow'd, I think, when he saw me.

> *Mrs Heegan and Susie come into the room.*

Mrs Foran He's makin' a hash of every little thing we have in the house, Mrs Heegan.

Mrs Heegan Go inside to the room, Mrs Foran, an' if he comes down again, we'll say you ran out to the street.

Mrs Foran (*going into room*) My poor little weddin' bowl that I might have had for generations!

Susie (*who has been looking out of the window, excitedly*) They're comin', they're comin': a crowd with a concertina; some of them carrying Harry on their shoulders, an' others are carrying that Jessie Taite too, holding a silver cup in her hands. Oh, look at the shameful way she's showing her legs to all who like to have a look at them!

Mrs Heegan Never mind Jessie's legs – what we have to do is to hurry him out in time to catch the boat.

> *The sound of a concertina playing in the street outside has been heard, and the noise of a marching crowd. The crowd stops at the house. Shouts are heard – 'Up the Avondales!'; 'Up Harry Heegan and the Avondales!' Then steps are heard coming up the stairs, and first Simon Norton enters, holding the door ceremoniously wide open to allow Harry to enter, with his arm around Jessie, who is carrying a silver cup joyously, rather than reverentially, elevated, as a priest would elevate a chalice. Harry is wearing khaki trousers, a military cap stained with trench mud, a vivid orange-coloured jersey with black collar and cuffs. He is twenty-three years of age, tall, with the sinewy muscles of a manual worker made flexible by athletic sport. He is a typical young worker, enthusiastic, very often boisterous, sensible by instinct rather than by reason. He has gone to the trenches as unthinkingly as he would go to the polling booth. He isn't naturally stupid; it is the stupidity of persons in high places that has stupefied him. He has*

*given all to his masters, strong heart, sound lungs,
healthy stomach, lusty limbs and the little mind that
education has permitted to develop sufficiently to make
all the rest a little more useful. He is excited now with
the sweet and innocent insanity of a fine achievement,
and the rapid lowering of a few drinks.*

*Jessie is twenty-two or so, responsive to all the animal
impulses of life. Ever dancing around, in and between
the world, the flesh, and the devil. She would be happy
climbing with a boy among the heather on Howth Hill,
and could play ball with young men on the swards of
the Phoenix Park. She gives her favour to the prominent
and popular. Harry is her favourite: his strength and
speed has won the Final for his club, he wears the
ribbon of the DCM. It is a time of spiritual and animal
exaltation for her.*

*Barney Bagnal, a soldier mate of Harry's, stands a
little shyly near the door, with a pleasant, good-
humoured grin on his rather broad face. He is the same
age as Harry, just as strong, but not so quick, less finely
formed, and not so sensitive; able to take most things
quietly, but savage and wild when he becomes enraged.
He is fully dressed, with topcoat buttoned on him, and
he carries Harry's on his arm.*

Harry (*joyous and excited*) Won, won, won, be-God; by
the odd goal in five. Lift it up, lift it up, Jessie, sign of
youth, sign of strength, sign of victory!

Mrs Heegan (*to Sylvester*) I knew, now, Harry would
come back in time to catch the boat.

Harry (*to Jessie*) Leave it here, leave it down here, Jessie,
under the picture, the picture of the boy that won the final.

Mrs Heegan A parcel of sandwiches, a bottle of whiskey,
an' some magazines to take away with you an' Barney,
Harry.

Harry Napoo sandwiches, an' napoo magazines: look at the cup, eh? The cup that Harry won, won by the odd goal in five! (*To Barney*) The song that the little Jock used to sing, Barney, what was it? The little Jock we left shrivellin' on the wire after the last push.

Barney 'Will ye no come back again?'

Harry No, no, the one we all used to sing with him, 'The Silver Tassie'. (*Pointing to cup*) There it is, the Silver Tassie, won by the odd goal in five, kicked by Harry Heegan.

Mrs Heegan Watch your time, Harry, watch your time.

Jessie He's watching it, he's watching it – for God's sake don't get fussy, Mrs Heegan.

Harry They couldn't take their beatin' like men . . . Play the game, play the game, why the hell couldn't they play the game? (*To Barney*) See the President of the Club, Dr Forby Maxwell, shaking hands with me, when he was giving me the cup, 'Well done, Heegan!' The way they yell'd and jump'd when they put in the equalizing goal in the first half!

Barney Ay, a fluke, that's what it was; a lowsey fluke.

Mrs Heegan (*holding Harry's coat up for him to put it on*) Here, your coat, Harry, slip it on while you're talkin'.

Harry (*putting it on*) Alright, keep smiling, don't fuss. (*To the rest*) Grousing the whole time they were chasing the ball; an' when they lost it, 'Referee, referee, offside, referee . . . foul there; ey, open your eyes, referee!'

Jessie And we scream'd and shout'd them down with 'Play the game, Primrose Rovers, play the game!'

Barney You ran them off their feet till they nearly stood still.

Mrs Foran (*has been peeping in twice timidly from the*

room and now comes in to the rest) Somebody run up an'
bring Teddy down for fear he'd be left behind.

Sylvester (*To Harry*) Your haversack an' trench tools,
Harry; haversack first, isn't it?

Harry (*fixing his haversack*) Haversack, haversack, don't
rush me. (*To the rest*) But when I got the ball, Barney,
once I got the ball, the rain began to fall on the others. An'
the last goal, the goal that put us one ahead, the winning
goal, that was a-a-eh-a stunner!

Barney A beauty, me boy, a hot beauty.

Harry Slipping by the back rushing at me like a mad bull,
steadying a moment for a drive, seeing in a flash the
goalie's hands sent with a shock to his chest by the force of
the shot, his half-stunned motion to clear, a charge, and
then carrying him, the ball and all with a rush into the
centre of the net!

Barney (*enthusiastically*) Be-God, I did get a thrill when I
seen you puttin' him sittin' on his arse in the middle of the
net!

Mrs Foran (*from the door*) One of yous do go up an' see if
Teddy's ready to go.

Mrs Heegan (*to Harry*) Your father 'll carry your kit-bag,
an' Jessie 'll carry your rifle as far as the boat.

Harry (*irritably*) Oh, damn it, woman, give your wailin'
over for a minute!

Mrs Heegan You've got only a few bare minutes to spare,
Harry.

Harry We'll make the most of them, then. (*To Barney*)
Out with one of them wine-virgins we got in 'The Mill in
the Field', Barney, and we'll rape her in a last hot moment
before we set out to kiss the guns!

Simon has gone into room and returned with a gun and a kit-bag. He crosses to where Barney is standing.

Barney (*taking a bottle of wine from his pocket*) Empty her of her virtues, eh?

Harry Spill it out, Barney, spill it out . . . . (*Seizing the silver cup, and holding it towards Barney*) Here, into the cup, be-God. A drink out of the cup, out of the Silver Tassie!

Barney (*who has removed the cap and taken out the cork*) Here she is now . . . Ready for anything, stripp'd to the skin!

Jessie No double-meaning talk, Barney.

Susie (*haughtily, to Jessie*) The men that are defending us have leave to bow themselves down in the House of Rimmon, for the men that go with the guns are going with God.

Barney pours wine into the cup for Harry and into a glass for himself.

Harry (*to Jessie*) Jessie, a sup for you.

Jessie drinks from the cup.

An' a drink for me. (*He drinks.*) Now a kiss while our lips are wet. (*He kisses her.*) Christ, Barney, how would you like to be retreating from the fairest face and (*lifting Jessie's skirt a little*) – and the trimmest, slimmest little leg in the parish? Napoo, Barney, to everyone but me!

Mrs Foran One of you go up, an' try to get my Teddy down.

Barney (*lifting Susie's skirt a little*) Napoo, Harry, to everyone but –

Susie (*angrily, pushing Barney away from her*) You khaki-cover'd ape, you, what are you trying to do? Man-handle the lassies of France, if you like, but put on your gloves when you touch a woman that seeketh not the things of the flesh.

Harry (*putting an arm round Susie to mollify her*) Now, Susie, Susie, lengthen your temper for a passing moment, so that we may bring away with us the breath of a kiss to the shell-bullied air of the trenches . . . . Besides, there's nothing to be ashamed of – it's not a bad little leggie at all.

Susie (*slipping her arm round Harry's neck, and looking defiantly at Barney*) I don't mind what Harry does; I know he means no harm, not like other people. Harry's different.

Jessie You'll not forget to send me the German helmet home from France, Harry?

Susie (*trying to rest her head on Harry's breast*) I know Harry, he's different. It's his way. I wouldn't let anyone else touch me, but in some way or another I can tell Harry's different.

Jessie (*putting her arm round Harry under Susie's in an effort to dislodge it*) Susie, Harry wants to be free to keep his arm round me during his last few moments here, so don't be pulling him about!

Susie (*shrinking back a little*) I was only saying that Harry was different.

Mrs Foran For God's sake, will someone go up for Teddy, or he won't go back at all!

Teddy (*appearing at door*) Damn anxious for Teddy to go back! Well, Teddy's goin' back, an' he's left everything tidy upstairs so that you'll not have much trouble sortin' things out. (*To Harry*) The Club an' a crowd's waitin' outside to bring us to the boat before they go to the spread in honour of the final. (*Bitterly*) A party for them while we muck off to the trenches!

Harry (*after a slight pause, to Barney*) Are you game, Barney?

Barney What for?

Harry To go to the spread and hang the latch for another night?

Barney (*taking his rifle from Simon and slinging it over his shoulder*) No, no, napoo desertin' on Active Service. Deprivation of pay an' the rest of your time in the front trenches. No, no. We must go back!

Mrs Heegan No, no, Harry. You must go back.

Simon,
Sylvester } (*together*) You must go back.
Susie

Voices of Crowd Outside They must go back!

The ship's siren is heard blowing.

Simon The warning signal.

Sylvester By the time they get there, they'll be unslinging the gangways!

Susie (*handing Harry his steel helmet*) Here's your helmet, Harry.

He puts it on.

Mrs Heegan You'll all nearly have to run for it now!

Sylvester I've got your kit-bag, Harry.

Susie I've got your rifle.

Simon I'll march in front with the cup, after Conroy with the concertina.

Teddy Come on: ong, avong to the trenches!

Harry (*recklessly*) Jesus, a last drink, then! (*He raises the silver cup. Singing*)
> Gae bring to me a pint of wine,
> And fill it in a silver tassie;

Barney (*joining in vigorously*)
> . . . a silver tassie.

Harry
> That I may drink before I go,
> A service to my bonnie lassie.

Barney
> . . . bonnie lassie.

Harry
> The boat rocks at the pier o' Leith,
> Full loud the wind blows from the ferry;
> The ship rides at the Berwick Law,
> An' I must leave my bonnie Mary!

Barney
> . . . leave my bonnie Mary!

Harry
> The trumpets sound, the banners fly,
> The glittering spears are ranked ready;

Barney
> . . . glittering spears are ranked ready;

Harry
> The shouts of war are heard afar,
> The battle closes thick and bloody.

Barney
> . . . closes thick and bloody.

Harry
> It's not the roar of sea or shore,
> That makes me longer wish to tarry,

Nor shouts of war that's heard afar –
It's leaving thee, my bonnie lassie!

Barney
. . . leaving thee, my bonnie lassie!

Teddy Come on, come on.

Simon, Sylvester and Susie go out.

Voices (*outside*)
Come on from your home to the boat;
Carry on from the boat to the camp.

*Teddy and Barney go out. Harry and Jessie follow; as
Harry reaches the door, he takes his arm from round
Jessie and comes back to Mrs Heegan.*

Voices (*outside*) From the camp up to the lines to the
trenches.

Harry (*shyly and hurriedly kissing Mrs Heegan*) Well,
goodbye, old woman.

Mrs Heegan Goodbye, my son.

*Harry goes out. The chorus of 'The Silver Tassie',
accompanied by a concertina, can be heard growing
fainter till it ceases. Mrs Foran goes out timidly. Mrs
Heegan pokes the fire, arranges the things in the room,
and then goes to the window and looks out. After a
pause, the loud and long blast of the ship's siren is
heard. The light on the masthead, seen through the
window, moves slowly away, and Mrs Heegan with a
sigh, 'Ah dear', goes over to the fire and sits down. A
slight pause, then Mrs Foran returns to the room.*

Mrs Foran Every little bit of china I had in the house is
lyin' above in a mad an' muddled heap like the flotsum an'
jetsum of the seashore!

Mrs Heegan (*with a deep sigh of satisfaction*) Thanks be to Christ that we're after managin' to get the three of them away safely.

End of Act One.

Act Two

In the war zone: a scene of jagged and lacerated ruin of
what was once a monastery. At back a lost wall and
window are indicated by an arched piece of broken coping
pointing from the left to the right, and a similar piece of
masonry pointing from the right to the left. Between these
two lacerated fingers of stone can be seen the country
stretching to the horizon where the front trenches are.
Here and there heaps of rubbish mark where houses
once stood. From some of these, lean, dead hands are
protruding. Further on, spiky stumps of trees which were
once a small wood. The ground is dotted with rayed and
shattered shell holes. Across the horizon in the red glare
can be seen the criss-cross pattern of the barbed wire
bordering the trenches. In the sky sometimes a green star,
sometimes a white star, burns. Within the broken archway
to the left is an arched entrance to another part of the
monastery, used now as a Red Cross Station. In the wall,
right, near the front is a stained-glass window,
background green, figure of the Virgin, white-faced,
wearing a black robe, lights inside making the figure
vividly apparent. Further up from this window is a life-size
crucifix. A shell has released an arm from the cross, which
has caused the upper part of the figure to lean forward
with the released arm outstretched towards the figure of
the Virgin. Underneath the crucifix on a pedestal, in red
letters, are the words: PRINCEPS PACIS. Almost opposite
the crucifix is a gunwheel to which Barney is tied. At the
back, in the centre, where the span of the arch should be,
is the shape of a big howitzer gun, squat, heavy underpart,
with a long, sinister barrel now pointing towards the front

at an angle of forty-five degrees. At the base of the gun a piece of wood is placed on which is chalked, HYDE PARK CORNER. *On another piece of wood near the entrance of the Red Cross Station is chalked,* NO HAWKERS OR STREET CRIES PERMITTED HERE. *In the near centre is a brazier in which a fire is burning. Crouching above, on a ramp, is a soldier whose clothes are covered with mud and splashed with blood. Every feature of the scene seems a little distorted from its original appearance. Rain is falling steadily; its fall worried now and again by fitful gusts of a cold wind. A small organ is heard playing slow and stately notes as the curtain rises.*

After a pause, the Croucher, without moving, intones dreamily:

Croucher

And the hand of the Lord was upon me, and carried me
   out in the spirit of the Lord, and set me down in the
   midst of a valley.

And I looked and saw a great multitude that stood upon
   their feet, an exceeding great army.

And he said unto me, Son of man, can this exceeding
   great army become a valley of dry bones?

The music ceases, and a voice, in the part of the monastery left standing, intones: Kyr . . . ie . . . e . . . eleison. Kyr . . . ie . . . e . . . eleison, followed by the answer: Christe . . . eleison.

(*Resuming*) And I answered, O Lord God, thou knowest.
And he said, prophesy and say unto the wind, come from
the four winds a breath and breathe upon these living that
they may die.

As he pauses the voice in the monastery is heard again: Gloria in excelsis Deo et in terra pax hominibus bonae voluntatis.

(*Resuming*) And I prophesied, and the breath came out of them, and the sinews came away from them, and behold a shaking, and their bones fell asunder, bone from his bone, and they died, and the exceeding great army became a valley of dry bones.

> *The voice from the monastery is heard, clearly for the first half of the sentence, then dying away towards the end: Accendat in nobis Dominus ignem sui amoris, et flammam aeternae caritatis.*
>
> *A group of soldiers comes in from fatigue, bunched together as if for comfort and warmth. They are wet and cold, and they are sullen-faced. They form a circle around the brazier and stretch their hands towards the blaze.*

1st Soldier Cold and wet and tir'd.

2nd Soldier Wet and tir'd and cold.

3rd Soldier Tir'd and cold and wet.

4th Soldier (*very like Teddy*) Twelve blasted hours of ammunition transport fatigue!

1st Soldier Twelve weary hours.

2nd Soldier And wasting hours.

3rd Soldier And hot and heavy hours.

1st Soldier Toiling and thinking to build the wall of force that blocks the way from here to home.

2nd Soldier Lifting shells.

3rd Soldier Carrying shells.

4th Soldier Piling shells.

1st Soldier In the falling, pissing rine and whistling wind.

2nd Soldier The whistling wind and falling, drenching rain.

3rd Soldier The God-damn rain and blasted whistling wind.

1st Soldier And the shirkers sife at home coil'd up at ease.

2nd Soldier Shells for us and pianos for them.

3rd Soldier Fur coats for them and winding-sheets for us.

4th Soldier Warm.

2nd Soldier And dry.

1st Soldier An' 'appy.

A slight pause.

Barney An' they call it re-cu-per-at-ing!

1st Soldier (*reclining near the fire*) Gawd, I'm sleepy.

2nd Soldier (*reclining*) Tir'd and lousey.

3rd Soldier (*reclining*) Damp and shaking.

4th Soldier (*murmuringly, the rest joining him*) Tir'd and lousey an' wet an' sleepy, but mother call me early in the morning.

1st Soldier (*dreamily*) Wen I thinks of 'ome, I thinks of a field of dysies.

The Rest (*dreamily*) Wen 'e thinks of 'ome, 'e thinks of a field of dysies.

1st Soldier (*chanting dreamily*)
I sees the missus paryding along Walham Green,
Through the jewels an' silks on the costers' carts,
Emmie a-pulling her skirt an' muttering,
'A balloon, a balloon, I wants a balloon',
The missus a-tugging 'er on, an' sying,
'A balloon, for shime, an' your father fighting:
You'll wait till 'e's 'ome, an' the bands a-plying!'

He pauses.

(*Suddenly*) But wy'r we 'ere, wy'r we 'ere – that's wot we wants to know!

2nd Soldier God only knows – or else, perhaps, a red-cap.

1st Soldier (*chanting*)
Tabs'll murmur, 'em an' 'aw, an' sy: 'You're 'ere because you're
Point nine double o, the sixth platoon an' forty-eight battalion,
The Yellow Plumes that pull'd a bow at Crecy,
And gave to fame a leg up on the path to glory;
Now with the howitzers of the Twenty-first Division,
Tiking life easy with the Army of the Marne,
An' all the time the battered Conchie squeals,
"It's one or two men looking after business"'

3rd Soldier An' saves his blasted skin!

1st Soldier (*chanting*) The padre gives a fag an' softly whispers

'Your king, your country an' your muvver 'as you 'ere.'
An' last time 'ome on leave, I awsks the missus:
'The good God up in heaven, Bill, 'e knows,
An' I gets the seperytion moneys reg'lar.'

He sits up suddenly.

But wy'r we 'ere, wy'r we 'ere, – that's wot I wants to know?

The Rest (*chanting sleepily*) Why 's 'e 'ere, why 's 'e 'ere – that's wot 'e wants to know!

Barney (*singing to the air of second bar in chorus of 'Auld Lang Syne'*) We're here because we're here, because we're here, because we're here!

Each slides into an attitude of sleep – even Barney's
head droops a little. The Corporal, followed by the
Visitor, appears at back. The Visitor is a portly man
with a rubicund face; he is smiling to demonstrate his
ease of mind, but the lines are a little distorted with
an ever-present sense of anxiety. He is dressed in a
semi-civilian, semi-military manner – dark worsted
suit, shrapnel helmet, a haversack slung round his
shoulder, a brown belt round his middle, black top
boots and spurs, and he carries a cane. His head is
bent between his shoulders, and his shoulders are
crouched a little.

Visitor Yes, tomorrow, I go a little further. Penetrate a
little deeper into danger. Foolish, yes, but then it's an
experience; by God, it's an experience. The military
authorities are damned strict – won't let a . . . man . . .
plunge!

Corporal In a manner of speakin', sir, only let you see the
arses of the guns.

Visitor (*not liking the remark*) Yes, no; no, oh yes.
Damned strict, won't let a . . . man . . . plunge! (*Suddenly,
with alarm*) What's that, what was that?

Corporal Wha' was what?

Visitor A buzz, I thought I heard a buzz.

Corporal A buzz?

Visitor Of an aeroplane.

Corporal Didn't hear. Might have been a bee.

Visitor No, no; don't think it was a bee. (*Arranging
helmet with his hands*) Damn shrapnel helmet; skin tight;
like a vice; hurts the head. Rather be without it; but,
regulations, you know. Military authorities damn

particular – won't let a . . . man . . . plunge! (*Seeing Barney*) Aha, what have we got here, what have we got here?

Corporal (*to Barney*) 'Tshun! (*To the Visitor*) Regimental misdemeanour, sir.

Visitor (*to Barney*) Nothing much, boy, nothing much?

Barney (*chanting softly*)
　A Brass-hat pullin' the bedroom curtains
　Between himself, the world an' the Estaminay's
　　daughter,
　In a pyjama'd hurry ran down an' phon'd
　A Tommy was chokin' an Estaminay cock,
　An' I was pinch'd as I was puttin' the bird
　Into a pot with a pint of peas.

Corporal (*chanting hoarsely*)
　And the hens all droop, for the loss has made
　The place a place of desolation!

Visitor (*reprovingly, to the Corporal*) Seriously, Corporal, seriously, please. Sacred, sacred: property of the citizen of a friendly State, sacred. On Active Service, serious to steal a fowl, a cock. (*To Barney*) The uniform, the cause, boy, the corps. Infra dignitatem, boy, infra dignitatem.

Barney Wee, wee.

Visitor (*pointing to reclining soldiers*) Taking it easy, eh?

Corporal Done in; transport fatigue; twelve hours.

Visitor Um, not too much rest, Corporal. Dangerous. Keep 'em moving much as possible. Too much rest – bad. Sap, sap, sap.

Corporal (*pointing to the left*) Bit of monastery left intact. Hold services there; troops off to front line. Little organ plays.

Visitor Splendid. Bucks 'em up. Gives 'em peace.

A Staff Officer enters suddenly, passing by the Visitor with a springing hop, so that he stands in the centre with the Visitor on his right and the Corporal on his left. He is prim, pert, and polished, superfine khaki uniform, gold braid, crimson tabs, and gleaming top boots. He speaks his sentences with a gasping importance.

Corporal (*stiffening*) 'Shun! Staff!

Soldiers (*springing to their feet – the Croucher remains as he is, with a sleepy alertness*) Staff! 'Shun!

Corporal (*bellowing at the Croucher*) Eh, you there: 'shun! Staff!

Croucher (*calmly*) Not able. Sick. Privilege. Excused duty.

Staff-Wallah (*reading document*)
Battery Brigade Orders, F.A., 31 D 2.
Units presently recuperating, parade eight o'clock p.m.
Attend Lecture organized by Society for amusement and
    mental development, soldiers at front.
Subject: Habits of those living between Frigid Zone and
    Arctic Circle.
Lecturer: Mr Melville Sprucer.
Supplementary Order: Units to wear gas masks.
As you were.

The Staff-Wallah departs as he came with a springing hop. The Visitor and the Corporal relax, and stroll down towards the RC Station. The soldiers relax too, seeking various positions of ease around the fire.

Visitor (*indicating RC Station*) Ah, in here. We'll just pop in here for a minute. And then pop out again.

He and the Corporal go into the RC Station. A pause.

1st Soldier (*chanting and indicating that he means the Visitor by looking in the direction of the RC Station*)
The perky bastard's cautious nibbling
In a safe, safe shelter at danger queers me.
Furiously feeling he's up to the neck in
The whirl and the sweep of the front-line fighting.

2nd Soldier (*chanting*)
In his full-blown, chin-strapp'd, shrapnel helmet,
He'll pat a mug on the back and murmur,
'Here's a stand-fast Tauntonshire before me',
And the mug, on his feet, 'll whisper 'yessir'.

3rd Soldier (*chanting*)
Like a bride, full-flush'd, 'e'll sit down and listen
To every word of the goddam sermon,
From the cushy-soul'd, word-spreading, yellow-streaked
    dud.

Barney (*chanting*)
Who wouldn't make a patch on a Tommy's backside.

A pause.

1st Soldier 'Ow long have we been resting 'ere?

2nd Soldier A month.

3rd Soldier Twenty-nine days, twenty-three hours and (*looking at watch*) twenty-three minutes.

4th Soldier Thirty-seven minutes more'll make it thirty days.

Croucher
Thirty days hath September, April, June, and
    November –
November – that's the month when I was born –
    November

Not the beginning, not the end, but the middle of
    November.
Near the valley of the Thames, in the middle of
    November.
Shall I die at the start, near the end, in the middle of
    November?

1st Soldier (*nodding towards the Croucher*) One more
scrap, an' 'e'll be Ay one in the kingdom of the bawmy.

2nd Soldier Perhaps they have forgotten.

3rd Soldier Forgotten.

4th Soldier Forgotten us.

1st Soldier If the blighters at the front would tame their
grousing.

The Rest Tame their grousing.

2nd Soldier And the wounded cease to stare their silent
scorning.

The Rest Passing by us, carried cushy on the stretchers.

3rd Soldier We have beaten out the time upon the duck-
board.

4th Soldier Stiff standing watch'd the sunrise from the
firestep.

2nd Soldier Stiff standing from the firestep watch'd the
sunset.

3rd Soldier Have bless'd the dark wiring of the top with
curses.

2nd Soldier And never a ray of leave.

3rd Soldier To have a quiet drunk.

1st Soldier Or a mad mowment to rustle a judy.

*3rd Soldier takes out a package of cigarettes; taking one
himself he hands the package round. Each takes one,
and the man nearest to Barney, kneeling up, puts one in
his mouth and lights it for him. They all smoke silently
for a few moments, sitting up round the fire.*

2nd Soldier (*chanting very earnestly and quietly*)
    Would God I smok'd an' walk'd an' watch'd th'
    Dance of a golden Brimstone butterfly,
    To the saucy pipe of a greenfinch resting
    In a drowsy, brambled lane in Cumberland.

1st Soldier
    Would God I smok'd and lifted cargoes
    From the laden shoulders of London's river-way;
    Then holiday'd, roaring out courage and movement
    To the muscled machines of Tottenham Hotspur.

3rd Soldier
    To hang here even a little longer,
    Lounging through fear-swell'd, anxious moments;
    The hinderparts of the god of battles
    Shading our war-tir'd eyes from his flaming face.

Barney
    If you creep to rest in a clos'd-up coffin,
    A tail of comrades seeing you safe home;
    Or be a kernel lost in a shell exploding –
    It's all, sure, only in a lifetime.

All (*together*)
    Each sparrow, hopping, irresponsible,
    Is indentur'd in God's mighty memory;
    And we, more than they all, shall not be lost
    In the forgetfulness of the Lord of Hosts.

*The Visitor and the Corporal come from the Red Cross
Station.*

Visitor (*taking out a cigarette case*) Nurses too gloomy.
Surgeons too serious. Doesn't do.

Corporal All lying-down cases, sir. Pretty bad.

Visitor (*who is now standing near the crucifix*) All the
more reason make things merry and bright. Lift them out
of themselves. (*To the soldiers*) See you all tomorrow at
lecture?

1st Soldier (*rising and standing a little sheepishly before
the Visitor*) Yessir, yessir.

The Rest Yessir, yessir.

Visitor Good. Make it interesting. (*Searching in pocket*)
Damn it, have I none? Ah, saved.

> He takes a match from his pocket and is about to strike
> it carelessly on the arm of the crucifix, when the 1st
> Soldier, with a rapid frightened movement, knocks it
> out of his hand.

1st Soldier (*roughly*) Blarst you, man, keep your peace-
white paws from that!

2nd Soldier The image of the Son of God.

3rd Soldier Jesus of Nazareth, the King of the Jews.

1st Soldier (*reclining by the fire again*) There's a Gawd
knocking abaht somewhere.

4th Soldier Wants Him to be sending us over a chit in the
shape of a bursting shell.

Visitor Sorry put it across you. (*To Corporal*) Too much
time to think. Nervy. Time to brood, brood; bad. Sap. Sap.
Sap. (*Walking towards where he came in*) Must return
quarters; rough and ready. Must stick it. There's a war on.
Cheerio. Straight down road instead of round hill: shorter?

Corporal Less than half as long.

Visitor Safe?

Corporal Yes. Only drop shells off and on, crossroads. Ration party wip'd out week ago.

Visitor Go round hill. No hurry. General Officer's orders, no unnecessary risks. Must obey. Military Authorities damned particular – won't let a . . . man . . . plunge!

He and the Corporal go off. The soldiers in various attitudes are asleep around the fire. After a few moments' pause, two Stretcher-Bearers come in slowly from left, carrying a casualty. They pass through the sleeping soldiers, going towards the Red Cross Station. As they go they chant a verse, and as the verse is ending, they are followed by another pair carrying a second casualty.

1st Bearers (*chanting*)
Oh, bear it gently, carry it softly –
A bullet or a shell said stop, stop, stop.
It's had it's day, and it's left the play,
Since it gamboll'd over the top, top, top.
It's had its day and it's left the play,
Since it gamboll'd over the top.

2nd Bearers (*chanting*)
Oh, carry it softly, bear it gently –
The beggar has seen it through, through, through.
If it 'adn't been 'im, if it 'adn't been 'im,
It might 'ave been me or you, you, you.
If it 'adn't been 'im, if it 'adn't been 'im,
It might 'ave been me or you.

Voice (*inside RC Station*) Easy, easy there; don't crowd.

1st Stretcher-Bearer (*to man behind*) Woa, woa there, Bill, 'ouse full.

Stretcher-Bearer (*behind, to those following*) Woa, woa; traffic blocked.

They leave the stretchers on the ground.

Wounded on the Stretchers (*chanting*)
Carry on, carry on to the place of pain,
Where the surgeon spreads his aid, aid, aid.
And we show man's wonderful work, well done,
To the image God hath made, made, made,
And we show man's wonderful work, well done,
To the image God hath made!

When the future hours have all been spent,
And the hand of death is near, near, near,
Then a few, few moments and we shall find
There'll be nothing left to fear, fear, fear,
Then a few, few moments and we shall find
There'll be nothing left to fear.

The power, the joy, the pull of life,
The laugh, the blow, and the dear kiss,
The pride and hope, the gain and loss,
Have been temper'd down to this, this, this,
The pride and hope, the gain and loss,
Have been temper'd down to this.

1st Stretcher-Bearer (*to Barney*) Oh, Barney, have they liced you up because you've kiss'd the Colonel's judy?

Barney They lit on me stealin' Estaminay poulthry.

1st Stretcher-Bearer A hen?

2nd Stretcher-Bearer A duck, again, Barney?

3rd Stretcher-Bearer A swan this time.

Barney (*chanting softly*)
A Brass-hat pullin' the bedroom curtains
Between himself, the world an' the Estaminay's daughter,

In a pyjama'd hurry ran down and phon'd
A Tommy was chokin' an Estaminay cock;
An' I was pinch'd as I was puttin' the bird
Into a pot with a pint of peas.

1st Stretcher-Bearer The red-tabb'd squit!

2nd Stretcher-Bearer The lousey map-scanner!

3rd Stretcher-Bearer We must keep up, we must keep up the morale of the awmy.

2nd Stretcher-Bearer (*loudly*) Does 'e eat well?

The Rest (*in chorus*) Yes, 'e eats well!

2nd Stretcher-Bearer Does 'e sleep well?

The Rest (*in chorus*) Yes, 'e sleeps well!

2nd Stretcher-Bearer Does 'e whore well?

The Rest (*in chorus*) Yes, 'e whores well!

2nd Stretcher-Bearer Does 'e fight well?

The Rest (*in chorus*) Napoo; 'e 'as to do the thinking for the Tommies!

Voice (*from the RC Station*) Stretcher Party – carry on!

The Bearers stoop with precision, attach their supports to the stretchers, lift them up and march slowly into the RC Station, chanting.

Stretcher-Bearers (*chanting*)
Carry on – we've one bugled reason why –
We've 'eard and answer'd the call, call, call.
There's no more to be said, for when we are dead,
We may understand it all, all, all.
There's no more to be said, for when we are dead,
We may understand it all.

They go out, leaving the scene occupied by the Croucher
and the Soldiers sleeping around the fire. The Corporal
re-enters. He is carrying two parcels. He pauses, looking
at the sleeping soldiers for a few moments, then shouts.

Corporal (*shouting*) Hallo, there, you sleepy blighters!
Number 2, a parcel; and for you, Number 3. Get a move
on – parcels!

The Soldiers wake up and spring to their feet.

For you, Number 2. (*He throws a parcel to 2nd Soldier.*)
Number 3. (*He throws the other parcel to 3rd Soldier.*)

3rd Soldier (*taking paper from around his parcel*) Looks
like a bundle of cigarettes.

1st Soldier Or a pack of cawds.

4th Soldier Or a prayer-book.

3rd Soldier (*astounded*) Holy Christ, it is!

The Rest What?

3rd Soldier A prayer-book!

4th Soldier In a green plush cover with a golden cross.

Croucher Open it at the Psalms and sing that we may be
saved from the life and death of the beasts that perish.

Barney *Per omnia saecula saeculorum.*

2nd Soldier (*who has opened his parcel*) A ball, be God!

4th Soldier A red and yellow coloured rubber ball.

1st Soldier And a note.

2nd Soldier (*reading*) To play your way to the enemies'
trenches when you all go over the top. Mollie.

1st Soldier See if it 'ops.

The 2nd Soldier hops the ball, and then kicks it from him. The Corporal intercepts it, and begins to dribble it across the stage. The 3rd Soldier tries to take it from him. The Corporal shouts 'Offside, there!' They play for a few minutes with the ball, when suddenly the Staff-Wallah springs in and stands rigidly in centre.

Corporal (*stiff to attention as he sees the Staff-Wallah*) 'Shun. Staff!

All the Soldiers stiffen. The Croucher remains motionless.

Corporal (*shouting to the Croucher*) You: 'shun. Staff!

Croucher Not able. Sick. Excused duty.

Staff-Wallah (*reading document*)
Brigade Orders, C/X 143. B/Y 341. Regarding gas-masks. Gas-masks to be worn round neck so as to lie in front $2\frac{1}{2}$ degrees from socket of left shoulder-blade, and $2\frac{3}{4}$ degrees from socket of right shoulder-blade, leaving bottom margin to reach $\frac{1}{4}$ of an inch from second button of lower end of tunic. Order to take effect from 6 a.m. following morning of date received. Dismiss!

He hops out again, followed by the Corporal.

1st Soldier (*derisively*) Comprenneemoy.

3rd Soldier Tray bong.

2nd Soldier (*who is standing in archway, back, looking scornfully after the Staff-Wallah, chanting*)
Jazzing back to his hotel he now goes gaily,
Shelter'd and safe where the clock ticks tamely.
His backside warming a cushion, downfill'd,
Green clad, well splash'd with gold birds redbeak'd.

1st Soldier
His last dim view of the front-line sinking

Into the white-flesh'd breasts of a judy;
Cuddling with proud, bright, amorous glances
The thing salved safe from the mud of the trenches.

2nd Soldier

His tunic reared in the lap of comfort,
Peeps at the blood-stain'd jackets passing,
Through colour-gay bars of ribbon jaunty,
Fresh from a posh shop snug in Bond Street.

Croucher

Shame and scorn play with and beat them,
Till we anchor in their company;
Then the decorations of security
Become the symbols of self-sacrifice.

A pause.

2nd Soldier

A warning this that we'll soon be exiles
From the freedom chance of life can give,
To the front where you wait to be hurried breathless,
Murmuring how, how do you do, to God.

3rd Soldier

Where hot with the sweat of mad endeavour,
Crouching to scrape a toy-deep shelter,
Quick-tim'd by hell's fast, frenzied drumfire
Exploding in flaming death around us.

2nd Soldier

God, unchanging, heart-sicken'd, shuddering,
Gathereth the darkness of the night sky
To mask His paling countenance from
The blood dance of His self-slaying children.

3rd Soldier

Stumbling, swiftly cursing, plodding,
Lumbering, loitering, stumbling, grousing,

Through mud and rain, and filth and danger,
Flesh and blood seek slow the front line.

2nd Soldier
Squeals of hidden laughter run through
The screaming medley of the wounded –
Christ, who bore the cross, still weary,
Now trails a rope tied to a field gun.

*As the last notes of the chanting are heard the Corporal
comes in rapidly; he is excited but steady; pale-faced
and grim.*

Corporal They attack. Along a wide front the enemy
attacks. If they break through it may reach us even here.

Soldiers (*in chorus as they all put on gas-masks*) They
attack. The enemy attacks.

Corporal Let us honour that in which we do put our trust.

Soldiers (*in chorus*) That it may not fail us in our time of
need.

*The Corporal goes over to the gun and faces towards it,
standing on the bottom step. The soldiers group around,
each falling upon one knee, their forms crouched in a
huddled act of obeisance. They are all facing the gun
with their backs to the audience. The Croucher rises and
joins them.*

Corporal (*singing*)
Hail cool-hardened tower of steel emboss'd
With the fever'd, figment thoughts of man;
Guardian of our love and hate and fear,
Speak for us to the inner ear of God!

Soldiers
We believe in God and we believe in thee.

Corporal

> Dreams of line, of colour, and of form;
> Dreams of music dead for ever now;
> Dreams in bronze and dreams in stone have gone
> To make thee delicate and strong to kill.

Soldier

> We believe in God and we believe in thee.

Corporal

> Jail'd in thy steel are hours of merriment
> Cadg'd from the pageant-dream of children's play;
> Too soon of the motley stripp'd that they may sweat
> With them that toil for the glory of thy kingdom.

Soldiers

> We believe in God and we believe in thee.

Corporal

> Remember our women, sad-hearted, proud-fac'd,
> Who've given the substance of their womb for shadows;
> Their shrivel'd, empty breasts war tinselléd
> For patient gifts of graves to thee.

Soldiers

> We believe in God and we believe in thee.

Corporal

> Dapple those who are shelter'd with disease,
> And women labouring with child,
> And children that play about the streets,
> With blood of youth expiring in its prime.

Soldiers

> We believe in God and we believe in thee.

Corporal

> Tear a gap through the soul of our mass'd enemies;
> Grant them all the peace of death;
> Blow them swiftly into Abram's bosom,

And mingle them with the joys of paradise!

Soldiers
For we believe in God and we believe in thee.

The sky has become vexed with a crimson glare, mixed with yellow streaks, and striped with pillars of rising brown and black smoke. The Staff-Wallah rushes in, turbulent and wild, with his uniform disordered.

Staff-Wallah
The enemy has broken through, broken through,
　　broken through!
Every man born of woman to the guns, to the guns.

Soldiers
To the guns, to the guns, to the guns!

Staff-Wallah
Those at prayer, all in bed, and the swillers drinking
　　deeply in the pubs.

Soldiers
To the guns, to the guns.

Staff-Wallah
All the batmen, every cook, every bitch's son that hides
A whiff of courage in his veins,
Shelter'd vigour in his body,
That can run, or can walk, even crawl –
Dig him out, dig him out, shove him on –

Soldiers
To the guns!

The Soldiers hurry to their places led by the Staff-Wallah to the gun. The gun swings around and points to the horizon; a shell is swung into the breech and a flash indicates the firing of the gun, searchlights move over the red glare of the sky; the scene darkens, stabbed with distant flashes and by the more vivid flash of the gun which the Soldiers load and fire with rhythmical movements while the scene is closing. Only flashes are seen; no noise is heard.

End of Act Two.

Act Three

The upper end of a hospital ward. At right angles from back wall are two beds, one covered with a red quilt and the other with a white one. From the centre of the head of each bed is an upright having at the top a piece like a swan's neck, curving out over the bed, from which hangs a chain with a wooden cross-piece to enable weak patients to pull themselves into a sitting posture. To the left of these beds is a large glass double-door which opens on to the ground: one of the doors is open and a lovely September sun, which is setting, gives a glow to the garden.

Through the door two poplar trees can be seen silhouetted against the sky. To the right of this door is another bed covered with a black quilt. Little white discs are fixed to the head of each bed: on the first is the number 26, on the second 27, and on the third 28. Medical charts hang over each on the wall. To the right is the fireplace, facing down the ward. Farther on, to the right of the fire, is a door of a bathroom. In the corner, between the glass door and the fire, is a pedestal on which stands a statue of the Blessed Virgin; under the statue is written, 'Mater Misericordiae, ora pro nobis'. An easy-chair, on which are rugs, is near the fire. In the centre is a white, glass-topped table on which are medicines, drugs, and surgical instruments. On one corner is a vase of flowers. A locker is beside the head, and a small chair by the foot of each bed. Two electric lights, green shaded, hang from the ceiling, and a bracket light with a red shade projects from the wall over the fireplace. It is dusk, and the two lights suspended from the ceiling are lighted. The walls are a brilliant white.

Sylvester is in the bed numbered '26'; he is leaning upon his elbow looking towards the glass door.

Simon, sitting down on the chair beside bed numbered '27', is looking into the grounds.

Sylvester (*after a pause*) Be God, isn't it a good one!

Simon Almost, almost, mind you, Sylvester, incomprehensible.

Sylvester To come here and find Susie Monican fashion'd like a Queen of Sheba. God moves in a mysterious way, Simon.

Simon There's Surgeon Maxwell prancing after her now.

Sylvester (*stretching to see*) Heads together, eh? Be God, he's kissing her behind the trees! Oh, Susannah, Susannah, how are the mighty fallen, and the weapons of war perished!

Harry Heegan enters crouched in a self-propelled invalid chair; he wheels himself up to the fire. Sylvester slides down into the bed, and Simon becomes interested in a book that he takes off the top of his locker. Harry remains for a few moments beside the fire, and then wheels himself round and goes out as he came in; Sylvester raises himself in the bed, and Simon leaves down the book to watch Harry.

Down and up, up and down.

Simon Up and down, down and up.

Sylvester Never quiet for a minute.

Simon Never able to hang on to an easy second.

Sylvester Trying to hold on to the little finger of life.

Simon Half-way up to heaven.

Sylvester And him always thinking of Jessie.

Simon And Jessie never thinking of him.

Susie Monican, in the uniform of a VAD nurse, enters the ward by the glass door. She is changed, for it is clear that she has made every detail of the costume as attractive as possible. She has the same assertive manner, but dignity and a sense of importance have been added. Her legs encased in silk stockings, are seen (and shown) to advantage by her short and smartly cut skirt. Altogether she is now a very handsome woman. Coming in she glances at the bed numbered '28', then pauses beside Sylvester and Simon.

Susie How is Twenty-eight?

Simon and Sylvester (*together*) Travelling again.

Susie Did he speak at all to you?

Sylvester Dumb, Susie, dumb.

Simon Brooding, Susie; brooding, brooding.

Sylvester Cogitatin', Susie; cogitatin', cogitatin'.

Susie (*sharply, to Sylvester*) It's rediculous, Twenty-six, for you to be in bed. The Sister's altogether too indulgent to you. Why didn't you pair of lazy devils entice him down to sit and cogitate under the warm wing of the sun in the garden?

Sylvester Considerin' the low state of his general health.

Simon Aided by a touch of frost in the air.

Sylvester Thinkin' it over we thought it might lead –

Simon To him getting an attack of double pneumonia.

Sylvester and Simon (*together*) An' then he'd go off like – (*they blow through their lips*) poof – the snuff of a candle!

Susie For the future, during the period you are patients here, I am to be addressed as 'Nurse Monican', and not as 'Susie'. Remember that, the pair of you, please.

Harry wheels himself in again, crossing by her, and, going over to the fire, looks out into grounds.

(*Irritatedly, to Sylvester*) Number Twenty-six, look at the state of your quilt. You must make an effort to keep it tidy. Dtch, dtch, dtch, what would the Matron say if she saw it!

Simon (*with a nervous giggle*) He's an uneasy divil, Nurse Monican.

Susie (*hotly, to Simon*) Yours is as bad as his, Twenty-seven. You mustn't lounge on your bed; it must be kept perfectly tidy (*she smoothes the quilts*). Please don't make it necessary to mention this again. (*To Harry*) Would you like to go down for a little while into the garden, Twenty-eight?

Harry crouches silent and moody.

(*Continuing*) After the sober rain of yesterday, it is good to feel the new grace of the yellowing trees, and to get the fresh smell of the grass.

Harry wheels himself round and goes out by the left.

(*To Sylvester as she goes out*) Remember, Twenty-six, if you're going to remain in a comatose condition, you'll have to keep your bed presentable.

A pause.

Sylvester (*mimicking Susie*) Twenty-six, if you're going to remeen in a comatowse condition, you'll have to keep your bed in a tidy an' awdahly mannah.

Simon Dtch, dtch, dtch, Twenty-seven, it's disgriceful. And as long as you're heah, in the capacity of a patient, please remember I'm not to be addressed as 'Susie', but as 'Nurse Monican'.

Sylvester Twenty-seven, did you tike the pills the doctah awdahed?

Voice of Susie (*left*) Twenty-six!

Sylvester Yes, Nurse?

Voice of Susie Sister says you're to have a bawth at once; and you, Twenty-seven, see about getting it ready for him.

A fairly long pause.

Sylvester (*angrily*) A bawth: well, be God, that's a good one! I'm not in a fit condition for a bath!

Another pause.

(*Earnestly, to Simon*) You haven't had a dip now for nearly a week, while I had one only the day before yesterday in the late evening: it must have been you she meant, Simon.

Simon Oh, there was no dubiety about her bellowing out Twenty-six, Syl.

Sylvester (*excitedly*) How the hell d'ye know, man, she didn't mix the numbers up?

Simon Mix the numbers up! How could the woman mix the numbers up?

Sylvester How could the woman mix the numbers up! What could be easier than to say Twenty-six instead of Twenty-seven? How could the woman mix the numbers up! Of course the woman could mix the numbers up!

Simon What d'ye expect me to do – hurl myself into a bath that was meant for you?

Sylvester I don't want you to hurl yourself into anything;

but you don't expect me to plunge into a bath that maybe
wasn't meant for me?

Simon Nurse Monican said Twenty-six, and when you
can alter that, ring me up and let me know. (*A pause; then
Simon gets up and goes towards bathroom door.*)

Sylvester (*snappily*) Where are you leppin' to now?

Simon I want to get the bath ready.

Sylvester You want to get the bawth ready! Turn the hot
cock on, and turn the cold cock on for Number Twenty-
six, mixin' them the way a chemist would mix his
medicines – sit still, man, till we hear the final verdict.

> *Simon sits down again. Susie comes in left, and, passing
> to the door leading to grounds, pauses beside Simon and
> Sylvester.*

Susie (*sharply*) What are the two of you doing? Didn't I
tell you, Twenty-six, that you were to take a bawth; and
you, Twenty-seven, that you were to get it ready for him?

Sylvester (*sitting brightly up in bed*) Oh, just goin' to
spring up, Nurse Monican, when you popped in.

Susie Well, up with you, then, and take it. (*To Simon*) You
go and get it ready for him.

> *Simon goes into the bathroom.*

Sylvester (*venturing a last hope as Susie goes towards the
entrance to grounds*) I had a dip, Nurse, only the day
before yesterday in the late evening.

Susie (*as she goes out*) Have another one now, please.

> *The water can be heard flowing in the bathroom, and a
> light cloud of steam comes out by the door which Simon
> has left open.*

Sylvester (*mimicking Susie*) Have another one, now,
please! One to be taken before and after meals. The
delicate audacity of the lip of that one since she draped her
shoulders with a crimson cape!

*Simon appears and stands leaning against the side of the
bathroom door.*

Simon (*gloating*) She's steaming away now, Sylvester, full
cock.

Sylvester (*scornfully, to Simon*) Music to you, the gurgling
of the thing, music to you. Gaugin' the temperature for
me. Dtch, dtch, dtch (*sitting up*), an hospital's the last
place that God made. Be damn it, I wouldn't let a stuffed
bird stay in one!

Simon Come on, man, before the hot strength bubbles out
of it.

Sylvester (*getting out of bed*) Have you the towels hot an'
everything ready for me to spring into?

Simon (*with a bow*) Everything's ready for your
enjoyment, sir.

Sylvester (*as he goes towards the bathroom*) Can't they be
content with an honest to God cleanliness, an' not be
tryin' to gild a man with soap and water.

Simon (*with a grin, as Sylvester passes*) Can I do anything
more for you, sir?

Sylvester (*almost inarticulate with indignation, as he goes
in*) Now I'm tellin' you, Simon Norton, our cordiality's
gettin' a little strained!

*Harry wheels himself in, goes again to the fireplace, and
looks into grounds. Simon watches him for a moment,
takes a package of cigarettes from his pocket and lights
one.*

Simon (*awkwardly, to Harry*) Have a fag, Harry, oul' son?

Harry Don't want one; tons of my own in the locker.

Simon Like me to get you one?

Harry I can get them myself if I want one. D'ye think my arms are lifeless as well as my legs?

Simon Far from that. Everybody's remarking what a great improvement has taken place in you during the last few days.

Harry Everybody but myself.

Simon What with the rubbing every morning and the rubbing every night, and now the operation tomorrow as a grand finally, you'll maybe be in the centre of the football field before many months are out.

Harry (*irritably*) Oh, shut up, man! It's a miracle I want – not an operation. The last operation was to give life to my limbs, but no life came, and again I felt the horrible sickness of life only from the waist up. (*Raising his voice*) Don't stand there gaping at me, man. Did you never before clap your eyes on a body dead from the belly down? Blast you, man, why don't you shout at me, 'While there's life there's hope!'

Simon edges away to his corner. Susie comes in by the glass door and goes over to the table.

(*To Susie*) A package of fags. Out of the locker. Will you, Susie?

Susie goes to Harry's locker, gets the cigarettes and gives them to him. As he lights the cigarette, his right arm gives a sudden jerk.

Susie Steady. What's this?

Harry (*with a nervous laugh*) Barred from my legs it's flowing back into my arms. I can feel it slyly creeping into my fingers.

Voice of Patient, out left (*plaintively*) Nurse!

Susie (*turning her head in direction of the voice*) Shush, you Twenty-three; go asleep, go asleep.

Harry A soft, velvety sense of distance between my fingers and the things I touch.

Susie Stop thinking of it. Brooding checks the chance of your recovery. A good deal may be imagination.

Harry (*peevishly*) Oh, I know the different touches of iron (*he touches the bed rail*); of wood (*he touches the chair*); of flesh (*he touches his cheek*); and to my fingers they're giving the same answers – a feeling of numb distance between me and the touches of them all.

Voice of Patient, out left Nurse!

Susie Dtch, dtch. Go asleep, Twenty-three.

Voice of Patient, out left The stab in the head is worse than ever, Nurse.

Susie You've got your dose of morphia, and you'll get no more. You'll just have to stick it.

> *Resident Surgeon Forby Maxwell enters from the grounds. He is about thirty years of age, and good-looking. His white overalls are unbuttoned, showing war ribbons on his waistcoat, flanked by the ribbon of the DSO. He has a careless, jaunty air, and evidently takes a decided interest in Susie. He comes in singing softly.*

Surgeon Maxwell (*singing*)
Stretched on the couch, Jessie fondled her dress,

That hid all her beauties just over the knee;
And I wondered and said, as I sigh'd, 'What a shame,
That there's no room at all on the couch there for me.'

Susie (*to Surgeon Maxwell*) Twenty-three's at it again.

Surgeon Maxwell Uh, hopeless case. Half his head in
Flanders. May go on like that for another month.

Susie He keeps the patients awake at night.

Simon With his 'God have mercys on me', running after
every third or fourth tick of the clock.

Harry 'Tisn't fair to me, 'tisn't fair to me; I must get my
bellyful of sleep if I'm ever going to get well.

Surgeon Maxwell Oh, the poor devil won't trouble any of
you much longer. (*Singing*)

Said Jess, with a light in the side of her eyes,
'A shrewd, mathematical fellow like you,
With an effort of thought should be able to make
The couch wide enough for the measure of two.'

Susie Dtch, dtch, Surgeon Maxwell.

Surgeon Maxwell (*singing*)
I fixed on a plan, and I carried it through,
And the eyes of Jess gleam'd as she whisper'd to me:
'The couch, made for one, that was made to hold two,
Has, maybe, been made big enough to hold three!'

*Surgeon Maxwell catches Susie's hand in his. Sylvester
bursts in from the bathroom, and rushes to his bed,
colliding with the Surgeon as he passes him.*

Hallo, hallo there, what's this?

Sylvester (*flinging himself into bed, covering himself
rapidly with the clothes, blowing himself warm*) Pooh,

pooh, I feel as if I was sittin' on the doorstep of
pneumonia! Pooh, oh!

Surgeon Maxwell (*to Sylvester*) We'll have a look at you
in a moment, Twenty-six, and see what's wrong with you.

*Sylvester subsides down into the bed, and Simon edges
towards the entrance to grounds, and stands looking
into the grounds, or watching Surgeon Maxwell
examining Sylvester.*

(*To Harry, who is looking intently out into the grounds*)
Well, how are we today, Heegan?

Harry I imagine I don't feel quite so dead in myself as I've
felt these last few days back.

Surgeon Maxwell Oh, well, that's something.

Harry Sometimes I think I feel a faint, fluttering kind of a
buzz in the tops of my thighs.

Surgeon Maxwell (*touching Harry's thigh*) Where, here?

Harry No; higher up, doctor; just where the line is that
leaves the one part living and the other part dead.

Surgeon Maxwell A buzz?

Harry A timid, faint, fluttering kind of a buzz.

Surgeon Maxwell That's good. There might be a lot in
that faint, fluttering kind of a buzz.

Harry (*after a pause*) I'm looking forward to the
operation tomorrow.

Surgeon Maxwell That's the way to take it. While there's
life there's hope (*with a grin and a wink at Susie*). And
now we'll have a look at Twenty-six.

*Harry, when he hears 'while there's life there's hope',
wheels himself madly out left; half-way out he turns his*

head and stretches to look out into the grounds, then he goes on.

Susie Will the operation tomorrow be successful?

Surgeon Maxwell Oh, of course; very successful.

Susie Do him any good, d'ye think?

Surgeon Maxwell Oh, blast the good it'll do him.

Susie goes over to Sylvester in the bed.

Susie (*to Sylvester*) Sit up, Twenty-six, Surgeon Maxwell wants to examine you.

Sylvester (*sitting up with a brave effort but a woeful smile*) Righto. In the pink!

Surgeon Maxwell comes over, twirling his stethoscope. Simon peeps round the corner of the glass door.

Susie (*to Surgeon Maxwell*) What was the cause of the row between the Matron and Nurse Jennings? (*To Sylvester*) Open your shirt, Twenty-six.

Surgeon Maxwell (*who has fixed the stethoscope in his ears, removing it to speak to Susie*) Caught doing the tango in the Resident's arms in the Resident's room. Naughty girl, naughty girl. (*To Sylvester*) Say 'ninety-nine'.

Sylvester Ninety-nine.

Susie Oh, I knew something like that would happen. Daughter of a Dean, too.

Surgeon Maxwell (*to Sylvester*) Say 'ninety-nine'.

Sylvester Ninety-nine. U-u-uh, it's gettin' very cold here, sitting up!

Surgeon Maxwell (*to Sylvester*) Again. Don't be frightened; breathe quietly.

Sylvester Ninety-nine. Cool as a cucumber, Doctor. Ninety-nine.

Surgeon Maxwell (*to Susie*) Damn pretty little piece. Not so pretty as you, though.

Sylvester (*to Surgeon Maxwell*) Yesterday Doctor Joyce, givin' me a run over, said to a couple of medical men that were with him lookin' for tips, that the thing was apparently yieldin' to treatment, and that an operation wouldn't be necessary.

Surgeon Maxwell Go on; ninety-nine, ninety-nine.

Sylvester Ninety-nine, ninety-nine.

Surgeon Maxwell (*to Susie*) Kicks higher than her head, and you should see her doing the splits.

Sylvester (*to Surgeon Maxwell*) Any way of gettin' rid of it'll do for me, for I'm not one of them that'll spend a night before an operation in a crowd of prayers.

Susie Not very useful things to be doing and poor patients awaiting attention.

Surgeon Maxwell (*putting stethoscope into pocket*) He'll do alright; quite fit. Great old skin. (*To Sylvester*) You can cover yourself up, now. (*To Susie*) And don't tell me, Nurse Susie, that you've never felt a thrill or left a bedside for a kiss in a corner. (*He tickles her under the arm.*) Kiss in a corner, Nurse!

Susie (*pleased, but coy*) Please don't, Doctor Maxwell, please.

Surgeon Maxwell (*tickling her again as they go out*) Kiss in a corner; ta-ra-ra-ra, kiss in a corner!

　　A pause.

Sylvester (*to Simon*) Simon, were you listenin' to that conversation?

Simon Indeed I was.

Sylvester We have our hands full, Simon, to keep alive. Think of sinkin' your body to the level of a hand that, ta-ra-ra-ra, would plunge a knife into your middle, haphazard, hurryin' up to run away after a thrill from a kiss in a corner. Did you see me dizzied an' wastin' me time pumpin' ninety-nines out of me, unrecognized, quiverin' with cold an' equivocation!

Simon Everybody says he's a very clever fellow with the knife.

Sylvester He'd gouge out your eye, saw off your arm, lift a load of vitals out of your middle, rub his hands, keep down a terrible desire to cheer lookin' at the ruin, an' say, 'Twenty-six, when you're a little better, you'll feel a new man!'

Mrs Heegan, Mrs Foran, and Teddy enter from the grounds. Mrs Foran is leading Teddy, who has a heavy bandage over his eyes, and is dressed in the blue clothes of military hospitals.

Mrs Foran (*to Teddy*) Just a little step here, Ted; upsh! That's it; now we're on the earth again, beside Simon and Sylvester. You'd better sit here. (*She puts him sitting on a chair.*)

Sylvester (*to Mrs Heegan, as she kisses him*) Well, how's the old woman, eh?

Mrs Heegan A little anxious about poor Harry.

Simon He'll be alright. Tomorrow'll tell a tale.

Susie (*coming in, annoyed*) Who let you up here at this hour? Twenty-eight's to have an operation tomorrow, and shouldn't be disturbed.

Mrs Heegan Sister Peter Alcantara said we might come up, Nurse.

Mrs Foran (*loftily*) Sister Peter Alcantara's authority ought to be good enough, I think.

Mrs Heegan Sister Peter Alcantara said a visit might buck him up a bit.

Mrs Foran Sister Peter Alcantara knows the responsibility she'd incur by keeping a wife from her husband and a mother from her son.

Susie Sister Peter Alcantara hasn't got to nurse him. And remember, nothing is to be said that would make his habit of introspection worse than it is.

Mrs Foran (*with dignity*) Thanks for the warnin', Nurse, but them kind of mistakes is unusual with us.

Susie goes out left, as Harry wheels himself rapidly in. Seeing the group, he stops suddenly, and a look of disappointment comes on to his face.

Mrs Heegan (*kissing Harry*) How are you, son?

Mrs Foran I brought Teddy, your brother in arms, up to see you, Harry.

Harry (*impatiently*) Where's Jessie? I thought you were to bring her with you?

Mrs Heegan She's comin' after us in a moment.

Harry Why isn't she here now?

Mrs Foran She stopped to have a word in the grounds with someone she knew.

Harry It was Barney Bagnal, was it? Was it Barney Bagnal?

Teddy Maybe she wanted to talk to him about gettin' the VC.

Harry What VC? Who's gettin' the VC?

Teddy Barney. Did he not tell you?

Mrs Foran prods his knee.

What's up?

Harry (*intensely, to Teddy*) What's he gettin' it for? What's he gettin' the VC for?

Teddy For carryin' you wounded out of the line of fire.

Mrs Foran prods his knee.

What's up?

Harry (*in anguish*) Christ Almighty, for carryin' me wounded out of the line of fire!

Mrs Heegan (*rapidly*) Harry, I wouldn't be thinkin' of anything till we see what the operation 'll do tomorrow.

Simon (*rapidly*) God, if it gave him back the use even of one of his legs.

Mrs Foran (*rapidly*) Look at all the places he could toddle to, an' all the things he could do then with the prop of a crutch.

Mrs Heegan Even at the worst, he'll never be dependin' on anyone, for he's bound to get the maximum allowance.

Simon Two quid a week, isn't it?

Sylvester Yes, a hundred per cent total incapacitation.

Harry She won't come up if one of you don't go down and bring her up.

Mrs Heegan She's bound to come up, for she's got your ukelele.

Harry Call her up, Simon, call her up – I must see Jessie.

Simon goes over to the door leading to the grounds, and looks out.

Mrs Foran (*bending over till her face is close to Harry's*) The drawn look on his face isn't half as bad as when I seen him last.

Mrs Heegan (*bending and looking into Harry's face*) Look, the hollows under his eyes is fillin' up, too.

Teddy I'm afraid he'll have to put Jessie out of his head, for when a man's hit in the spine . . .

Mrs Foran prods his knee.

What's up, woman?

Harry (*impatiently, to Simon*) Is she coming? Can you see her anywhere?

Simon I see someone like her in the distance, under the trees.

Harry Call her; can't you give her a shout, man?

Simon (*calling*) Jessie. Is that you, Jessie! Jessie-e!

Mrs Heegan (*to Harry*) What time are you goin' under the operation?

Harry (*to Simon*) Call her again, call her again, can't you!

Simon (*calling*) Jessie; Jessie-e!

Teddy Not much of a chance for an injury to the spine, for . . .

Mrs Foran (*putting her face close to Teddy's*) Oh, shut up, you!

Harry Why did you leave her in the grounds? Why didn't you wait till she came up with you?

Mrs Foran (*going over to Simon and calling*) Jessie, Jessie-e!

Jessie's Voice (*in distance*) Yehess!

Mrs Foran (*calling*) Come up here at once; we're all waitin' for you!

Jessie's Voice I'm not going up!

Mrs Foran (*calling*) Bring up that ukelele here at once, miss!

Jessie's Voice Barney'll bring it up!

> *Harry, who has been listening intently, wheels himself rapidly to where Simon and Mrs Foran are, pushing through them hurriedly.*

Harry (*calling loudly*) Jessie! Jessie! Jessie-e!

Mrs Foran Look at that, now; she's runnin' away, the young rip!

Harry (*appealingly*) Jessie! Jessie-e!

> *Susie enters quickly from left. She goes over to Harry and pulls him back from the door.*

Susie (*indignantly*) Disgraceful! Rousing the whole ward with this commotion! Dear, dear, dear, look at the state of Twenty-eight. Come along, come along, please; you must all go at once.

Harry Jessie's coming up for a minute, Nurse.

Susie No more to come up. We've had enough for one night, and you for a serious operation tomorrow. Come on, all out, please. (*She conducts Mrs Heegan, Mrs Foran, and Teddy out left.*)

Mrs Foran (*going out*) We're goin', we're goin', thank you. A nice way to treat the flotsum and jetsum of the battlefields!

Susie (*to Harry*) To bed now, Twenty-eight, please. (*To

235

Simon) Help me get him to bed, Twenty-seven.

> *Susie pushes Harry to his bed, right; Simon brings portion of a bed-screen which he places around Harry, hiding him from view.*

(*Turning to speak to Sylvester, who is sitting up in bed, as she arranges screen*) You're going to have your little operation in the morning, so you'd better go to sleep too.

> *Sylvester goes pale and a look of dismay and fear crawls over his face.*

Don't funk it now. They're not going to turn you inside out. It'll be over in ten minutes.

Sylvester (*with a groan*) When they once get you down your only hope is in the infinite mercy of God!

Simon If I was you, Sylvester, I wouldn't take this operation too seriously. You know th' oul' song – 'Let Me Like a Soldier Fall'! If I was you, I'd put it completely out of me mind.

Sylvester (*subsiding on to the pillow – with an agonized look on his face*) Let me like a soldier fall! Did anyone ever hear th' equal o' that! Put it out of me mind completely! (*He sits up, and glares at Simon.*) Eh, you, look! If you can't think sensibly, then thry to think without talkin'! (*He sinks back on the pillow again.*) Let me like a soldier fall. Oh, it's not a fair trial for a sensible man to be stuck down in a world like this!

> *Sylvester slides down till he lies prone and motionless on the bed. Harry is in bed now. Simon removes the screen, and Susie arranges Harry's quilt for the night.*

Susie (*to Simon*) Now run and help get the things together for supper.

> *Simon goes out left.*

(*Encouragingly to Harry*) After the operation, a stay in the air of the Convalescent may work wonders.

Harry If I could mingle my breath with the breeze that blows from every sea, and over every land, they wouldn't widen me into anything more than the shrivell'd thing I am.

Susie (*switching off the two hanging lights, so that the red light over the fireplace alone remains*) Don't be foolish, Twenty-eight. Wheeling yourself about among the beeches and the pines, when the daffodils are hanging out their blossoms, you'll deepen your chance in the courage and renewal of the country.

> *The bell of a Convent in the grounds begins to ring for Compline.*

Harry (*with intense bitterness*) I'll say to the pine, 'Give me the grace and beauty of the beech'; I'll say to the beech, 'Give me the strength and stature of the pine'. In a net I'll catch butterflies in bunches; twist and mangle them between my fingers and fix them wriggling on to mercy's banner. I'll make my chair a Juggernaut, and wheel it over the neck and spine of every daffodil that looks at me, and strew them dead to manifest the mercy of God and the justice of man!

Susie (*shocked*) Shush, Harry, Harry!

Harry To hell with you, your country, trees, and things, you jibbering jay!

Susie (*as she is going out*) Twenty-eight!

Harry (*vehemently*) To hell with you, your country, trees, and things, you jibbering jay!

> *Susie looks at him, pauses for a few moments, as if to speak, and then goes out.*

A pause; then Barney comes in by door from grounds.
An overcoat covers his military hospital uniform of
blue. His left arm is in a sling. Under his right arm he
carries a ukelele, and in his hand he has a bunch of
flowers. Embarrassed, he goes slowly to Harry's bed,
drops the flowers at the foot, then he drops the ukelele
there.

Barney (*awkwardly*) Your ukelele. An' a bunch of flowers
from Jessie.

Harry remains motionless on the bed.

A bunch of flowers from Jessie, and . . . your . . . ukelele.

The Sister of the Ward enters, left, going to the chapel
for Compline. She wears a cream habit with a white
coif; a large set of Rosary beads hangs from her girdle.
She pauses on her way, and a brass Crucifix flashes on
her bosom.

Sister (*to Harry*) Keeping brave and hopeful, Twenty-
eight?

Harry (*softly*) Yes, Sister.

Sister Splendid. And we've got a ukelele too. Can you play
it, my child?

Harry Yes, Sister.

Sister Splendid. You must play me something when you're
well over the operation. (*To Barney*) Standing guard over
your comrade, Twenty-two, eh?

Barney (*softly and shyly*) Yes, Sister.

Sister Grand. Forasmuch as ye do it unto the least of these
my brethren, ye do it unto me. Well, God be with you
both, my children. (*To Harry*) And Twenty-eight, pray to
God, for wonderful He is in His doing toward the children

of men. (*Calm and dignified she goes out into the grounds.*)

Barney (*pausing as he goes out left*) They're on the bed; the ukelele, and the bunch of flowers from . . . Jessie.

The Sisters are heard singing in the convent the hymn of Salve Regina.

Sisters (*singing*)
Salve Regina, mater misericordiae;
Vitae dulcedo et spes nostra, salve!
Ad te clamamus, exules filii Hevae;
Ad te suspiramus, gementes et flentes in hac lacrymarum valle.
Eia ergo Advocata nostra,
Illos tuos misericordes oculos ad nos converte,
Et Jesum, benedictum fructum ventris tui –

Harry God of the miracles, give a poor devil a chance, give a poor devil a chance!

Sisters (*singing*)
Nobis post hoc exsilium ostende,
O clemens, o pia, o dulcis Virgo Maria!

End of Act Three.

Act Four

A room of the dance hall of the Avondale Football Club.
At back, left, cutting corners of the back and side walls, is
the arched entrance, divided by a slim pillar, to the dance
hall. This entrance is hung with crimson and black striped
curtains; whenever these are parted the dancers can be
seen swinging or gliding past the entrance if a dance be
taking place at the time. Over the entrance is a scroll on
which is printed: 'Up the Avondales!' The wall back has a
wide, tall window which opens to the garden, in which the
shrubs and some sycamore trees can be seen. It is hung
with apple-green casement curtains, which are pulled to
the side to allow the window to be open as it is at present.
Between the entrance to hall and the window is a Roll of
Honour containing the names of five members of the Club
killed in the war. Underneath the Roll of Honour a wreath
of laurel tied with red and black ribbon. To the front left is
the fireplace. Between the fireplace and the hall entrance is
a door on which is an oval white enamel disc with
'Caretaker' painted on it. To the right a long table,
covered with a green cloth, on which are numerous bottles
of wine and a dozen glasses. On the table, too, is a
telephone. A brown carpet covers the floor. Two easy
chairs and one ordinary are in the room. Hanging from
the ceiling are three lanterns; the centre one is four times
the length of its width, the ones at the side are less than
half as long as the centre lantern and hang horizontally;
the lanterns are black, with a broad red stripe running
down the centre of the largest and across those hanging at
each side, so that, when they are lighted, they suggest an
illuminated black cross with an inner one of gleaming red.

*The hall is vividly decorated with many coloured lanterns,
looped with coloured streamers.*

*When the scene is revealed the curtains are drawn, and
the band can be heard playing a fox-trot. Outside in the
garden, near the window, Simon and Sylvester can be seen
smoking, and Teddy is walking slowly up and down the
path. The band is heard playing for a few moments, then
the curtains are pulled aside, and Jessie, with Barney
holding her hand, comes in and walks rapidly to the table
where the wine is standing. They are quickly followed by
Harry, who wheels himself a little forward, then stops,
watching them. The curtains part again, and Mrs Heegan
is seen watching Harry. Simon and Sylvester, outside,
watch those in the room through the window. Barney
wears a neat navy-blue suit, with a rather high, stiff collar
and black tie. Pinned on the breast of his waistcoat are his
war medals, flanked by the Victoria Cross. Harry is also
wearing his medals. Jessie has on a very pretty, rather
tight-fitting dance frock, with the sleeves falling widely to
the elbow, and cut fairly low on her breast. All the
dancers, and Harry too, wear coloured, fantastically
shaped paper hats.*

Jessie (*hot, excited, and uneasy, as with a rapid glance
back she sees the curtains parted by Harry*) Here he comes
prowling after us again! His watching of us is pulling all
the enjoyment out of the night. It makes me shiver to feel
him wheeling after us.

Barney We'll watch for a chance to shake him off, an' if
he starts again we'll make him take his tangled body
somewhere else.

As Harry moves forward from the curtained entrance.

Shush, he's comin' near us. (*In a louder tone to Jessie*) Red
wine, Jessie, for you, or white wine?

Harry Red wine first, Jessie, to the passion and the power and the pain of life, an' then a drink of white wine to the melody that is in them all!

Jessie I'm so hot.

Harry I'm so cold; white wine for the woman warm to make her cold; red wine for the man that's cold to make him warm!

Jessie White wine for me.

Harry For me the red wine till I drink to men puffed up with pride of strength, for even creeping things can praise the Lord!

Barney (*gently to Harry, as he gives a glass of wine to Jessie*) No more for you now, Harry.

Harry (*mockingly*) Oh, please, your lusty lordship, just another, an' if I seek a second, smack me well. (*Wheeling his chair viciously against Barney*) Get out, you trimm'd-up clod. There's medals on my breast as well as yours! (*He fills a glass.*)

Jessie Let us go back to the dancing, Barney.

Barney hesitates.

Please, Barney, let us go back to the dancing!

Harry To the dancing, for the day cometh when no man can play. And legs were made to dance, to run, to jump, to carry you from one place to another; but mine can neither walk, nor run, nor jump, nor feel the merry motion of a dance. But stretch me on the floor fair on my belly, and I will turn over on my back, then wriggle back again on to my belly; and that's more than a dead, dead man can do!

Barney Jessie wants to dance, an' so we'll go, and leave you here a little.

Harry Cram pain with pain, and pleasure cram with pleasure. I'm going too. You'd cage me in from seeing you dance, and dance, and dance, with Jessie close to you, and you so close to Jessie. Though you wouldn't think it, yes, I have – I've hammer'd out many a merry measure upon a polish'd floor with a sweet, sweet heifer. (*As Barney and Jessie are moving away he catches hold of Jessie's dress.*) Her name? Oh, any name will do – we'll call her Jessie!

Jessie Oh, let me go. (*To Barney*) Barney, make him let me go, please.

> *Barney, without a word, removes Harry's hand from Jessie's dress. Jessie and Barney then go out to the dance hall through the curtained entrance. After a while Mrs Heegan slips away from the entrance into the hall. After a moment's pause Harry follows them into the hall. Simon and Sylvester come in from the garden, leaving Teddy still outside smoking and walking to and fro in the cautious manner of the blind. Simon and Sylvester sit down near the fire and puff in silence for a few moments.*

Sylvester (*earnestly*) I knew it. I knew it, Simon – strainin', an' strainin' his nerves; driftin', an' driftin' towards an hallucination!

Simon Jessie might try to let him down a little more gently, but it would have been better, I think, if Harry hadn't come here tonight.

Sylvester I concur in that, Simon. What's a decoration to an hospital is an anxiety here.

Simon To carry life and colour to where there's nothing but the sick and helpless is right; but to carry the sick and helpless to where there's nothing but life and colour is wrong.

The telephone bell rings.

Sylvester There's the telephone bell ringing.

Simon Oh, someone 'll come in and answer it in a second.

Sylvester To join a little strength to a lot of weakness is what I call sensible; but to join a little weakness to a lot of strength is what I call a . . .

Simon A cod.

Sylvester Exactly.

The telephone continues to ring.

There's that telephone ringin' still.

Simon Oh, someone 'll come in and answer it in a second.

Teddy has groped his way to French window.

Teddy The telephone's tinklin', boys.

Sylvester Thanks, Teddy. We hear it, thanks. (*To Simon*) When he got the invitation from the Committay to come, wearin' his decorations, me an' the old woman tried to persuade him that, seein' his condition, it was better to stop at home, an' let me represent him, but (*with a gesture*) no use!

Teddy resumes his walk to and fro.

Simon It was natural he'd want to come, since he was the means of winning the Cup twice before for them, leading up to their keeping the trophy for ever by the win of a year ago.

Sylvester To bring a boy so helpless as him, whose memory of agility an' strength time hasn't flattened down, to a place wavin' with joy an' dancin', is simply, simply –

Simon Devastating, I'd say.

Sylvester Of course it is! Is that God-damn telephone goin'
to keep ringin' all night?

Mrs Foran enters from hall quickly.

Mrs Foran Miss Monican says that one of you is to
answer the telephone, an' call her if it's anything
important.

Sylvester (*nervously*) I never handled a telephone in my
life.

Simon I chanced it once and got so hot and quivery that I
couldn't hear a word, and didn't know what I was saying
myself.

Mrs Foran Have a shot at it and see.

The three of them drift over to the telephone.

Sylvester Chance it again, Simon, an' try to keep steady.

As Simon stretches his hand to the receiver.

Don't rush, don't rush, man, an' make a mess of it. Take it
in your stride.

Simon (*pointing to receiver*) When you lift this down,
you're connected, I think.

Sylvester No use of thinkin' on this job. Don't you turn
the handle first?

Simon (*irritably*) No, you don't turn no handle, man!

Mrs Foran Let Simon do it now; Simon knows.

*Simon tremblingly lifts down the receiver, almost letting
it fall.*

Sylvester Woa, woa, Simon; careful, careful!

Simon (*speaking in receiver*) Eh, hallo! Eh, listen there.
Eh, hallo! listen.

Sylvester You listen, man, an' give the fellow at the other end a chance to speak.

Simon If you want me to manipulate the thing, let me manipulate it in tranquillity.

Mrs Foran (*to Sylvester*) Oh, don't be puttin' him out, Sylvester.

Simon (*waving them back*) Don't be crushing in on me; give me room to manipulate the thing.

Dead silence for some moments.

Mrs Foran Are you hearin' anything from the other end?

Simon A kind of a buzzing and a roaring noise.

Sylvester suddenly gives the cord a jerk and pulls the receiver out of Simon's hand.

(*Angrily*) What the hell are you trying to do, man? You're after pulling it right out of my mit.

Sylvester (*heatedly*) There was a knot or a twist an' a tangle in it that was keepin' the sound from travellin'.

Simon If you want me to work the thing properly, you'll have to keep yourself from interfering. (*Resuming surlily*) Eh, hallo, listen, yes? Ha! ha! ha! ha! Yes, yes, yes. No, no, no. Cheerio! Yes. Eh, hallo, listen, eh. Hallo.

Sylvester What is it? What're they sayin'?

Simon (*hopelessly, taking the receiver from his ear*) I don't seem to be able to hear a damn sound.

Sylvester An' Holy God, what are you yessin' and noin' and cheerioin' out of you for then?

Simon You couldn't stand here like a fool and say nothing, could you?

Sylvester Show it to me, Simon, show it to me – you're not holdin' it at the proper angle.

Mrs Foran Give it to Syl, Simon; it's a delicate contrivance that needs a knack in handlin'.

Sylvester (*as he is taking the receiver from Simon and carefully placing it to his ear*) You have always to preserve an eqwee-balance between the speakin' mouth and the hearin' ear. (*Speaking into receiver*) Hallo! Anybody there at the other end of this? Eh, wha's that? Yes, yes, I've got you (*taking the receiver from his ear and speaking to Simon and Mrs Foran*): something like wine, or dine, or shine, or something – an' a thing that's hummin'.

Simon I can see no magnificent meaning jumping out of that!

Mrs Foran They couldn't be talkin' about bees, could they?

Sylvester (*scornfully*) Bees! No, they couldn't be talkin' about bees! That kind of talk, Mrs Foran, only tends to confuse matters. Bees! Dtch, dtch, dtch – the stupidity of some persons is . . . terrifyin'!

Simon Ask them quietly what they want.

Sylvester (*indignantly*) What the hell's the use of askin' them that, when I can hear something only like a thing that's hummin'?

Mrs Foran It wouldn't be, now, comin', or even bummin'?

Sylvester It might even possibly be drummin'. Personally, Mrs Foran, I think, since you can't help, you might try to keep from hinderin'.

Simon Put it back, Syl, where it was, an' if it rings again, we'll only have to slip quietly out of this.

Mrs Foran Yes, put it back, an' say it never rang.

Sylvester Where was it? Where do I put it back?

Simon On that thing stickin' out there. Nice and gently now.

Sylvester cautiously puts receiver back. They look at the telephone for a few moments, then go back to the fire, one by one. Sylvester stands with his back to it; Simon sits in a chair, over the back of which Mrs Foran leans.

Mrs Foran Curious those at the other end of the telephone couldn't make themselves understood.

Simon Likely they're not accustomed to it, and it's a bit difficult if you're not fully conscious of its manipulation.

Sylvester Well, let them study an' study it then, or abide by the consequences, for we can't be wastin' time teachin' them.

The curtains at entrance of dance hall are pulled aside, and Teddy, who has disappeared from the garden a little time before, comes in. As he leaves the curtains apart, the dancers can be seen gliding past the entrance in the movements of a tango. Teddy comes down, looks steadily but vacantly towards the group around the fire, then goes over carefully to the table, where he moves his hand about till it touches a bottle, which he takes up in one hand, feeling it questioningly from the other.

Simon How goes it, Teddy?

Teddy (*with a vacant look towards them*) Sylvester – Simon – well. What seest thou, Teddy? Thou seest not as man seeth. In the garden the trees stand up; the green things showeth themselves and fling out flowers of divers hues. In the sky the sun by day and the moon and the stars by night – nothing. In the hall the sound of dancing, the eyes of women, grey and blue and brown and black, do sparkle and dim and sparkle again. Their white breasts rise and fall, and rise again. Slender legs, from red and black, and white and green, come out, go in again – nothing. Strain as you may, it stretches from the throne of God to the end of the hearth of hell.

Simon What?

Teddy The darkness.

Simon (*knowing not what to say*) Yes, oh yes.

Teddy (*holding up a bottle of wine*) What colour, Syl? It's all the same, but I like the red the best.

Mrs Foran (*going over to Teddy*) Just one glass, dear, and you'll sit down quietly an' take it in sips.

Mrs Foran fills a glass of wine for Teddy, leads him to a chair, puts him sitting down, and gives the glass of wine carefully to him. The band in the hall has been playing, and through the parted curtains the dancers are seen gliding past. Jessie moves by now in the arms of Barney, and in a few moments is followed along the side of the hall by Harry wheeling himself in his chair and watching them. Mrs Foran and the two men look on and become more attentive when among the dancers Susie, in the arms of Surgeon Maxwell, Jessie partnered with Barney, and Harry move past.

Sylvester (*as Susie goes by*) Susie Monican's lookin' game enough tonight for anything.

Simon Hardly remindful of her one-time fear of God.

Sylvester (*as Jessie goes by followed by Harry*) There he goes, still followin' them.

Simon And Jessie's looking as if she was tired of her maidenhood, too.

Mrs Foran The thin threads holdin' her dress up sidelin' down over her shoulders, an' her catchin' them up again at the tail end of the second before it was too late.

Simon (*grinning*) And Barney's hand inching up, inching up to pull them a little lower when they're sliding down.

Mrs Foran Astonishin' the way girls are advertisin' their immodesty. Whenever one of them sits down, in my heart I pity the poor men havin' to view the disedifyin' sight of the full length of one leg couched over another.

Teddy (*forgetful*) A damn nice sight, all the same, I think.

Mrs Foran (*indignantly*) One would imagine such a thought would jar a man's mind that had kissed goodbye to the sight of his eyes.

Teddy Oh, don't be tickin' off every word I say!

Mrs Foran (*after an astonished pause, whipping the glass out of Teddy's hand*) Damn the drop more, now, you'll get for the rest of the evenin'.

> *The band suddenly stops playing, and the couples seen just then through the doorway stop dancing and look attentively up the hall. After a slight pause, Harry in his chair, pushed by Susie, comes in through the entrance; his face is pale and drawn, his breath comes in quick faint gasps, and his head is leaning sideways on the back of the chair. Mrs Heegan is on one side of Harry, and Surgeon Maxwell, who is in dinner-jacket style of evening dress, wearing his medals, including the DSO, walks on the other. Harry is wheeled over near the open window. Barney and Jessie, standing in the entrance, look on and listen.*

Surgeon Maxwell Here near the window. (*To Mrs Heegan*) He'll be all right, Mrs Heegan, in a second; a

little faint – too much excitement. When he recovers a
little, I'd get him home.

Harry (*faintly but doggedly*) Napoo home, napoo. Not
yet. I'm all right. I'll spend a little time longer in the belly
of an hour bulgin' out with merriment. Carry on.

Surgeon Maxwell Better for you to go home, Heegan.

Harry When they drink to the Club from the Cup – the
Silver Tassie – that I won three times, three times for them
– that first was filled to wet the lips of Jessie and of me –
I'll go, but not yet. I'm all right; my name is yet only a
shadow on the Roll of Honour.

Mrs Heegan Come home, Harry; you're gettin' your
allowance only on the understandin' that you take care of
yourself.

Harry Get the Cup. I'll mind it here till you're ready to
send it round to drink to the Avondales – on the table here
beside me. Bring the Cup; I'll mind it here on the table
beside me.

Surgeon Maxwell Get the Cup for him, someone.

> *Simon goes to the hall and returns with the Cup, which
> he gives to Harry.*

Harry (*holding the Cup out*) A first drink again for me,
for me alone this time, for the shell that hit me bursts for
ever between Jessie and me. (*To Simon*) Go on, man, fill
out the wine!

Surgeon Maxwell (*to Simon*) A little – just a glass. Won't
do him any harm. (*To Harry*) Then you'll have to remain
perfectly quiet, Heegan.

Harry The wine – fill out the wine!

Simon (*to Harry*) Red wine or white?

Harry Red wine, red like the faint remembrance of the fires in France; red wine like the poppies that spill their petals on the breasts of the dead men. No, white wine, white like the stillness of the millions that have removed their clamours from the crowd of life. No, red wine; red like the blood that was shed for you and for many for the commission of sin! (*He drinks the wine.*) Steady, Harry, and lift up thine eyes unto the hills. (*Roughly to those around him*) What are you all gaping at?

Surgeon Maxwell Now, now, Heegan – you must try to keep quiet.

Susie And when you've rested and feel better, you will sing for us a Negro Spiritual, and point the melody with the ukelele.

Mrs Heegan Just as he used to do.

Sylvester Behind the trenches.

Simon In the Rest Camps.

Mrs Foran Out in France.

Harry Push your sympathy away from me, for I'll have none of it. (*He wheels his chair quickly towards the dance hall.*) Go on with the dancing and keep the ball a-rolling. (*Calling loudly at the entrance*) Trumpets and drum begin!

The band begins to play.

Dance and dance and dance. (*He listens for a moment.*) Sink into merriment again, and sling your cares to God!

He whirls round in the chair to the beat of the tune. Dancers are seen gliding past entrance.

Dear God, I can't. (*He sinks sideways on his chair.*) I must, must rest. (*He quietly recites.*)

For a spell here I will stay,
Then pack up my body and go –
For mine is a life on the ebb,
Yours a full life on the flow!

*Harry goes over to far side of window and looks out
into garden. Mrs Heegan is on his right and Teddy on
his left; Simon and Sylvester a little behind, looking on.
Mrs Foran to the right of Mrs Heegan. Surgeon
Maxwell and Susie, who are a little to the front, watch
for a moment, then the Surgeon puts his arm round
Susie and the pair glide off into the dance hall.*
  *When Surgeon Maxwell and Susie glide in to the
motions of the dance through the entrance into the
dance hall, the curtains are pulled together. A few
moments' pause. Teddy silently puts his hand on
Harry's shoulder, and they both stare into the garden.*

Simon The air'll do him good.

Sylvester An' give him breath to sing his song an' play the
ukelele.

Mrs Heegan Just as he used to do.

Sylvester Behind the trenches.

Simon In the Rest Camps.

Mrs Foran Out in France.

Harry I can see, but I cannot dance.

Teddy I can dance, but I cannot see.

Harry Would that I had the strength to do the things I see.

Teddy Would that I could see the things I've strength to
do.

Harry The Lord hath given and the Lord hath taken
away.

Teddy　Blessed be the name of the Lord.

Mrs Foran　I do love the ukelele, especially when it goes tinkle, tinkle, tinkle in the night-time.

Sylvester　Bringin' before you glistenin' bodies of blacks, coilin' themselves an' shufflin' an' prancin' in a great jungle dance; shakin' assegais an' spears to the rattle, rattle, rattle an' thud, thud, thud of the tom-toms.

Mrs Foran　There's only one possible musical trimmin' to the air of a Negro Spiritual, an' that's the tinkle, tinkle, tinkle of a ukelele.

Harry　The rising sap in trees I'll never feel.

Teddy　The hues of branch or leaf I'll never see.

Harry　There's something wrong with life when men can walk.

Teddy　There's something wrong with life when men can see.

Harry　I never felt the hand that made me helpless.

Teddy　I never saw the hand that made me blind.

Harry　Life came and took away the half of life.

Teddy　Life took from me the half he left with you.

Harry　The Lord hath given and the Lord hath taken away.

Teddy　Blessed be the name of the Lord.

> *Susie comes quickly in by entrance, goes over to the table and, looking at several bottles of wine, selects one. She is going hurriedly back, when, seeing Harry, she goes over to him.*

Susie　(*kindly*) How are you now, Harry?

Harry All right, thank you.

Susie That's good.

Susie is about to hurry away, when Mrs Foran stops her with a remark.

Mrs Foran (*with a meaning gesture*) He's takin' it cushy till you're ready to hear him singin' his Negro Spiritual, Miss.

Susie Oh, God, I'd nearly forgotten that. They'll be giving out the balloons at the next dance, and when that fox-trot's over he'll have to come in and sing us the Spiritual.

Mrs Heegan Just as he used to do.

Simon Behind the trenches.

Sylvester In the Rest Camps.

Mrs Foran Out of France.

Susie As soon as the Balloon Dance is over, Harry, out through the garden and in by the front entrance with you, so that you'll be ready to start as they all sit down. And after the song, we'll drink to the Club from the Silver Tassie. (*She hurries back to the hall with the bottle of wine.*)

Mrs Foran I'm longin' to hear Harry on the ukelele.

Harry I hope I'll be able to do justice to it.

Mrs Heegan Of course you will, Harry.

Harry (*nervously*) Before a crowd. Forget a word and it's all up with you.

Simon Try it over now, softly; the sound couldn't carry as far as the hall.

Sylvester It'll give you confidence in yourself.

Harry (*to Simon*) Show us the ukelele, Simon.

Simon gets the ukelele and gives it to Harry.

Teddy If I knew the ukelele it might wean me a little way from the darkness.

Harry pulls a few notes, tuning the ukelele, then he softly sings.

Harry (*singing*)
Swing low, sweet chariot, comin' for to carry me home,
Swing low, sweet chariot, comin' for to carry me home,
I looked over Jordan, what did I see, comin' for to carry
    me home?
A band of angels comin' after me – comin' for to carry
    me home.

A voice in the hall is heard shouting through a megaphone.

Voice Balloons will be given out now! Given out now – the balloons!

Mrs Foran (*excitedly*) They're goin' to send up the balloons! They're going to let the balloons fly now!

Harry (*singing*)
Swing low, sweet chariot, comin' for to carry me home,
Swing low, sweet chariot, comin' for to carry me home.

Mrs Foran (*as Harry is singing*) Miss Monican wants us all to see the flyin' balloons.

She catches Teddy's arm and runs with him into the hall.

Simon We must all see the flyin' balloons.

Mrs Heegan (*running into hall*) Red balloons and black balloons.

Simon (*following Mrs Heegan*) Green balloons and blue balloons.

Sylvester (*following Simon*) Yellow balloons and puce balloons.

All troop into the hall, leaving the curtains apart, and Harry alone with his ukelele. Through the entrance various coloured balloons that have been tossed into the air can be seen, mid sounds of merriment and excitement.

Harry (*softly and slowly*) Comin' for to carry me home.

He throws the ukelele into an armchair, sits still for a moment, then goes to the table, takes up the silver cup, and wheels himself into the garden.
After a pause Barney looks in, then enters pulling Jessie by the hand, letting the curtains fall together again. Then he goes quickly to window, shuts and bolts it, drawing-to one half of the curtains, goes back to Jessie, catches her hand again, and tries to draw her towards room on the left. During the actions that follow the dance goes merrily on in the hall.

Jessie (*holding up a broken shoulder-strap and pulling back towards the hall*) Barney, no. God, I'd be afraid he might come in on us alone.

Hands part the curtains and throw in coloured streamers that encircle Jessie and Barney.

Barney Damn them! . . . He's gone, I tell you, to sing the song an' play the ukelele.

Jessie (*excited and afraid*) See, they're watching us. No, Barney. You mustn't. I'll not go!

Barney seizes Jessie in his arms and forces her towards the door on the left.

You wouldn't be good. I'll not go into that room.

Barney I will be good, I tell you! I just want to be alone with you for a minute. (*He loosens Jessie's other shoulder-strap, so that her dress leaves her shoulders and bosom bare.*)

Jessie (*near the door left, as Barney opens it*) You've loosened my dress – I knew you weren't going to be good. (*As she kisses him passionately.*) Barney, Barney – you shouldn't be making me do what I don't want to do!

Barney (*holding her and trying to pull her into room*) Come on, Jessie, you needn't be afraid of Barney – we'll just rest a few minutes from the dancing.

> At that part of the window uncurtained Harry is seen peering in. He then wheels his chair back and comes on to the centre of the window-frame with a rush, bursting the catch and speeding into the room, coming to a halt, angry and savage, before Barney and Jessie.

Harry So you'd make merry over my helplessness in front of my face, in front of my face, you pair of cheats! You couldn't wait till I'd gone, so that my eyes wouldn't see the joy I wanted hurrying away from me over to another? Hurt her breast pulling your hand quick out of her bodice, did you? (*To Jessie*) Saved you in the nick of time, my lady, did I? (*To Barney*) Going to enjoy yourself on the same little couch where she, before you formed an image in her eye, acted the part of an amateur wife, and I acted the part of an amateur husband – the black couch with the green and crimson butterflies, in the yellow bushes, where she and me often tired of the things you're dangling after now!

Jessie He's a liar, he's a liar, Barney! He often tried it on with coaxing first and temper afterwards, but it always ended in a halt that left him where he started.

Harry If I had my hands on your white neck I'd leave marks there that crowds of kisses from your Barney wouldn't moisten away.

Barney You half-baked Lazarus, I've put up with you all the evening, so don't force me now to rough-handle the bit of life the Jerries left you as a souvenir!

Harry When I wanted to slip away from life, you brought me back with your whispered 'Think of the tears of Jess, think of the tears of Jess', but Jess has wiped away her tears in the ribbon of your Cross, and this poor crippled jest gives a flame of joy to the change; but when you get her, may you find in her the pressed down emptiness of a whore!

Barney (*running over and seizing Harry*) I'll tilt the leaking life out of you, you jealous, peering pimp!

Jessie (*trying to hold Barney back*) Barney, Barney, don't! don't!

Harry (*appealingly*) Barney, Barney! My heart – you're stopping it!

Jessie (*running to entrance and shouting in*) Help! help! They're killing each other!

In the hall the dance stops. Surgeon Maxwell runs in, followed by Susie, Simon, Sylvester, Mrs Foran, Mrs Heegan, and lastly Teddy finding his way over to the window. Dancers gather around entrance and look on.
Surgeon Maxwell, running over, separates Barney from Harry.

Surgeon Maxwell What's this? Come, come – we can't have this sort of thing going on.

Mrs Heegan He was throttlin' him, throttlin' a poor helpless creature, an' if anything happens, he and that painted slug Jessie Taite 'll be held accountable!

Surgeon Maxwell This can't be allowed to go on. You'll have to bring him home. Any more excitement would be dangerous.

Mrs Heegan This is what he gets from Jessie Taite for sittin' on the stairs through the yawnin' hours of the night, racin' her off to the play an' the pictures, an' plungin' every penny he could keep from me into presents for the consolidation of the courtship!

Surgeon Maxwell Bring the boy home, woman, bring the boy home.

Sylvester (*fiercely to Jessie*) And money of mine in one of the gewgaws scintillatin' in her hair!

Jessie What gewgaw? What gewgaw?

Coloured streamers are thrown in by those standing at entrance, which fall on and encircle some of the group around Harry.

Sylvester The tiarara I gave you two Christmases ago with the yellow berries and the three flutterin' crimson swallows.

Harry (*faintly and bitterly, with a hard little laugh*) Napoo Barney Bagnal and napoo Jessie Taite. A merry heart throbs coldly in my bosom; a merry heart in a cold bosom – or is it a cold heart in a merry bosom? (*He gathers a number of the coloured streamers and winds them round himself and chair.*) Teddy! (*Harry catches Teddy by the sleeve and winds some more streamers round him.*) Sing a song, man, and show the stuff you're made of!

Surgeon Maxwell (*catching hold of Mrs Heegan's arm*) Bring him home, woman. (*He catches Sylvester's arm.*) Get him home, man.

Harry Dear God, this crippled form is still your child. (*To Mrs Heegan*) Dear mother, this helpless thing is still your son. Harry Heegan, me, who, on the football field, could crash a twelve-stone flyer off his feet. For this dear Club three times I won the Cup, and grieve in reason I was just too weak this year to play again. And now, before I go, I give you all the Cup, the Silver Tassie, to have and to hold for ever, evermore. (*From his chair he takes the Cup with the two sides hammered close together, and holds it out to them.*) Mangled and bruised as I am bruised and mangled. Hammered free from all its comely shape. Look, there is Jessie writ, and here is Harry, the one name safely separated from the other. (*He flings it on the floor.*) Treat it kindly. With care it may be opened out, for Barney there to drink to Jess, and Jess there to drink to Barney.

Teddy Come, Harry, home to where the air is soft. No longer can you stand upon a hill-top; these empty eyes of mine can never see from one. Our best is all behind us – what's in front we'll face like men, dear comrade of the blood-fight and the battle-front!

Harry What's in front we'll face like men!

Harry goes out by the window, Sylvester pushing the chair, Teddy's hand on Harry's shoulder, Mrs Heegan slowly following. Those left in the room watch them going out through the garden, turning to the right till they are all out of sight.

(*As he goes out of window*) The Lord hath given and man hath taken away!

Teddy (*heard from the garden*) Blessed be the name of the Lord!

The band in the hall begins to play again. Those in hall begin to dance.

Surgeon Maxwell Come on, all, we've wasted too much time already.

Susie (*to Jessie, who is sitting quietly in a chair*) Come on, Jessie – get your partner; (*roguishly*) you can have a quiet time with Barney later on.

Jessie Poor Harry!

Susie Oh nonsense! If you'd passed as many through your hands as I, you'd hardly notice one. (*To Jessie*) Jessie, Teddy Foran and Harry Heegan have gone to live their own way in another world. Neither I nor you can lift them out of it. No longer can they do the things we do. We can't give sight to the blind or make the lame walk. We would if we could. It is the misfortune of war. As long as wars are waged, we shall be vexed by woe; strong legs shall be made useless and bright eyes made dark. But we, who have come through the fire unharmed, must go on living. (*Pulling Jessie from the chair*) Come along, and take your part in life! (*To Barney*) Come along, Barney, and take your partner into the dance!

> *Barney comes over, puts his arm round Jessie, and they dance into the hall. Susie and Surgeon Maxwell dance together. As they dance the waltz 'Over the Waves', some remain behind drinking. Two of these sing the song to the same tune as the dance.*

Surgeon Maxwell
Swing into the dance,
Take joy when it comes, ere it go;
For the full flavour of life
Is either a kiss or a blow.
He to whom joy is a foe,
Let him wrap himself up in his woe;
For he is a life on the ebb,
We a full life on the flow!

All in the hall dance away with streamers and balloons flying. Simon and Mrs Foran sit down and watch the fun through the entrance. Mrs Foran lights a cigarette and smokes. A pause as they look on.

Mrs Foran It's a terrible pity Harry was too weak to stay an' sing his song, for there's nothing I love more than the ukelele's tinkle, tinkle in the night-time.

Curtain

SONGS AND CHANTS IN THE SILVER TASSIE

1st CHANT

THE SILVER TASSIE

2nd CHANT

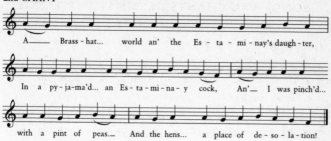

A —— Brass – hat... world an' the Es – ta – mi – nay's daugh – ter,

In a py – ja – ma'd... an Es – ta – mi – na – y cock, An'—— I was pinch'd...

with a pint of peas.—— And the hens... a place of de – so – la – tion!

3rd CHANT

The—— per – ky... queers me, Furi – ous – ly feel – ing... front – line fight – ing.

In his full – blown,... mur – mur, 'Here's a stand – fast... whis – per 'yes – sir'.

Like a bride,... ser – mon, From the cush – y... Tom – my's back – side.

4th CHANT

Jazz-ing back to his ho-tel he now goes gai-ly, Shel-ter'd
and safe where the clock ticks tame-ly. His— back-side warm-ing
a cu-shion, down-fill'd, Green-clad, well splash'd with gold birds red-beak'd.
His— last dim... ju-dy; Cud-dling with proud... the mud of the tren-ches.
His— tu-nic... pass-ing, Through col-our... shop snug in Bond Street.
Shame and scorn... com-pa-ny; Then— the decor-a-tions... of self-sac-ri-fice.

5th CHANT

A— warn-ing... give,— To the front... do, to God.—
God, un-chang-ing,... night sky To— mask... His self-slay-ing chil-dren.
Stum-bling, swift-ly... grous-ing, Through mud... seek slow the front line.
Squeals of hid-den... wound-ed— Christ who bore... tied to a field gun.

THE SILVER TASSIE

THE ENEMY HAS BROKEN THROUGH

The e-ne-my has bro-ken through, bro-ken through, bro-ken through! Ev-ery man born of wo-man to the guns, to the guns. To the guns, to the guns, to the guns! Those at prayer, all in bed and the swil-lers drink-ing deep-ly in the pubs. To the guns, to the guns. All the bat-men, ev-ery cook, ev-ery bit-ch's son that hides A whiff of cour-age in his veins, Shel-ter'd vig-our in his bo-dy, That can run, or can walk, ev-en crawl— Dig him out, dig him out, shove him on— To the guns!

SONG TO THE GUN

Hail, cool-hard-en'd tow'r of steel em-boss'd With the fev-er'd, fig-ment thoughts of man; Guard-ian of our love and hate and fear, Speak for us to the in-ner ear of God! We be-lieve in God and we be-lieve in thee.—

267

SEAN O'CASEY

WOULD GOD, I SMOK'D

Would God, I smok'd___ and walk'd and
Would God, I smok'd___ and lift—ed
To hang here ev—en a lit—tle
If you creep to rest___ in a clos'd—up
Each spar—row, hop———ping, ir—re—

watch'd___ The dance of a gol—den Brim—stone but—ter—
car—goes___ From the la—den shoul—ders of Lon—don's riv—er—
lon—ger Loung—ing___ through___ fear—swell'd, anx—ious
cof—fin, A tail of com—rades see—ing you safe
—spon—si—ble, Is in—den—tur'd___ in God's migh—ty mem—o—

—fly,___ To the sau—cy pipe___ of a
—way; The ho—li—day'd, roar—ing out___
mo—ments; The___ hin—der—parts___ of The
home;___ Or a ker—nal lost___ in a
—ry; And we, more than they all, shall___

green—finch rest—ing In a drow—sy, bram—bl'd lane in
cour—age and move—ment To the___ mus—cl'd ma—chines of
God of bat—tles Sha—ding our war—tir'd eyes from his
shell ex—plod—ing It's all, sure,___ on—ly in a
not be lost___ In the for—get—ful—ness of the

Cum—ber—land.___ In Cum—ber—land.___
Tot—ten—ham Hot—spur. Of Tot—ten—ham Hot—spur.
flam—ing face. From his flam—ing face.
life——time.___ A life——time.___
Lord of Hosts.___ Of the Lord of Hosts.___

SURGEON'S SONG

Stret - ched on the couch, Jess - ie fon - dl'd her dress, That hid all her beau - ties just o - ver the knee; And I won - der'd and said, as I sigh'd, 'What a shame, that there's no room at all on the couch there for me.'

STRETCHER-BEARER'S SONG

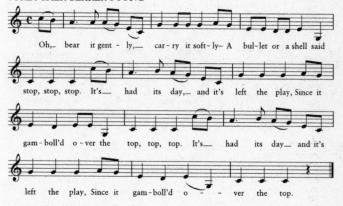

Oh, bear it gent - ly, car - ry it soft - ly— A bul - let or a shell said stop, stop, stop. It's had its day, and it's left the play, Since it gam - boll'd o - ver the top, top, top. It's had its day and it's left the play, Since it gam - boll'd o - ver the top.

PURPLE DUST

A WAYWARD COMEDY IN THREE ACTS

To Shivaun

Characters

Cyril Poges
Basil Stoke
Souhaun, Cyril's mistress
Avril, Basil's mistress
Barney, their manservant
Cloyne, their maidservant
O'Killigain, a foreman stonemason
1st Workman
2nd Workman
3rd Workman
Reverend George Canon Chreehewel, P.P. of Clune na Geera
Postmaster
Yellow-bearded Man
The Figure
The Bull

Time – The present.

Act One

A wide, deep, gloomy room that was once part of the
assembly or living-room of a Tudor-Elizabethan mansion.
The floor is paved with broad black and dull red
flagstones. The walls are timbered with oak beams, and
beams of the same wood criss-cross each other, forming
the roof, so that the room looks somewhat like a gigantic
cage. The beams are painted, alternately, black and white
so as to show they are there and to draw attention to their
beauty; but the paint makes them too conspicuous and,
therefore, ugly.

On the right is a huge open fireplace, overhung by a
huge hood. In the centre of the fireplace is a big iron arm
with a swinging cross-piece thrust out like a crane; from
this cross-piece hangs a thick chain to which a big shining
copper kettle is attached. At the back are two rather
narrow arched doorways, one towards the right, the other
towards the left. Between these are two long, deep,
mullioned windows. At the right, nearly opposite the
fireplace, is a wider arched doorway leading to the
entrance hall. Near the fireplace are two straight-backed
seats, like infantile church pews, each big enough only to
hold one person. A small Elizabethan or Jacobean table is
somewhere near the centre of the room. On this table is a
vase in which are a collection of violets and primroses,
mostly primroses.

It is about seven o'clock of an autumn morning, fine,
crisp, and fair.

Three workmen are seen in the room, two with shovels
and one with a pickaxe. One with a shovel and the one
with the pickaxe are standing near the archway leading to

*the entrance hall; the other, with a shovel, is beside the
wide fireplace, looking curiously at it. The 1st Workman is
a tall, lean man with a foxy face; the 2nd Workman is tall
too, and strongly built; he has a dreamy look, and has a
dark trim beard faintly touched with grey; the 3rd
Workman is stouter than the others, and not so tall. They
are all roughly dressed in soiled clothes, and wear high
rubber boots.*

1st Workman (*near the fireplace*) Well, of all th'
wondhers, to come to live in a house that's half down and
it's wanin' over. Thrickin' th' rotten beams into a look o'
sturdiness with a coat o' white and black paint, an' they
for long a dismal dwellin', even for the gnawin' beetle an'
th' borin' worm.

3rd Workman (*with the pickaxe*) They like that sort of
thing.

1st Workman An' th' maid was tellin' me they're goin' to
invest in hins an' cows, an' make th' place self-supportin'.

3rd Workman An' th' two o' them business men, rollin' in
money.

1st Workman Women you're not married to cost a lot to
keep; an' th' two with them'll dip deep into the oul' men's
revenue. Goin' over to London done them a world o'
good.

3rd Workman Irish, too, an' not a bit ashamed o'
themselves.

1st Workman Ashamed is it? Isn't th' oulder one
proclaimin' she's straight derived from th' Duke of
Ormond?

3rd Workman An' we knowin' th' two o' them well as
kids with patched petticoats an' broken shoes, runnin'
round th' lanes o' Killnageera.

1st Workman God be good to her, anyway, for bringin' a bit o' th' doddherers' money to where it's needed.

3rd Workman Th' two poor English omadhauns won't have much when th' lasses decide it's time for partin'.

2nd Workman (*who has been silently leaning on his shovel, looking dreamily ahead of him*) That day'll hasten, for God is good. Our poets of old have said it often: time'll see th' Irish again with wine an' ale on th' table before them; an' th' English, barefoot, beggin' a crust in a lonely sthreet, an' th' weather frosty.

1st Workman Afther a reckless life, they need th' peace o' th' country.

3rd Workman (*assuming a listening attitude*) They're stirrin'.

Mr Cyril Poges, Souhaun and Barney come in by one entrance at the back; Avril, Basil Stoke, and Cloyne from the other; they dance in what they think to be a country style, and meet in the centre, throwing their legs about while they sing. Avril has a garland of moonfaced daisies round her neck and carries a dainty little shepherd's crook in her hand; Cyril Poges, a little wooden rake with a gaily-coloured handle; Souhaun has a little hoe, garlanded with ribbons; Cloyne, a dainty little hayfork; Barney, a little reaping-hook; and Basil Stoke, a slim-handled little spade. Each wears a white smock having on it the stylized picture of an animal; on Poges's, a pig; on Basil's, a hen; on Souhaun's, a cow; on Avril's, a duck; on Cloyne's, a sheep; on Barney's, a cock.

Poges is a man of sixty-five years of age. He was, when young, a rather good-looking man, but age has altered him a lot. He is now inclined to be too stout, with a broad chest and too prominent belly; his face is a little too broad, too ruddy, and there are perceptible bags of flesh under his eyes. He has a large head; getting bald in front; though behind and over his ears the hair is long, fairly thick, and tinged with grey. He has a fussy manner, all business over little things; wants his own way at all times; and persuades himself that whatever he thinks of doing must be for the best, and expects everyone else to agree with him. He is apt to lose his temper easily, and to shout in the belief that that is the only way to make other people fall in with his opinions. He has now persuaded himself that in the country peace and goodwill are to be found; and expects that everyone else should find them there too. Under the smock he is dressed in morning clothes, and he wears a tall hat.

Basil Stoke is a long, thin man of thirty, with a rather gloomy face which he thinks betokens dignity, made gloomier still by believing that he is something of a philosopher. His cheeks are thin and their upper bones are as sharp as a hatchet. He is clean-shaven, and the thin hair on his half-bald head is trimly brushed back from his forehead. His eyes are covered with a pair of large horn-rimmed glasses. Under the smock he is dressed in jacket, plus-fours, and he wears a cap.

Souhaun is a woman of thirty-three years of age. She must have been a very handsome girl and she is still very good-looking, in a more matronly way. She has the fine figure of her young friend Avril, but her arms and her legs have grown a little plumper. She is still attractive enough to find attention from a good many men, when her young friend is out of the way. She wears, under the smock, what a lady would usually wear in the morning.

Cloyne is a stoutly built, fine-looking girl of twenty-six or so, and wears the servant's dress under her smock, and has a smart servant's cap on her head.

Barney is a middle-aged man with a discontented face

and a muttering manner. Under his smock he wears the
usual dress of a butler.
    Avril is dressed, under her smock, in gay pyjamas.

Poges (*singing*)
    Rural scenes are now our joy:
    Farmer's boy,
    Milkmaid coy,
    Each like a newly painted toy,

All
    In the bosky countrie!

Avril (*singing*)
    By poor little man the town was made,
    To degrade
    Man and maid;
    God's green thought in a little green shade
    Made the bosky countrie!

All (*chorus*)
    Hey, hey, the country's here,
    The country's there,
    It's everywhere!
    We'll have it, now, last thing at night,
    And the very first thing in the morning!

Basil (*singing*)
    Our music, now, is the cow's sweet moo,
    The pigeon's coo,
    The lark's song too,
    And the cock's shrill cock-a-doodle-doo,

All
    In the bosky countrie!

(*chorus*)
    Hey, hey, the country's here,
    The country's there,

It's everywhere!
We'll have it, now, last thing at night,
And the very first thing in the morning!

As they are singing the last lines of the chorus for the second time, those who have come in by the left entrance go out by the right one; and those who have come in by the right entrance go out by the left one. The workmen stand silent for a few moments, watching the places where the singers disappeared.

1st Workman Well, God help the poor omadhauns! It's a bad sign to see people actin' like that, an' they sober.

3rd Workman A sthrange crowd, they are, to come gallivantin' outa the city to a lonely an' inconsiderate place like this.

1st Workman At home, now, they'd be sinkin' into their first sleep; but because they're in the counthry they think the thing to do is to get up at the crack o' dawn.

3rd Workman An' they killin' themselves thryin' to look as if the counthry loved them all their life.

1st Workman With the young heifer gaddin' round with next to nothin' on, goadin' the decency an' circumspection of the place.

3rd Workman An' her eyes wiltin' when she sees what she calls her husband, an' widenin' wondherfully whenever they happen to light on O'Killigain.

1st Workman A handsome, hefty young sthripling, with a big seam in his arm that he got from a bullet fired in Spain.

3rd Workman For ever fillin' the place with reckless talk against the composure of the Church in the midst of the way things are now.

2nd Workman Ay, an' right he is, if ears didn't shut when his mind was speakin'.

1st Workman (*to 2nd Workman*) If I was you I'd be dumb as well, for Canon Chreehewel's mad to dhrive him outa th' place, with all who hear him.

2nd Workman (*fervently*) There's ne'er another man to be found as thrue or as clever as him till you touch the city's centre; an' if he goes, I'll go too.

1st Workman (*a little derisively*) Me brave fella.

3rd Workman It's what but they're thryin' to be something else beside themselves.

1st Workman They'd plunge through any hardship to make themselves believe they are what they never can become.

2nd Workman (*dolorously*) An' to think of two such soilifyin' females bein' born in Ireland, an' denizenin' themselves here among decent people!

3rd Workman Whissht; here's the boss, O'Killigain.

O'Killigain comes in from the side entrance, with a short straight-edge in his hand. He is a tall, fair young man twenty-five or twenty-six years old. He has a rough, clearly cut face; dogged-looking when he is roused, and handsome when he is in a good humour, which is often enough. He is clean-shaven, showing rather thick but finely formed lips. His hair, though cut short, is thick and striking. When he speaks of something interesting him, his hands make graceful gestures. He has had a pretty rough life, which has given him a great confidence in himself; and wide reading has strengthened that confidence considerably. He is dressed in blue dungarees and wears a deep yellow muffler, marked with blue decoration, round his neck. He is

*humming a tune as he comes in, and goes over towards
the men.*

O'Killigain (*lilting, as he comes in*)
They may rail at this life, from the hour I began it,
I found it a life full of kindness and bliss;
And until they can show me some happier planet,
More social and bright, I'll content me with this.

(*To the men*) 'Morra, boys.

All the Men 'Morra, Jack.

O'Killigain (*with a gesture pointing to where he thinks the
people of the house may be*) Up yet?

1st Workman Up is it? Ay, an' dancin' all about the place.

O'Killigain Bright colours, in cloth and paint, th' ladies
want, they say; jazz pastherns, if possible, say the two dear
young ladies: well, they'll want pretty bright colours to
cheer up this morgue.

3rd Workman It's a strange thing, now, that a man with
money would like to live in a place lonesome an' cold
enough to send a shiver through a year-old dead man!

O'Killigain Because they think it has what they call a
history. Everything old is sacred in every country. Give a
house a history, weave a legend round it, let some titled
tomfool live or die in it – and some fool mind will see
loveliness in rottenness and ruin.

1st Workman A nephew of the Duke of Ormond, they
say, dhrank himself to death in it, and the supernumary
wife of the older codger says she's a direct descendant of
the nephew; and she says they've come from the darkness
an' danger of England to settle down in what is really their
proper home.

O'Killigain And they're goin' to have the spoons and

forks an' knives done with what they say is the Ormond crest; Ormond's motto will shine out from their notepaper; and this tumble-down oul' shack is to be christened Ormond Manor.

2nd Workman (*savagely*) The English gett, hurryin' off with the ensign privilege of an Irish gentleman!

3rd Workman Isn't it sthrange how many'll fall for a mere name? Remember oul' Miss MacWilliam who used to faint with ecstasy the times she told the story of sittin' for a second in the King o' Denmark's chair; an' oul' Tom Mulligan who swaggered round for years afther the son o' the Earl of Skibbereen had accidentally spit in his eye!

O'Killigain Well, men, we'd better make a start.

1st Workman (*warningly*) Shush! Here's the flower o' Finea!

Avril comes in from the left entrance. She is a pretty girl of twenty-one or so, inclined, at times, to be a little romantic, and is very much aware of her good looks. She is far from being unintelligent, but does little and cares less about developing her natural talents. Her eyes are large and expressive, but sometimes sink into a hardened lustre. She is inclined to think that every good-looking young fellow, rich or poor, should fall for her pretty face and figure, and is a little worried if one of them doesn't. She adopts a free-and-easy and very unnatural attitude when she is talking to workmen. She is dressed now in gay scarlet trousers, widening at the ends, and very tight around her hips and bottom; low-cut black silk bodice, slashed with crimson, half hidden by a red-and-white striped scarf thrown carelessly round her shoulders – and black shoes. She trips over in a slow dancing way to where the workmen are standing, and as she comes in she lilts the first verse of 'The Maid of Bunclody'.

Avril (*close to the workmen*) Top o' the mornin', boys!

O'Killigain (*humouring her*) Same to you, miss, an' many of them, each of them fairer an' finer than the finest of all that ever brought the soft light o' the dawn at the peep o' day into your openin' eyes.

Avril It's meself that hopes you like the lovely house you're renovatin'?

O'Killigain An' tell me who wouldn't like the lovely house we're renovatin'? It's a dark man he'd be, without a stim o' light, an' destitute o' feelin'.

1st Workman (*enthusiastically*) Sure, miss, it's dumb with many wondhers we've all been for years that no one o' the well-to-do laid hands suddenly on the house to give it the glory again that musta been here throughout the jewell'd days of the times gone by!

Avril When it's thoroughly restored it'll be a pleasure an' a pride to the whole district.

O'Killigain (*with just a touch of sarcasm in his voice*) Sure, when we're done with it wouldn't it be fit for the shelter an' ayse an' comfort of Nuad of the Silver Hand, were he with us now, or of the great Fergus himself of the bright bronze chariots?

Avril Or even the nephew of Ormond's great Duke, the warlike ancestor of my very own friend an' distant cousin?

O'Killigain An' all the people here who are anything'll be mad with envy that they hadn't seized holt of it to make it what it'll soon be shown to be!

Avril lilts a reel and dances lightly about the room. The 1st and 3rd Workmen join in the lilting of the air. As she is passing O'Killigain he catches her excitedly and whirls her recklessly round the room till she is

*breathless, while the two men quicken the time of the
lilting.*

(*To Avril while she stands breathlessly before him*) Bow to
your partner.

> *Avril bows to him and he bows to her.*

(*Indicating the two men who lilted the tune of the reel*)
Bow, bow to the bards.

> *She bows to the two men, and when she has bent to the
> bow, O'Killigain gives her a sharp skelp on the behind.
> She straightens herself with a little squeal of pain and a
> sharp cry of indignation, and faces him angrily.*

Avril (*indignantly*) You low fellow, what did you dare do
that for! How dare you lay your dirty hands on a real
lady! That's the danger of being friendly with a
guttersnipe! Wait till you hear what Mr Basil Stoke'll say
when he hears what you've done. Get out of the room, get
out of the house – go away, and never let your ugly face be
seen here again!

O'Killigain (*with some mockery in his voice*) Sure, I
meant no harm, miss; it was simply done in the excitement
of the game. (*To 3rd Workman*) Wasn't it, now, Bill?

3rd Workman Ay was it, miss. Sure, th' poor man lost his
caution in the gaiety and the gayer tune.

O'Killigain I did it all in play; I thought you'd like it.

Avril (*sarcastically*) Oh, did you? Well, I didn't like it, and
I don't allow anyone to take advantage of any effort I
make to treat workmen as human beings.

2nd Workman (*maliciously*) If I was asked anything, I'd
say I saw a spark of pleasure in the flame of pain that
came into her eyes when she was hot!

Avril (*furiously – to the men*) Be off, you, and let me speak alone to this young man! I don't require any explanation from such as you; so be off, and I'll deal with this fellow!

The three workmen slide away out of the scene.

(*With a gentler tone in her voice*) Never, never do a thing like that again, young man.

O'Killigain (*with mocking earnestness*) Never again, young lady. You looked so handsome, gay, and young that my thoughts became as jaunty an' hilarious as your little dancin' feet.

Avril Never again, mind you – especially when others are here to stand and gape. (*She goes over and feels the muscle of his arm.*) There's too much power in that arm to give a safe and gentle blow to a poor young girl.

O'Killigain Ashamed I am of the force that sent a hand to hit a girl of grace, fit to find herself walkin' beside all the beauty that ever shone before the eyes o' man since Helen herself unbound her thresses to dance her wild an' willin' way through the sthreets o' Throy!

Avril It's I that know the truth is only in the shine o' the words you shower on me, as ready to you as the wild flowers a love-shaken, innocent young girl would pick in a hurry outa the hedges, an' she on her way to Mass.

O'Killigain Is it afther tellin' me that you are, an' your own words dancin' out as fair an' fine as the best o' mine?

Avril An' why wouldn't they, now, an' me that sang me song, first runnin' me years in, an' runnin' them out, in th' fields an' roads that skirted the threes an' hills o' Killnageera? But is there an Irishman goin' who hasn't a dint o' wondher in his talkin'?

O'Killigain I never met many who had it; but I got the touch of makin' a song from me mother, who – (*proudly*) – once won a grand gold medal at a Feis for a song of her own, put together between the times of bringin' up six children an' puttin' an odd flower on the grave of the one that died.

Avril You must sing me a few of your songs sometime.

O'Killigain Now, if you'd like to listen, an' you think that the time is handy.

Avril Not now; we might be disturbed; but some evening, somewhere away from here.

O'Killigain I will, an' welcome; some of them, too, that have been set in a little book, lookin' gay an' grand, for all the world to see. Come; listen – (*in a mocking whisper*) – and brave the wrath of the gouty, doughty Basil Stoke.

Avril (*with a toss of her head*) That thing! (*With bitter contempt*) A toddler thricking with a woman's legs; a thief without the power to thieve the thing he covets; a louse burrowing in a young lioness's belly; a perjurer in passion; a gutted soldier bee whose job is done, and still hangs on to life!

O'Killigain (*embracing her tightly*) Tonight, or tomorrow night, then, beside the blasted thorn three.

Avril (*with fright in her voice*) The blasted thorn tree! Oh, not there, not there – for evil things sit high, sit low in its twisty branches; and lovers, long ago, who leaned against it lost their love or died. No, no, not there: a saint himself would shudder if he had to pass it on a dusky night, with only a sly chit of a moon in the sky to show the way.

O'Killigain Oh, foolish girl, there never can be evil things where love is living. Between the evil things an' us we'll make the sign of the rosy cross, an' it's blossomin' again the dead an' dhry thing will be, an' fruit will follow. We are no' saints, and so can abide by things that wither, without shudder or sigh, let the night be dark or dusky. It is for us to make dying things live once more, and things that wither, leaf and bloom again. Fix your arm in mine, young and fair one, and face for life.

Avril (*after a little hesitation*) Undher the thorn three then, with you.

> *As the sound of voices is heard he holds her tight for a few moments, kisses her several times, then lets her go. He goes over and examines a wall where a telephone is evidently being put in.*
>
> *Avril, all demure, stands at the other end of the room watching him.*
>
> *Souhaun, followed by Poges and Basil, comes into the room. She is carrying a large two-handled earthenware jug in her right hand, and two coloured cushions under her left arm. Cyril Poges is carrying a large coloured picture of himself in a gold frame; and Basil Stoke too is bearing a picture of himself in a silver frame; he has a hammer sticking out of his side pocket. Cloyne follows them in with a six-step A ladder. Poges and Stokes are wearing gum-boots reaching to their thighs, and bright scarves round their necks.*
>
> *Poges and Basil rest the pictures against a wall.*

Souhaun (*to Avril*) Oh, here you are, with Mr O'Killigain. We were wondering where you were. We've a lot to do, dear, before we can get the house comfortable, so don't keep Mr O'Killigain from his work.

> *She leaves the jug down in a corner.*

Filled with gay flowers, Cyril, this jug'll be just the thing on your quattrocento desk-bureau.

Poges Lovely, darling. (*To O'Killigain*) We've been for a
run over the fields, O'Killigain; lovely; feel as fresh as a
daisy after it. (*Indicating the boots*) Great comfort, these
boots, in the long damp grass. Saw a swarm of rabbits –
quaint creatures.

Basil With these and rubber hats and rubber coats, we'll
be able to weather anything. I've got the hammer. Have
you got the nails?

Poges I forgot them. I'll get them now.

Basil And I'll get the string.

One goes out left, and the other right.

Souhaun (*to Cloyne*) Hold this curtain stuff end, Cloyne,
till we see its width.

*Cloyne holds one end of the stuff while Souhaun holds
the other. O'Killigain, pretending to be interested, bends
over Cloyne and, stretching out a hand to handle the
stuff, half puts his arm around Cloyne's neck, who is
very well pleased.*

O'Killigain Finely woven as a plover's wing, it is. No way
odd it ud look as a cloak for the lovely Emer; an', if it
hung from th' sturdy shouldhers of Queen Maev herself,
she'd find a second glory!

Souhaun (*displeased at his covert attention to Cloyne*)
Over here, Cloyne, please; hold this end.

*Souhaun and Cloyne change places, and O'Killigain
bends over Souhaun.*

Avril (*to O'Killigain*) I must have a chat with that man
working for you who knows everything worth knowing
about Ireland's past and present, Mr O'Killigain.

O'Killigain (*very seriously*) And please, miss, don't try to make fun of him. Touch him not with a jibe, for he's a wandherin' king holdin' th' ages be th' hand.

Souhaun How could a common worker be a king, O'Killigain?

O'Killigain Easier than for a king to be a common worker. Th' king o' a world that doesn't exist was a carpenter.

Avril Where is the real world to be found, then?

O'Killigain Where I have found it often, an' seek to find it still.

Avril And where's that place to be found?

O'Killigain With the bittherness an' joy blendin' in a pretty woman's hand; with the pity in her breast; in th' battlin' beauty of her claspin' arms; an' rest beside her when th' heart is tired.

Cloyne Sure, it's only makin' fun of us all he is.

O'Killigain Softer an' safer than St Patrick's breastplate is a woman's breast to save a man from the slings of life. (*Singing softly, moving a little away. Slyly towards the women:*)

Come in, or go out, or just stay at the door,
With a girl on each arm an' one standin' before;
Sure, the more that I have, the more I adore,
For there's life with the lasses,
Says Rory O'More!

Oh, courtin's an illigant, gorgeous affray,
When it's done in the night, or just done in the day;
When joy has been spent, sure, there's joy still in store;
For there's life with the lasses,
Says Rory O'More!

When all has been done, though nothin's been said,

Deep in the green grass, or at home in the bed;
To ev'ry brave effort we'll yield an encore;
For there's life with the lasses,
Says Rory O'More!

*As he ends his song, Poges and Basil return, the one
with the nails, the other with the string-wire.*

Poges (*to O'Killigain – briskly*) The garage is well in
hand, isn't it, O'Killigain?

O'Killigain (*who has tapped the wall, and is shaking his
head*) Yes, well in hands.

Poges (*enthusiastically*) Good man; when it's done I'll get
a first-class artist over from London to paint and make it
exactly like a little Tudor dwelling, so that it won't in any
way distort the beauty of the fine old house. What do you
say, O'Killigain?

O'Killigain is silent.

Eh?

O'Killigain I didn't speak.

Basil (*who has moved over, and is looking ecstatically up
at an end wall*) Early Tudor, I think; yes, Early Tudor, I'll
swear. A great period, a great period. Full of flow, energy,
colour, power, imagination, and hilarity.

O'Killigain (*tapping the wall beside him – ironically*) And
this is Middle Tudor – not a doubt about it.

Poges (*looking ecstatically at the other end wall*) Late
Tudor this one, I'm sure. Ah, England had no equal then.
Look at the Lionheart, eh? Smashed the infidel, smashed
him out of Jerusalem into the desert places. What was his
name, follower of the Prophet? You remember, Hegira, the
white stone, or was it a black stone? – oh, what was the
bounder's name?

Souhaun (*helpfully*) Tuttuttankamen, dear?

Poges (*scornfully*) Tuttuttankamen! My God, woman, he was only the other day!

Avril (*more helpfully*) The Mahdi, dear?

Poges (*more scornfully*) The Mahdi! (*Plaintively*) Is there no one here knows a line of the history of his country!

Basil (*with complacent confidence*) Genghis Khan.

Poges (*emphatically*) Genghis Khan! That was the name of the bounder driven from Jerusalem by the Lionhearted Richard. A warrior, a hero. And maybe he was actually in this very house. It's all very moving. (*To O'Killigain*) I imagine I hear the clank, clank, clank of armour when I walk the rooms, and see the banners and banneroles, with their quaint designs, fluttering from the walls! Don't you feel the lovely sensation of – er – er – er – old, unhappy, far-off things, and battles long ago?

O'Killigain is silent.

(*Insistently*) Don't you feel something of all that, O'Killigain, eh?

O'Killigain (*quietly*) I let the dead bury their dead.

Souhaun Oh, don't worry Mr O'Killigain, Cyril; he's a workaday worker, and neither understands nor takes an interest in these things.

Poges Nonsense; O'Killigain's an intelligent man, and is only too glad to learn a little about the finer things of life; and to think of great things past and gone is good – isn't that so?

O'Killigain Occasionally, perhaps; but not to live among them. Life as it is, and will be, moves me more.

Poges Come, come; we mustn't be always brooding upon

the present and the future. Life is too much with us,
O'Killigain; late and soon, getting and spending, we lay
waste our powers. But you've never read good old
Wordsworth, I suppose?

O'Killigain As a matter of fact, I have.

Poges You have? Well, that promotes a fellowship
between us, eh? Great man, great man; but a greater poet,
eh?

O'Killigain (*with some vehemence*) A tired-out oul'
blatherer; a tumble-down thinker; a man who made a
hiding-place of his own life; a shadow parading about as
the sun; a poet, sensitive to everything but man; a bladder
blown that sometimes gave a note of music; a fool who
thought the womb of the world was Wordsworth; a poet
who jailed the striving of man in a moral lullaby; a snail to
whom God gave the gleam of the glowworm; a poet
singing the song of safety first!

Poges (*irritated*) Oh! Is that the result of the new
schooling? I'm afraid very few will agree with you, my
friend. Well, well, we've more to do than discuss the merit
of a poet; so hasten on the work of building the garage,
like a good man.

O'Killigain (*bowing ironically*) I go, sir. (*He goes out.*)

Poges (*to the others*) Isn't that a shocking example of bad
taste and ignorance? (*To Souhaun*) There's one of your
fine countrymen for you, dear.

Souhaun Well, Cyril dear, you know you were just trying
to show off to him. A few little quotations, drummed into
you at school, is all you know of Wordsworth. You're
never tired of saying that poetry isn't your cup of tea.

Poges (*angry*) Modern poetry, modern poetry isn't my cup
of tea; and I don't care who knows it. But I don't deny the

past. Tradition – that is our strength in time of trouble; tradition, follow the traditions, the only things that count in a cultured man's life. Keep as close as we can to the beauties of the past – the, the glory that was Rome and the grandeur that was Greece – Shakespeare knew what he was talking about when he said that.

Basil Well, by living in this old historic house we're keeping close to the old traditions.

Souhaun (*dubiously*) It's beginning to feel a little cold and damp to me.

Poges (*astonished and indignant*) Cold? What are you talking about? Damp? Nonsense. Were it warmer, it would begin to feel uncomfortable. What do you say, Cloyne?

Cloyne (*who has been dusting the walls with a long-handled duster*) I feel quite cosy, sir; though there is a bit of a breeze blowing down the chimney.

Poges (*shivering a little*) Eh? Cosy, eh? Of course you do; we all do. Think, too, of the loveliness all round us: river, lake, valley, and hill. (*Lilting*) Angels, often pausing here, doubt if Eden were more fair. Here we have the peace of Eden.

Souhaun And you must admit, dear, that we Irish are a simple, hearty, honest, and obliging people.

Basil (*enthusiastically*) They're dears. All I've met of them are dears; so quaint and charming – they are sweet. They need control, though; they need control.

Poges I agree. All the Irish are the same. Bit backward perhaps, like all primitive peoples, especially now, for they're missing the example and influence of the gentry; but delightful people all the same. They need control, though; oh yes, they need it badly.

Basil We must get to really know the country; it's one thing to be sensitive about the country scene, and quite another to understand it.

Poges (*heartily*) Quite right, Basil. We must get to know the country so that everything in it is natural to us. (*Lilting*) To plough and to sow, to reap and to mow, and to be a farmer's boy-oy-oy. The different trees, for example, to call them by their names the instant we see them.

Avril In winter or summer.

Poges Quite. In the summer by their fruits.

Avril Trees don't have fruits, Cyril.

Poges Of course not. I mean barks and branches. It will be a joy to say to some ignorant visitor from the city: That tree? Oh, that's just an oak; and that one there by the river is a – a –

Avril Gooseberry tree, Cyril.

Poges A lilac, or something. (*To Avril*) Don't be funny. This is a serious matter.

Cloyne We mustn't forget the hens, either, sir.

Poges Hens? Yes, of course – the hens. A fine idea. Yes, we'll have to have hens; a first-class strain, though: nothing else would be of any use.

Cloyne A first-class strain, of course.

Poges And a cow as well.

Avril A cow might be dangerous.

Poges Dangerous? Nonsense; if he was, then we'd simply have to keep him in a cage. (*He sets up the step-ladder, mounts it, and holds up his picture against the wall.*) How does that look?

Souhaun (*taking no notice*) First of all, we must get to know the nature and names of all the wild flowers of the district.

Poges (*letting the picture rest on the ground, and turning to the rest*) Especially the wild flowers that Shakespeare loved – the – the – er – er – (*his eye catches sight of primroses in a little vase on the table*) – the primrose, for instance; you know – the primrose by the river's brim, a yellow primrose was to him, but it was nothing more; though we all actually know all there is to be known about the little primrose.

Basil (*letting his picture rest on the ground, leaning over the top so that he at one end of the room and Poges at the other look like preachers in pulpits, panelled with their own portraits*) That's just ignorant complacency, Cyril. Of course, if we regard, assume, or look at the plant purely as a single entity, then a primrose is a primrose, and there's nothing more to be said about it.

Poges Well, you can't assume or regard the primrose as an elm tree, can you, old boy?

Basil (*quickly*) Don't interrupt me for a minute, please. If we take the primrose, however, into our synthetical consideration, as a whole, or, *a priori*, as a part, with the rest of the whole of natural objects or phenomena, then there is, or may be, or can be a possibility of thinking of the flower as of above the status, or substance, or quality of a fragment; and, consequently, correlating it with the whole, so that, to a rational thinker, or logical mind, the simple primrose is, or may become, what we may venture to call a universal. See?

Poges (*bewildered*) Eh? Oh yes, yes; no, no; yes, yes: eh, what?

Souhaun (*to Cloyne*) Cloyne, you'd better go and look after the fires in our room.

Cloyne rises and goes out.

Avril (*with mockery in her voice*) Hush, listen all – great men are speaking!

Poges (*to Basil*) Eh, what the devil are you trying to say, man?

Avril (*with triumphant mockery*) Ah, Cyril, you're caught!

Poges (*indignantly*) Caught? Who's caught? Me? Nonsense, girl. He has simply compounded a fact with a fallacy. Can I see? Have I eyes? Yes. Very well, then. I see a flower with a root, leaves and a blossom; I ask myself, What is it? I answer, A flower; I ask, What is it called? I answer, A primrose.

Basil (*languidly*) So you say, sir.

Poges (*vehemently*) So everyone says, sir!

Basil (*leaning forward towards Poges*) And what is a flower, sir?

Poges (*furiously*) A flower? Good God, sir, a plant; a contrivance springing out of the earth; a vegetating combination of root, leaves, and blossom.

Souhaun Calmly, Cyril, calmly.

Basil (*leaning back and closing his eyes wearily*) I knew you'd just say that, sir. Words; you're merely using words. Try to think, sir, of a primrose, not as a primrose, but as a simple object, and as a substance outside of yourself.

Poges (*half frantic*) Damn it, man, don't I know that a primrose isn't a substance inside of myself! Tell us how a man is to think of a primrose except as a primrose. He can't think of it as the dear little, sweet little shamrock of Ireland, can he? It is indeed a pitiful humiliation to have to listen to a half-educated fool!

Basil (*angry at last – setting the picture aside and taking a threatening step towards Poges, Avril stepping in front to restrain him*) A fool! Do you say I am a fool, sir? Is a man versed in all the philosophies of the world to be called a fool!

Avril Basil, dear!

Souhaun (*getting in front of Poges*) Cyril, darling, do remember that we are having just a little friendly discussion about a common country flower!

Avril (*ironically*) Basil is only trying to share his great knowledge with us.

Poges He calls that knowledge, does he?

Souhaun We must remember that Basil passed through Oxford, dear.

Poges I don't care if he crept under it or flew over it; he's not going to punish me with what he picked up there.

Basil (*a little tearfully*) Considering that I have read every word written by Hume, Spinoza, Aristotle, Locke, Bacon, Plato, Socrates, and Kant, among others, I think my views ought to receive some respect from an ignorant man.

Poges (*boastfully*) I was reared any old how; and here I am today, a money'd man, able to say to almost any man, come, and he cometh, and to almost any other man, go, and he goeth – and quick too; able to shake hands with lords and earls, and call them by their Christian names. This – (*he touches his forehead*) – and these – (*he holds out his hands*) – did it all, without an inherited penny to help! (*He looks balefully at Basil.*) And that's more than some of them can say. And I never passed through Oxford!

Souhaun (*soothingly – to Basil*) Come, now, go away for a few minutes, till he's calm again.

Basil (*tearfully and wrathfully*) Souhaun and you can see, Avril, that the virtue of respect and ready veneration that every right-minded Englishman has for the classic colleges has gone completely out of him.

Souhaun (*soothingly*) There now, there now; it'll all come back soon.

Basil (*almost weeping*) Whenever we got the chance he hurried me down to Oxford to meet this professor and that doctor, itching all over to obtain a degree *honoris causa*, in any faculty of Divinity, Science, Literature, Medicine, or Law!

Poges (*scornfully*) And most of them anxious for tips from the Stock Exchange. Go away, man, and weep in silence. (*He lifts his picture up against the wall.*) We have something else to do. Here, how does that look there?

Souhaun (*gently pushing Basil out of the room*) There, go, dear, till you recover yourself.

Basil (*going out – loudly*) *Quisabit grunniodem expectio porcum* – what can one expect from a pig but a grunt?

Poges (*with the picture against the wall*) There, how does that look here? (*Pityingly*) Poor fool; juvenile mind, Souhaun, juvenile mind. But snappy enough, when he likes, and I, by cunning investment, having doubled his income for him. Ingratitude. (*Impatiently*) Well, how does this look here?

Souhaun I think the opposite wall would be more suitable, dear.

Avril Where it is, is best, mother.

Poges Make up your minds, make up your minds!

Souhaun Where it is, dear.

Poges How is it for height?

Souhaun A little higher.

Avril A little lower.

Poges One of you, one of you!

Souhaun A little to the right, now.

Avril A little to the left, now.

Poges (*lowering the picture to the ground*) Which is it? How is it? What is it!

Cloyne comes in with a newspaper in her hand.

Cloyne (*to Poges*) Your newspaper, sir – the *Financial Universe*.

She leaves it on the table, and goes out again. Poges breaks open his paper, and is about to look at it when Barney appears at the left entrance. A sound of cackling is heard outside, and the loud lowing of a cow, and the crowing of cocks.

Poges (*with the paper half spread before him*) What the hell's that?

Barney There's a man outside wants to know if you want any entherprisin' hins?

Poges Any what?

Barney Any hins, entherprisin' hins?

Poges (*impatiently*) What the devil would I want with hins enterprising or unenterprising?

Barney He says it's all over the counthry that you're searchin' high an' low for entherprisin' hins.

Cloyne (*appearing at the right entrance*) There's two men

here wantin' to know if you'd buy some prime an' startlin'
cocks, goin' cheap?

1st Workman (*appearing beside Barney, and shoving him
aside to get in front*) Excuse me, sir, but there's a friend o'
mine just arrived with a cow that ud do any man good to
see; a baste with a skin on her as shiny an' soft as the
down on a first-class angel's wing; an' uddhers that'll
make any man hard put to it to fetch enough pails to get
the milk she gives!

Poges Hins, cocks, and cows! (*To 1st Workman*) What
the hell do you take me for – a farmer's boy, or what?

Souhaun It's all out of what you said about having hens
and a cow in the place. (*To Cloyne*) And you, you little
fool, must have gossiped it all over the district!

Cloyne The only one I mentioned it to was Mr O'Killigain.

1st Workman (*coming over to Poges*) Listen, sir, whisper,
now: sthrike for th' honour of St Patrick, while the iron's
hot, for the cow. An' whisper, don't, for the love o' God,
have anything to do with the hins an' cocks they're thryin'
to palm off on you – there isn't one o' them that isn't th'
essence of a false pretendher!

Souhaun (*angrily – to Cloyne*) I won't have you gossiping
to O'Killigain, spending time with him you ought to give
getting the house in shape! The idea of discussing our
private affairs with O'Killigain! If you think that
O'Killigain has taken a fancy to you, you never made a
bigger mistake, my girl.

Cloyne (*indignantly*) Indeed, ma'am? Well, if Mr
O'Killigain bids me the time o' day, I'll do the same,
without any permission from you, ma'am!

Barney (*impatiently*) An' what am I goin' to say to the
man who's brought th' entherprisin' hins?

Poges (*shouting*) Pack him off about his business!

Barney goes out.

(*To Cloyne*) And you do the same to the man who brought the startling cocks!

Souhaun (*to Cloyne*) And no more trespassing on the good nature of O'Killigain, either!

Cloyne (*turning and facing Souhaun swiftly as she is going out*) There's a withering old woman, not a hundred miles from where I am, who ought to take her own advice, an' keep from thryin' her well-faded thricks of charm on poor Mr O'Killigain herself! (*She goes out.*)

Poges (*loudly and complainingly*) Oh, stop these unseemly disputes in a house that ought to know only peace and dignity! Can't you try to act as the *les grand dames* and the *les grander monsieurs* must have acted when they moved about here in this beautiful Tudor house. While we're in it, let us forget the vile world and all its ways. (*Angrily – to 1st Workman, who has been tugging at his sleeve for the last few moments*) What the hell do you want, man?

1st Workman (*earnestly, almost into Poges' ear*) Listen, whisper, sir; take the bull be th' horns, an' get the cow, before she's gone. An' as for entherprisin' hins, or cocks that'll do you credit, leave it to me, sir, an' you'll go about with a hilarious look in your eyes!

Poges (*catching 1st Workman by the shoulders, in a rage, and pushing him out of the room, and down the passage*) Get out, get out, you fool, with your hins and cocks and cows!

Souhaun (*quickly – to Avril, when Poges has disappeared round the entrance*) Go on up, and flatter and comfort your old fool by ridiculing my old fool; and, when he's half himself again, wanting still more comfort and flattery, wheedle a cheque out of the old prattler.

Avril (*jumping up*) Splendid idea! (*She runs off out.*)

Souhaun (*calling after her*) A good one, mind you!

Poges comes back fuming, and brushing his coat where it touched the 1st Workman.

Poges Are we to have no peace down here where peace was born? (*He takes up the paper again and begins to read it.*) Uum. Ha, tin shares up again. Good. (*He buries his face in the paper.*) If it weren't for the damned taxes.

1st and 3rd Workmen peer around corner of the left entrance; then they come over quickly and smoothly to where Poges is buried in his paper, the 1st Workman standing on his left hand and the 3rd Workman on his right.

1st Workman (*persuasively – towards Poges' paper*) Listen, here, sir: if it's genuine poulthry you want, that lay with pride an' animation, an' not poor, insignificant fowls that set about th' business o' layin' like a member o' Doyle Eireann makin' his maiden speech, I have a sthrain o' pullets that'll give you eggs as if you were gettin' them be steam!

Poges (*angrily – glancing over the top of his paper*) Go away, go away, man, and don't be driving me mad!

3rd Workman (*towards Poges' paper*) Oh, the lies that some can tell to gain their own ends! Sure, sir, everyone knows that his poor hins are harmless; only venturin' to lay when heavy thundher frightens them into a hasty sign o' life! But it's meself can give you what you want, with a few lively cocks thrown in, to help them on with the work of furnishing nourishment to the whole world.

Poges Go away; when I want poultry, I'll get into touch with the experts in the Department of Agriculture.

1st Workman (*horrified – partly to Poges and partly to Souhaun*) Oh, listen to that, now! Didja hear that, ma'am? The Department of Agriculture, is it? Wisha, God help your innocence, sir. Sure, it's only a tiny time ago that the same Department sent down a special sthrong covey o' cocks to improve the sthrain, an' only afther a short probation, didn't they give the hins hysterics?

Poges Hysterics? Good God!

3rd Workman Ay, an' hadn't the frightened farmers to bring guns to bear on the cocks when they found their hins scatthered over hill an' dale, lyin' on their backs with their legs in the air, givin' their last gasp, an' glad to get outa the world they knew so well! The few mighty ones who survived were that stunned that there wasn't an egg in th' place for years!

Poges (*good-humouredly catching the men by the arm and leading them to the left entrance*) Now, now, men, I'm busy; I've some very important business to think about and can't be bothered with hins!

1st Workman (*as they go out*) Another time, sir; but don't think of the Department in this important matther: they'll send you hins'll paralyse the cocks, or cocks that'll paralyse the hins!

They go out.

Poges (*returning and reading the paper*) Childlike people, the Irish, aren't they? Hysterical hins! Dr What's-his-name, the fellow who said all man is moved by streams of thought that never enter his head – well, he'd find something to study down here. Well, it's delightful to be in a lovely house, in a lovely country, with nothing to think of but hysterical hins! (*He suddenly concentrates on something in the paper.*) I must have some of those shares. (*He runs to the telephone and joggles and shakes it.*) What can be the matter with this Exchange? – I can't hear a sound! (*To Souhaun*) Call one of the workmen, will you? I must get through to London at once.

> *Souhaun runs out to call a workman. In a moment or two the 2nd Workman comes into the room.*

2nd Workman Is it me you want, sir?

Poges Not you especially; I just want to know if you know, or anyone in the county knows, why I can't connect with the Exchange.

2nd Workman Oh, is that all, sir?

Poges (*snappily*) Is that all! Isn't it enough, fool!

2nd Workman (*sharply*) Who th' hell are you callin' a fool to?

Poges (*placatingly but with some impatience*) My good man, please let me know if you can say why the Exchange doesn't answer my call.

2nd Workman Ask anyone from one end o' the counthry to the other, or even O'Killigain himself, if Philib O'Dempsey's a fool, an' see what they'll say. A sound mind, armed with a firm education for seven long years in a steady school, an' now well fit to stand his ground in any argument, barrin' th' highest philosophies of the greatest minds mendin' th' world!

Poges My good man, I only asked you a simple question.

2nd Workman (*ignoring the remark*) Comin' over here, thinkin' that all the glory an' grandeur of the world, an' all the might of man, was stuffed into a bulgin' purse, an' stickin' their tongue out at a race that's oldher than themselves by a little like a thousand years, greater in their beginnin' than they are in their prime; with us speakin' with ayse the mighty languages o' the world when they could barely gurgle a few sounds, sayin' the rest in the movement of their fingers.

Poges (*almost in rage*) Go to the devil, man, and learn manners!

2nd Workman (*going on vehemently, but moving slowly to one of the entrances*) Hammerin' out handsome golden ornaments for flowin' cloak an' tidy tunic we were, while you were busy gatherin' dhried grass, an' dyin' it blue, to hide the consternation of your middle parts; decoratin' eminent books with glowin' colour an' audacious beauty were we, as O'Killigain himself will tell you, when you were still a hundhred score o' years away from even hearin' of the alphabet. (*Beside the entrance*) Fool? It's yourself's the fool, I'm sayin', settlin' down in a place that's only fit for the housin' o' dead men! Settlin' here, are you? Wait till God sends the heavy rain, and the floods come! (*He goes out.*)

Poges (*to Souhaun*) There's Erin, the tear and the smile in her eye for you! The unmannerly ruffian! Venomous, too – wanting me to wait till the floods come! Cheeking me up to my very face!

Souhaun Well, it's not a royal face, is it? You'll have to learn to be respectful to the people if you want them to be respectful to you.

Poges (*sarcastically*) I'll be most deferential in the future. (*Stormily – to 1st Workman appearing at the entrance*) Well, what do you want?

1st Workman Excuse, but I sailed in, hearin' you were in a difficulty, an' I wanted to see if I could help.

Poges Well, I want to know where's the man who is responsible for putting in this 'phone?

1st Workman Why, is there anything wrong with it, sir?

Poges (*stormily*) Everything's wrong with it, man! I can't get on to the Exchange.

1st Workman Sure, that's aysily explained: it's not connected yet.

Poges It was to be connected first thing this morning. When will it be connected?

1st Workman (*cautiously*) Oh, now, that depends, sir.

Poges Depends? Depends on what?

1st Workman On how long it'll take to get the sthrame o' sound from here flowin' safely to whatever other end there may be fixed for it to be heard in.

Poges (*impatiently*) Get O'Killigain, get him to come here at once.

1st Workman Sure, that's the Postmaster's job – Mr O'Killigain has nothing to do with it.

Poges (*shouting*) Then get me the man that has something to do with it!

Souhaun (*who has been looking at the coloured curtain stuff and spreading it out*) Now, Cyril, see what you think: is the red with the green stripe or the green with the red stripe the most suitable to go with the walls?

The sound of horses trotting is heard outside, becoming plainer, till the sound ceases somewhere close to the house.

Poges (*to Souhaun – with irritation*) For goodness' sake, one thing at a time. (*To 1st Workman*) Go and get the man that's doing this job.

1st Workman I'm afraid you'll have to thravel a long way
if you want to get him, sir; you see, he had to go to pay his
last respects to a dead cousin; but never fear, he won't be
gone beyond a couple of hours, unless something out o'
the ordinary keeps him away the whole o' the evenin' an'
th' strongest part o' th' night.

*Poges sinks down on one of the seats, silent and
confounded.*

Cloyne (*appearing at back entrance*) Th' horses are here
now, sir.

Poges (*sitting up*) Horses? What horses?

Cloyne The horses Mr Basil an' Miss Avril ordhered to
come here.

Souhaun Basil and Avril are going out for a little canter,
Cyril.

Poges (*peevishly*) But this is not the time to be thinking of
amusement; we have to get the house into some shape.
Ask O'Killigain to come here.

Souhaun (*to Cloyne*) Yes, get O'Killigain, Cloyne; he has
a good eye, and will be able to judge which of these
curtain stuffs should go on the windows.

*Cloyne goes. O'Killigain appears at the left entrance
with an anxious look on his face.*

O'Killigain Who's going to ride these horses that are
outside?

Souhaun (*haughtily*) Miss Avril and her friend Mr Basil
Stoke are going to ride them.

O'Killigain I suppose you know these horses are
mettlesome creatures, and need riders at home in the
saddle?

Souhaun (*more haughtily still*) Miss Avril and her friend learned the art in a London riding-school, and exercised frequently in Richmond Park; so your kind solicitude is unnecessary, sir.

O'Killigain (*viciously*) Richmond Park isn't Clune na Geera, ma'am. The horses there are animals; the horses here are horses.

Avril comes tripping in, dressed in jersey and jodhpurs, and is followed by Basil, dressed in a dark green kind of hunting coat, buckskin breeches, and big gleaming top-boots with spurs; he carries a whip in his hand, and a high, handsome, shining tall hat on his head.

(*With a frightened look at Basil*) Good God! (*He turns on his heel and walks out again.*)

Basil (*with complacent conceit – to Souhaun*) The old ways coming back again to the old house, Souhaun.

Souhaun (*rapturously*) Isn't it grand, dear? Don't forget to go through the village.

Avril (*joyously*) Basil has been so kind, Souhaun, dear; he has given me a grand cheque.

Souhaun (*giving Basil a kiss and winking at Avril*) Basil, you're a darling!

Poges (*grumpily*) Be careful how you handle those horses.

Basil (*haughtily – to Poges*) Did you say anything, sir?

Poges (*with some heat*) I said be careful how you handle those horses!

Basil (*with a mocking bow*) Thank you, sir; we'll do our best. (*To Avril*) Come, darling.

Avril trips out, and Basil follows her in a way that he deems to be stately.

Poges I hope they'll do no damage, now.

Souhaun Oh, never fear; Basil sits the saddle like a centaur.

The movement of horses' hooves is heard, then a trot, getting fainter till it dies away.

Poges (*exasperated*) God send he doesn't frighten the horse. More decent of him had he remained here to get this telephone going. They all seem to be determined here to keep us away from every semblance of civilization! (*To Souhaun – stormily*) Will you, for God's sake, try to get O'Killigain to do something to get this thing in order? (*He goes over to where Souhaun is busy with the curtains and pulls the curtains out of her hands, then flings them on the floor.*) D'ye hear, d'ye hear what I'm saying to you, woman?

Souhaun (*losing patience and seizing him, and shaking him roughly*) What d'ye think you're doing, you old dim-eyed, old half-dead old fool! I'll disconnect you as well as the telephone if you don't learn to behave yourself! You settled on coming here, and you'll put up with the annoyances!

Poges (*protestingly*) Eh, eh, there! It was you who persuaded me to come to this god-forsaken hole!

Souhaun (*shaking him more fiercely*) You're a liar, I didn't! It was you yourself who were always pining to see the little squirrels jigging about on the trees, and see the violets and primroses dreaming in the budding stir of spring! (*She pushes him violently from her.*) Another snarly sound out of you, and I'm off to live alone.

Poges (*gloomily*) You can well afford to be independent now, since, like a fool, I settled five hundred a year on you.

During this contest Cloyne has appeared at the left

entrance and now gives a judicious cough.

Souhaun (*quickly – to cover dispute from Cloyne*) We'll decide on this stuff, then, for the curtains, Cyril, dear.

Poges It'll look delightful, darling. (*Pretending to see Cloyne for the first time*) Oh, what do you want?

Cloyne Canon Chreehewel's outside an' would like to have a few words with you, if you're not too busy.

Poges (*showing irritation*) Oh, these priests, these priests! Thick as weeds in this poor country. Opposed to every decent thought that happens not to have come from them. Ever on guard to keep the people from growing out of infancy. No one should give them the slightest encouragement. Oh, if the misguided people would only go back to the veneration of the old Celtic gods, what a stir we'd have here! To the delightful, if legendary, loveliness of – er – er – er – what's his name, what's her name, what's their name? I have so often said it, so often in my mind, the chief, or one of the chief gods of the ancient Celts?

Souhaun Was it Gog or Magog, dear?

Poges (*with fierce scorn*) Oh, no, no, no; try to think a little, if you really want to assist me. Can't you remember that Gog and Magog were two Philistinian giants killed by David, or Jonathan, or Joshua, or Joab, or Samson, or someone? It's the old Celtic god I have in mind, the one – what was his name?

Souhaun Gulliver?

Poges Oh no; not Gulliver!

Souhaun Well, I don't know the hell who it was.

Poges (*slapping his thigh exultantly*) Brobdingnag! That was the fellow – the fellow that ate the nine nuts – or was it seven? – plucked from the tree hanging over the well near the world's end.

Cloyne What am I to say to the Canon, sir?

Poges What does he want; did you ask him what he wants?

Cloyne He says he just wants to drop a word or two of thanks for the fifty pounds you sent him.

A murmur of voices is heard outside. It comes nearer and the sound seems excited.

Poges (*listening*) What's that, now?

1st Workman (*outside*) Keep his head up.

3rd Workman (*outside*) You're home, sir, you're home now.

They come in supporting Basil by the arms, followed by the 2nd Workman, holding Basil's coat-tail. Basil is pale, and has a frightened look on his face. His lovely coat is spattered with mud and, in some places, torn. The 1st Workman is carrying the tall hat, now looking like a battered concertina.

Poges (*anxiously*) What's this; what's happened?

1st Workman (*soothingly*) He's all right, sir; just a little shock. We seen him crawling towards the house an' went to his help. His horse flung him. (*Whispering to Poges*) He shouldn't be let on anything more mettlesome than a rocking-horse, sir.

Souhaun (*running to Basil*) Are you much hurt, Basil, dear?

Basil (*brokenly*) Bruised, bruised from head to foot.

Poges (*with irritation*) Well, why the hell didn't you stay here and help me to get the telephone fixed?

Basil Why didn't you hold me back by force? Oh, why did you let me go!

Souhaun (*anxiously*) Where's Avril?

Basil (*ignoring her query*) Oh, I should never have ventured upon an Irish horse! Irresponsible, irresponsible, like the people. When he wouldn't go, I gave him just a little jab with the spur – (*moaningly*) – and the brute behaved like a wild animal, just like a wild animal!

1st Workman (*soothingly – to Souhaun*) He's not hurt much, ma'am; came down in th' grass on his poor bum.

Souhaun But where's Avril? (*Shaking Basil's shoulder*) Where's Avril?

Basil Gone!

Souhaun Gone?

Basil Away with O'Killigain. He came bounding up to help Avril and abused me for falling off. Then they cantered away together. (*Loudly and a little shrilly*) Naked and unashamed, the vixen went away with O'Killigain!

Plaster falls and a hole appears in the ceiling, almost directly over the fireplace; then a thin rope, with a bulb attached to its end, comes dangling down, followed by the face of a heavily Yellow-bearded Man, who thrusts his head as far as it can go through the hole.

Yellow-bearded Man (*to those below*) Hay, hay there; is this where yous want the light to go?

Poges (*with a vexatious yell when he sees where the rope hangs*) No it isn't, no it isn't, you fool! (*Indicating a place near the centre and towards the back*) There, there's where it's wanted! Where my desk will be! Oh, they're knocking down more than they're building up!

Yellow-bearded Man (*soothingly*) Don't worry; just a little mistake in measurement, sir. Never fear, we'll hit th' right spot one o' these days! The one thing to do, sir, is to keep cool.

He takes his head out of the hole and disappears, leaving Poges furious.

Poges (*shouting up at the hole*) Who are you to order me to keep cool? I won't keep cool. I refuse to keep cool!

Souhaun (*to Poges*) Here, help me in with poor Basil till he drinks some brandy and lies down for a little.

Poges takes one arm, Souhaun takes the other, and they lead Basil out of the room.

Poges (*to Basil – helping him out*) I hope you realize the sterling trouble you give people by your damned refusal to recognize your limitations!

Basil (*petulantly*) Carry me out, man; carry me out!

Cloyne (*as they pass*) What am I to do with the Canon, sir?

Poges (*ferociously*) Tell him I'll give him another cheque if he gets the telephone fixed for me before the night is out!

Basil, Souhaun and Poges go out by the left entrance; Cloyne by that on the right, leaving the men standing together in a corner of the room.

2nd Workman (*pensively*) Th' spirit of th' Grey o' Macha's in our Irish horses yet!

1st Workman (*excitedly*) Did yous hear that, eh? Did yous hear what he just let dhrop? That the lassie o' th' house went off with O'Killigain riding naked through the locality!

2nd Workman Stark naked she was, too. Didn't I know

314

well be th' cut of her jib that she was a hop, step, an' lep
of a lassie! An' right well she looked too!

1st Workman Th' sight near left me eyes when I seen her
go prancin' out without as much as a garther on her to
keep her modesty from catchin' cold.

3rd Workman This'll denude the disthrict of all its self-
denyin' decency.

1st Workman (*excitedly jumping upon a seat to get nearer
to the hole in the ceiling*) Cornelius, eh, there, Cornelius!

*The yellow-bearded head is thrust through the hole
again.*

Yellow-bearded Man What's up?

1st Workman Didja hear th' terrible thing that's afther
happenin'?

Yellow-bearded Man No; what terrible thing?

1st Workman The lassie o' th' house's gone careerin' all
over th' counthry on horseback with only her skin as a
coverin'!

Yellow-bearded Man (*horrified*) G'way!

3rd Workman (*up to him*) An' th' poor men workin' in th'
fields had to flee to th' ditches to save th' sight of their eyes
from th' shock o' seein' her!

Yellow-bearded Man (*with aggravated anguish in his
voice*) Oh, isn't it like me to be up here outa sight o' th'
world, an' great things happenin'!

Curtain.

Act Two

The same as in the preceding Act.

The two portraits, one of Stoke, the other of Poges, are now hanging on the wall at back, between the windows. Bright green curtains, broadly striped with red, are on the windows. A Jacobean armchair has been added to the two stiff pew-like seats beside the fireplace. The table is to the left, so that two mattresses, one beside the other, can be seen, with their heads against the wall and their feet towards the front. On these, wrapped round with rugs and blankets, are Poges and Stoke. Some thick rolled-up floor rugs are lying against the wall. A bunch of pampas grass is in the earthenware jug standing on the table. The rejected crimson curtain stuff is lying over one of the pew-like seats. A walking-stick – Basil's – is leaning against the wall, near to where he is lying.

It is about half-past seven on a cold and misty morning. A few misty beams of sunlight are coming in through the windows, paling the light of a lighted lantern standing between the two beds.

The two men are twisting about uneasily on the mattresses; when Poges twists to the right, Basil twists to the left, and vice versa. Then Poges, wearing a blue beret with a black bow at the side, lifts his head a little and glances over at Basil. He is in that drowsy state felt by a man who has spent long hours of the night trying to get to sleep and failing to do so.

Before the scene is disclosed, the hooting of owls is heard first; then the faint lowing of cattle, grunting of swine, crowing of cocks, bleating of sheep; then, vigorously from various directions the whistling of the *chorus of 'The Farmer's Boy'.*

Poges (*after he has twisted about several times – half to himself, half to Basil*) Good God, isn't it cold!

  Basil is silent.

Eh, Basil, are you awake? How d'ye feel now?

Basil (*with a faint groan*) Stiff as hell still! It's a mercy I'm alive. And, on the top of it, Avril to make a laughing-stock of me by enjoying herself with O'Killigain.

Poges (*sympathetically*) It was damned mean of her, Basil. She's inclined that way, I'm afraid. You'll have to keep a strong hand over her, my boy.

Basil (*with a deep groan*) I can't – now.

Poges Why can't you, man?

Basil A month before we came here I did a very foolish thing.

Poges Oh?

Basil (*mournfully*) Settled five hundred a year on her for life.

Poges Oh! (*a fairly long pause*) Basil, Basil, I did the same to Souhaun!

Basil We're done for, Cyril.

Poges (*in a sprightly way*) No, no; a month in the country'll make us young again. We'll be as lively as goats in no time. Besides, we can always cautiously hint at an increase in the settlement.

Basil (*gloomily*) With the workers always striking for higher wages, it'll have to remain a hint.

Poges (*as gloomily*) It's damnable, Basil. If much more is given to them, how's a poor man to live?

> *He sinks back on the mattress and pulls the clothes over*
> *his head. Outside a cock crows loudly, followed by the*
> *call of a cuckoo.*

(*Clicking his tongue exasperatedly – from under the*
clothes) Dtch, dtch, dtch! Isn't it a good thing those birds
aren't in the house!

> *The cock crows again, much louder this time, and the*
> *cuckoo calls again.*

(*Popping his head from under the clothes*) Damn that cock
and cuckoo! Did you hear that cock crowing, Basil, and
the cuckoo calling?

Basil Deafening, aren't they! And the owls, too, all the
night. Jungle noises!

Poges The country's not going to be so quiet as I thought.
Still, I'm glad we came.

Basil So am I, really. These sounds are just part of the
country's attractions – pleasant and homely.

Poges And stimulating, Basil, stimulating. Look at the
sunlight coming in through the windows – another dawn,
Basil; another life. Every day in the country brings another
chance of living a new life.

Basil (*enthusiastically*) And we're going to live it, eh,
what, Cyril?

Poges (*enthusiastically*) Oh, boy, ay!

> *Souhaun appears at the back entrance, left, and Avril at*
> *entrance to the right. Both are wearing fur coats over*
> *their nightdresses, and shiver a little.*

Souhaun (*plaintively*) For goodness' sake, will you two
men get up and do something. Cloyne's fallen down in a
dark passage and hurt her wrist, and she can't do much.

Poges Oh?

Avril And something will have to be done to heat the rooms – we were almost frozen last night.

Poges Ah! Well, we weren't scorched with the heat either.

Souhaun Well, stir yourselves, and you'll soon get warm. O'Killigain and his men are already at work, and will want to be coming in and out of here.

The cock crows louder than ever, and is joined by many more, a few of them at a great distance, so that the sounds are heard but faintly; these are mingled with the barking of dogs, the lowing of cattle, the bleating of sheep, the twittering of birds, the grunting of pigs, and the cackling of hens.

Avril There, you here; everything's alive but you two.

Poges Well, we'll be in the midst of them all in a second.

The two women withdraw. Basil and Poges, with the clothes wrapped round them, sit up, and dive down again. After a second or two they sit bolt-upright again, and again dive down.

(*Shivering*) Ooooh, Basil, cold!

Basil (*shivering*) Bitter, bitter! What would I not give now for a cosy flat; a cosier bed; and a blazing hot-water bottle!

They lay quiet for a short time.

Poges There's nothing for it but to plunge out of the summer into the black and bitter winter.

Basil You say the word.

Poges Ready! Steady! Go!

They climb laboriously out of the beds. When they get

*out, it can be seen that they have been fully dressed,
even to their heavy topcoats and scarves wound round
their necks.*

(*Blowing on to his hands and rubbing them*) Ooooh, crisp,
isn't it? Healthy, though. Ooooh! Where the hell's that
Barney, that he hasn't a fire lighted for us? Oooh! One
would want to be on his tail all day. (*Shouting*) Barney,
Barney!

*Barney comes in holding some logs in the crook of his
right arm, and a lantern in his left hand. Cloyne follows,
with some paper and a bellows. Her left wrist is
bandaged. Barney is wearing a topcoat, and has a
muffler round his neck. Cloyne, too, is wearing a heavy
coat. They both go over to the fireplace.*

(*As they come in*) Ah, here we are. Bit nippy, Barney;
sharp, but beneficial. (*To Cloyne*) You'll have to be more
careful with the steps and passages. Mind your feet
coming in, mind your head going out. Oooooh! (*To Basil*)
You better slip off, and give the others any help you can.
(*As Basil is going*) What about your walking-stick?

Basil (*moving stiffly*) I must try to do without it – about
the house, anyway. (*He takes the lantern that is beside his
bed, and goes out, limping a little.*)

Poges (*to the other two*) Well, what do the pair of you
think of the country, eh? And the house? Better than any
your old Kings of Tarara had, eh?

Cloyne (*effusively*) I'm sure it'll be lovely, sir, when we
settle down.

*Poges has been jerking his arms about in an effort to
drive the cold from his body. Cloyne begins to fold the
clothes on the beds, and tidy them up.*

Poges Of course it will. We'll enjoy it all; we'll feel

younger; we will *be* younger. The air, fresh air, pure air, exhilarating air, will be able to get at us. (*He sucks in his breath and blows it out again.*) Ooooh! Soon we won't know ourselves. We'll eat better, sleep better; flabby muscles will become firm, and we'll realize that we are alive, alive, alive-O. Think of the walks we'll have; so much to see, so much to hear, so much to smell; and then to come back, nicely tired, to such a lovely house. A life for the gods!

Cloyne Wondherful, wondherful, sir.

Poges Now I must be off to swallow down a cup of tea, for there's a lot to be done, a lot to be done yet. (*He hurries off out of the room.*)

Cloyne The poor oul' codger!

Barney Comin' down to this back o' God-speed place for rest an' quietness! Afther all that science has thried to do for us, goin' back to lantherns an' candles. Th' only electric light he'll allow in a Tudor house is one over his own desk! Runnin' in the face o' God Almighty's goodness – that's what it is.

Cloyne They'll get tired of it before us.

Barney I can tell you, I'm tired of it already. Looka the place we're livin' in: doors everywhere shaped like doors o' dungeons; passages dark as hell when it was first formed; crackin' your head when you're goin' in, and breakin' your toe when you're goin' out; an' I'm tellin' you, it's only beginnin'.

Cloyne It might be worse.

Barney (*striking a match to light the paper*) We're goin' to be worse, I'm tellin' you.

Cloyne We can't be worse than we are.

Barney (*as the flames of the paper die down*) There's no chance o' kindlin' here. Why did you say, then, that we might be worse?

Cloyne Well, so, indeed, an' we might.

Barney How can we be worse, woman, when we're as bad as we can be?

Cloyne Simply be bein' worse than we were.

Barney How can we be worse than we were, when we're as bad as we can be, now.

Cloyne You'll see we'll be worse before we're betther.

Barney Damn these logs! Isn't that what I'm sthrivin' to dhrive into your head?

Cloyne What are you sthrivin' to dhrive into me head?

Barney That we'll be worse than we were before we're as bad as we are now, an' in a week's time we'll be lookin' back with a sigh to a time, bad as it could be then, that was betther than the worst that was on top of us now.

Poges bustles in again. The heavy topcoat is gone and he is now dressed in bright blue shorts, emerald-green jersey, brown shoes, and the scarf is still round his neck. He has a cup of tea in his hand, and he is sipping it as he comes into the room. He is miserably cold, but he puts on a brisk air, sorting it out in his mind that to be cold in the country is natural, to be ignored as far as possible, and to be countered by a smiling face, a brisk manner, and the wearing of brilliant clothes denoting freedom of movement and utter disregard of the common rules of convention. He is feeling far from comfortable, but thinks this shouldn't be shown; for the colder you are, and the more uncomfortable you feel, the brisker you must be, and the hardier you'll get.

Poges Here we are again! Ready for anything now. (*losing his gay attitude when he sees that the fire isn't lighted*) Isn't the fire lighted yet? What are you doing, Barney? Being in the country's no reason why we should be frozen to death.

Barney I can't get a spark out of it, afther all me sthrivin'.

Poges (*testily*) You can't light logs with a bit of paper, man. Oh, use your brains, Barney, use your brains.

Barney An' what else have I got to light them with?

Poges Small sticks, man; put some small sticks under them.

Barney An' will you tell me where I'm goin' to get the small sticks? Isn't the nearest shop a dozen miles away?

Poges Well, if there's no sticks, sprinkle a little paraffin on them.

Barney (*sarcastically*) An' where am I goin' to get the paraffin? There's no oil wells knockin' about here.

Poges (*severely*) Don't be funny. You've got to remember you're in the country now.

Barney Isn't it meself that's gettin' to know it well!

Poges We've got to do things for ourselves: there's no chance of pushing a button to get things done here.

Barney Sure, I'm beginnin' to think you're right.

Poges Can't you see that those logs are too big?

Barney I think I do, unless me sight's goin' curious.

Poges (*hotly*) Well, then, why don't you do it!

Barney Arra, do what?

Poges (*loudly*) Make them smaller, man!

Barney (*calmly and sarcastically*) An' how?

Poges And how? Why, with an axe, of course.

Barney (*losing his temper – loudly*) An' where's the axe, an' where's the axe?

Poges There must be an axe knocking about somewhere.

Barney There's nothin' knockin' about here but a bitther breeze whirlin' through the passages that ud make the very legs of a nun numb!

Cloyne (*trying to mollify things*) Sure, the poor man's back-broken an' heart-broken thryin' to kindle it, sir.

Poges (*who has been waving his arms and stamping his feet while his teeth chatter – turning fiercely on Cloyne*) You mind your own business, girl! (*Seeing her putting the mattresses by the wall*) Have we got to sleep down here again tonight?

Cloyne Ay, an' yous have. Th' other rooms are too damp still. Sure, Mr O'Killigain says that it'll take a month of fierce fires to dhry them out.

Poges (*testily*) Mr O'Killigain says this, and Mr O'Killigain says that! I'm getting tired of what Mr O'Killigain says. If we have to sleep here, you or Barney'll have to stay up all night keeping the fire going, or we'll be frozen in our sleep. (*His eye catches sight of the telephone. He goes over to it and lifts the receiver.*) Not a sound! No, oh no; not a bit of a hurry. (*Angrily to Cloyne*) Go out, girl, and send in the boy who's working at this telephone. (*With a low moan*) Ireland!

> *Cloyne goes out by the doorway on the right leading to the entrance hall. After a few seconds the loud lowing of a cow is heard, followed by a scream from Cloyne, who rushes frantically back into the room, pale and trembling.*

Cloyne (*breathlessly rushing back into the room, falling on the floor, and catching Poges wildly by the legs*) Save me! Stuck his head into me face, th' minute I opened the door. Mother o' God, I'll never see th' light of another day with th' fright I got!

Poges (*alarmed*) What is it, what is it, woman?

Cloyne (*almost incoherent*) A bull, a wild bull, out in th' enthrance hall!

Barney (*frantically*) A wild bull! We're all desthroyed.

Poges (*trying to release himself from Cloyne's hold*) Let me go, girl! Let me go, or I can't defend myself. If he comes in here, the whole of us'll be horned!

Cloyne (*frantically*) My legs have given undher me. Let me hold on to you, sir – it's me only hope!

Poges (*to Barney*) Put the table to the doorway, man, and help to bar him out – quick, quick, man! And a mattress. (*To Cloyne while Barney is pushing the table and a mattress to the door*) Why didn't you clap the door in his face, you fool!

Cloyne Wasn't he half into the hall before I'd the door half open! Oh, sir, what are we goin' to do? Oh, please go, sir, an' thry an' shove him out!

The bellow of the animal is heard outside in the hall.

Poges (*half dead with panic*) My God, woman, you can't shove bullocks about! (*Shouting*) Souhaun, there's a wild bull in the house! Help, O'Killigain, help. (*To Barney*) Run, run, man, and get Mr Stoke to bring down the gun. Oh, go quick, man! An' keep well out of range.

Barney runs off.

(*Shouting*) O'Killigain, help! Can't you let me go, girl?

Cloyne (*still clinging to him*) Carry me off, sir, please. Don't leave me here to die alone! Maybe he won't be able to climb the stairs afther us. Oh, when I came to th' counthry, I never thought there'd be wild animals on th' door-step!

Basil appears at one of the entrances at the back; he moves forward stealthily and extends a gun to Poges.

Basil (*nervous*) What is it, what is it?

Poges A bull, out in the hall.

Basil Who let him in? Damn it, such carelessness! You must be on guard in the country, you know. Here, take the gun, man.

Poges (*angrily – to Basil*) Come out, come out in the open, man, and be ready to use the gun if he comes into the room! (*Shoving the gun from him*) You use it, man; weren't you an ARP man?

Basil (*indignantly*) I never did anything more than clay-pigeon shooting! Let whoever let the damned animal in, let the damned animal out! (*He pokes Poges with the gun.*) Here, take this, and down him – you're nearer the bull than I am.

Poges (*angrily*) I'm not a toreador, am I? And don't point, don't point the gun at me! Lower the barrel, man; oh, lower the barrel! D'ye want me to die two deaths at once? What's the advantage of your passing through Oxford if you can't face a bull with a gun in your hand? Be a man, man, and not a mouse.

Basil (*keeping well in the passage, and only showing his nose*) Telephone the police, the fire brigade, or something.

Poges (*violently*) Don't you know the kind of a country we're in! There's no police, no fire brigade, no telephone!

Come here, if you won't use the gun, and help me carry this girl away out of danger.

The cow puts a stylized head, with long curving horns, over the barricade and lets out a loud bellow. Cloyne spasmodically tugs the legs of Poges, making him lose his balance so that he topples to the floor, after a frantic effort to save himself.

Cloyne Oooh, sir, save me!

Poges (*with a wild shout as he is falling*) My God, he's on top of us! We're done for! Help!

Basil throws the gun into the room and runs for his life.

Barney (*in the far distance*) Sing out, sir, if you want any assistance.

Someone is heard stirring outside where the animal is; this stir is followed by the voice of the 1st Workman shooing the cow out of the hall. After a few moments, Poges slowly sits up and listens.

1st Workman (*shouting outside*) Eh, oick, oick, eh, yeh gett; ay, ay, oick, oick!

Poges gets up on to his feet, shaking a little, and going over, picks up the gun and, steadying himself on it, stands over the prostrate Cloyne, who is almost in a faint, bundled up on the floor, with her face hidden in her hands. Shortly after, the 1st Workman appears at the entrance with a bucket of coal and some sticks. He looks over the table, astonished to see the prostrate Cloyne, and Poges standing near with a gun in his hand.

Poges (*stormily*) Where the hell did that bull come from? Who owns her? Who let that bull come tearing into a private house?

1st Workman Bull, sir? Oh, that wasn't a bull, sir. (*He* *pushes the table back to its place.*) Jest a harmless innocent cow, sir. Frightened the poor girl, now, did it? (*Cunningly*) But I see it didn't frighten you, sir.

Poges (*flattered*) No, no, not me. (*To Cloyne*) Here, girl, get up on your feet. (*Loudly*) It wasn't a bull; I knew it couldn't be a bull! and it's gone, so get up. (*Putting down the gun*) Get up!

> With the help of the 1st Workman and Poges, Cloyne gets up on her feet.

There now, be off with you. Get Miss Avril to give you a stiff glass of whiskey, and you'll be all right. And take this gun back to Mr Basil. (*He picks up the gun and hands it to the shaking Cloyne.*)

Cloyne Oh, sir, this place is worse than a jungle in th' desert!

Poges Go on, go on! I thought you Irish were a brave people. (*He is shaky himself, but he stiffens himself to conceal the tremors.*)

Cloyne (*going out with the gun*) For ages now, it's bulls I'll be dhreamin' of, an' there's ne-er a lock on me door either!

Poges Fainting, shouting, screaming, and running about for nothing! No nerves, no nerves, no spirit; no coolness in a crisis.

1st Workman (*craftily*) An' did they all think it was a bull, sir? An' you stood your ground. Looka that now. Prepared for anything, sir.

Poges (*taking it all in*) The other fellow, Mr Basil, ran for his life; think of that – ran for his life!

1st Workman Did he, now?

Poges British, too, think of that; surprising and disappointing, very. (*Briskly and a little anxiously*) Still, I must acquaint the police. I can't have cows or bulls wandering about the rooms of Ormond Manor.

1st Workman (*who has started to light the fire*) One o' th' ladies sent me in to light a fire for you. (*Placatingly*) Sure, sir, she was only the cow me friend brought this mornin' so that, when you had a minute, you could run out an' look her over. A fine animal, sir. She got loose an' wandhered in when she found th' door open. She's betther than th' best that was in th' cattle raid o' Cooley.

Souhaun comes in by a back entrance followed by Avril. She is carrying a black vase, striped with blue, and has a jazzy overall on one of her arms. Avril carries a blue bowl, striped with black. They are carrying them very carefully, as if they were very precious indeed.

Souhaun What's all this commotion about a bull? We had to stop Basil from trying to throw himself out of a window!

Avril And Barney got out on top of the roof.

Poges Oh, nothing, nothing at all; a stray cow in the garden mooed, and Basil lost his head and Cloyne lost her feet.

Avril But Barney, when he was rushing past, said that you were out here roaring for help!

1st Workman Roarin' for help, is it? Indeed an' he wasn't, for I can testify to that, but standin' here, cool as you like, he was, waitin' for the worst.

Souhaun Well, if we're to stay in the country, we'll have to get used to all kinds of animals, big and small.

Poges (*shaking his head*) I'm convinced now that poor

Basil can't be wholly English. There's a weak joint somewhere.

Souhaun (*leaving the overall on a seat*) There's your overall, dear, to wear when you're working, and we're taking your precious Annamese vase and Cambodian bowl to our room for safety, till everything's straight.

Poges Oh, that's right, if anything happened to either of them, I'd pass out. Lift the vase up, dear, till I see it a second. (*She lifts it up.*) Oh, Lord, isn't it lovely? (*To Avril*) The Cambodian bowl too. (*She lifts it over her head.*) A little too high, dear; just go down on one knee. (*She does so.*) Aaah! Precious, precious! The chaste form, the tender planes, the refined colouring; the exquisite design, the *tout ensemble* – they go down into the undiscoverable deeps of the heart!

1st Workman Arra, be God, indeed an' they do, sir.

Avril (*languishingly*) A background of eau-de-nil would set them off to their full advantage.

Souhaun (*cocking her eye at them*) Oh no, Avril; Chinese white's the pure and proper background for them.

Avril Eau-de-nil.

Souhaun Chinese white, dear.

Poges Neither. Chrome yellow's the tone. A warm and pure cloak, as it were, for the chaste bodies of the vase and the bowl. (*He goes over and touches them tenderly.*) My darling treasures! Take them off, and lay them down with circumspection. Mind the step going out.

> *Souhaun and Avril go slowly and stately out, carrying the vase and the bowl as if they were precious relics.*

1st Workman (*to Poges who has come over to the*

fireplace where a fine fire is blazing now) There y'are, sir; a
fire that'll warm y' up an' make your mind easy.

Poges (*stretching out his hands to the fire*) Good, great,
grand! Are you the workman who knows all the stories
and legends of Ireland since the world began?

1st Workman No, no, not me, sir; it's Philib you mean –
th' powerful man with th' powerful beard. (*Touching his
forehead*) Some say he isn't all there, but a wondherful
man, ay, indeed, is Philib. Does a man good to talk to him.

Poges I'll have a chat with him, the first chance I get.

1st Workman (*looking round the room with a ravishing
air*) This is a wondherful house, so it is. It's an honour to
be workin' in it. Afther hundhreds o' years standin' in
frost, rain, an' snow, frontin' th' winds o' the world, it's a
marvel it isn't flat on its face, furnishin' only an odd
shelther for a sthray fox; but here it stands, an' we all
waitin' for a windy winther ud stagger it an' send it
tottherin' down.

Poges (*indignantly*) Tottherin' down! What d'ye mean,
tottherin' down? The place is as firm as a lighthouse.
Tottherin' down, indeed!

1st Workman (*repelling the idea that he thought of such a
thing*) Tottherin' down, is it? Now who, in th' name o'
God, save a sure an' safe fool ud think it was tottherin'
down? Not me, now; oh no, not me. Tottherin' down me
neck! Isn't the grand oul' house goin' to show, soon an'
sudden, a sign of what a fine residence it was when the
quality harnessed their horses for a hunt be the risin' rim
o' th' dawn, or sat down in their silks an' satins to their
evenin' meal in the shadowy shine o' th' golden candles!

Poges Purple nights and golden days, my friend. (*He
sighs.*) Aah!

1st Workman (*with a long, deep, imitative sigh*) Ah! We'll never set eyes on the like o' them again, sir; th' sparklin' carriages comin' an' goin', th' steeds throttin' nicely an' neatly, or movin' at a gallop, always elegant, on a visit to me lord here, or me lady there, with th' sky above in a fair swoon o' pride for th' fine things movin' about below; an' they full o' grace, an' decked out in the grandeur o' th' West Indies an' th' East Indies, sobered down a thrifle for use in a Christian counthry, the women's bosoms asway with jewels, like a tendher evenin' sky, alive with stars. An' th' gentlemen, just a dim step down, but elegant too, in finery fair, with ruffles an' lace, with cutaway coats an' vests embroidhered, each holdin' a cane to keep them steady, an' all halo'd with scents to ring them round from th' smell o' th' poor an' dingier world at work or play!

Poges (*enthusiastically*) Those were handsome days. (*He fixes a plume of pampas grass in his beret.*) When shall we look upon their like again? (*He folds the crimson curtain stuff round him as if it were a cavalier's cloak.*) The lawns and ramparts still are here, and we shall be the men! (*He snatches up Basil's walking-stick.*) The plume in the hat, the velvet cloak over the shoulder, the tapering rapier in the hand! (*He makes a vicious lunge at the 1st Workman, who narrowly dodges the pass.*) Die, varlet!

1st Workman (*remonstratively*) Eh, eh, there; careful, sir, be careful! Be careful how yeh prod!

Poges (*leaning on the stick as if it were a sword – sorrowfully*) Where are the kings and queens and warriors now? Gone with all their glory! The present day and present men? Paltry, mean, tight, and tedious. (*Disgustedly*) Bah!

1st Workman What are we now, what are we all, but a tired thribe thryin' to do nothin' in th' shortest possible time? Worn away we are, I'm sayin', to shreds and shaddas mouldin' machines to do everything for us. Tired, is it? Ay, tired an' thremblin' towards th' edge of th' end of a life hardly worth livin'!

Poges (*gloomily pacing up and down*) Not worth living, not worth living.

1st Workman (*with greater energy*) Time ago, an' we gave a ready ear to one speakin' his faith in God an' his neighbour; but now, there's so many gabbers goin' that there's hardly a listener left. Sure, that in itself is as sharp a punishment as a lease o' hell for a long vacation. It's meself is sayin' ourselves came late, but soon enough to see the finery fade to purple dust, an' the glow o' th' quality turn to murmurin' ashes.

Poges (*striking the attitude of a clumsy cavalier*) We won't let them perish completely! We'll keep the stern old walls standing. We'll walk where they walked, sit where they sat, and sleep where they slept!

1st Workman An' talk as they talked too.

Poges (*wildly*) Our pride shall be their pride, our elegance their elegance, and the banner of the Ormonds shall fly from the battlements again! The King, the King, God bless him!

1st Workman (*warningly*) I wouldn't say too much about the King, sir; we're a little touchy about kings down here in Clune na Geera.

> *From outside is heard a scream from Souhaun and a squeal from Avril; then the sound of running feet, and the crash of breaking chinaware. After a moment or so, Souhaun pitches into the room from the left entrance at back, and Avril from the right one. Souhaun is holding the top rim of the vase in her hand, and Avril the butt of the bowl. When he see the damage, the 1st Workman slinks off.*

Poges (*furiously*) What the hell's all this?

Avril (*breathlessly*) Rats!

Souhaun (*breathlessly*) Gigantic creatures!

Avril Here.

Souhaun There.

Both (*together*) Everywhere!

Poges (*in anguish*) Oh, look at what's left of my Annamese vase and Cambodian bowl! A hundred pounds of the best for each, and then only when I happened to catch the cunning Keeper drunk in the Bazaar of Singapore. What the hell were the pair of you thinking of?

Souhaun Rats

Avril Here, there, and everywhere.

Poges (*wildly*) You evil-handed dolts to destroy my two best treasures! You'll pay for them, you'll pay for them!

Avril (*scornfully*) We'd look well thinking of them, and we running for our lives.

Souhaun You can imagine what it was when Basil is up there now on guard with the gun.

Poges (*mockingly*) Oh, he's the boy to shoot down wild animals. (*Imploringly*) For God's sake go up and take the gun off him or he'll send a bullet through the body of some human being! And for the future, you and your friend keep your awkward hands off any treasures I may have left.

Souhaun (*scornfully*) Treasures! Who told you that the Annamese vase and your old Cambodian bowl were treasures?

Poges Everyone who saw them, woman!

Souhaun Ay, to humour you. Well, let me tell you they weren't more valuable than a second-hand vase or bowl bought at a Woolworth sale. That's the fact, and it's best to know it.

Poges (*with quiet emphasis*) And who gave you that information?

Avril Couldn't anyone, not a fool, see what they were the minute they saw them?

Souhaun The minute Mr O'Killigain set eyes on them, he said that they went from Derby in thousands to Singapore and Saigon for suckers to buy them!

Poges (*with furious scorn*) Oh, indeed, did he? Oh, an authority on what kind of art d'ye call it in Clune na Geera? I'll test them. I'll send them to the Curator of the Wallace Collection. We'll see. Mr O'Killigain – good God!

He takes the pieces from Avril and Souhaun and puts them on the table. Cloyne appears at an entrance at back with a troubled look on her face.

Cloyne Here, they've gone and dumped the garden tools an' the roller right in front of the hall door! And the roller's so close that when you want to go out or come in you have to climb over it.

Poges Tell whoever brought them to bring them to the back and put them in the shed, fool!

Cloyne How can I tell him when him an' the lorry's gone?

Poges (*furiously*) And why didn't you tell him before he went?

Cloyne An' didn't I now? He just said that the back was threnched be the workmen an' he hadn't time to build pontoon bridges.

Poges What a country! What a people! (*Viciously – to Souhaun*) And you encourage them, because you and your friend Avril are Irish too!

Souhaun If you ask me, you're not such a shining paragon of goodness yourself.

Poges (*explosively*) I believe in efficiency! I demand efficiency from myself, from everyone. Do the thing thoroughly and do it well: that's English. The word given, and the word kept: that's English. (*Roaring*) And I'm an Englishman!

Souhaun You are indeed, God help you!

Cloyne An' what are we goin' to do about the garden tools an' th' roller?

Souhaun (*in a bustling and dominant way, catching up the jazz-patterned overall and putting it on Poges*) Here, if we waste any more time talking, the house will never be ready to live in. Put this on, and go and bring the roller from the front door through here, out of the way, to the back. When you've done that, bring the garden tools to the back too, and let us see your grand English efficiency at work while I and Avril do some of the hundred things remaining to be done.

She gives him a push from her, and she and Avril hurry away out by one of the back entrances.

Cloyne (*warningly*) It seems a heavy roller, sir, so mind you don't sthrain yourself when you're pullin' it.

Poges (*testily*) Go away, go away, girl; I'm not an invalid.

Cloyne goes. Poges moves over to the blazing fire and stretches out his hands to the flame. The 2nd Workman comes in by left entrance at back wheeling a barrow filled with bricks. He is a powerful man of fifty, with

336

*gleaming eyes and wide and strong beard. As he comes
nearer, Poges turns to give him greeting.*

(*Warmly*) Good day, good sir; it's a cold day that's in it,
surely.

2nd Workman (*eyeing Poges curiously*) Ay is it, for them
who has to brave it, an' can't stand all day in front of a
sturdy fire like a kingly Pharaoh.

Poges (*a little nonplussed*) Quite, yes, yes, quite. Everyone
tells me the place round here is a rich storehouse of
history, legend, and myth?

2nd Workman (*with a little scorn in his voice*) It's a little
they know an' little they care about those things. But the
place has her share o' histhory an' her share o' wondhers.

Poges (*flatteringly*) And I'm told you have a rare stock of
them yourself.

2nd Workman Ay, indeed, I have me share o' wondhers,
new an' old.

Poges (*trying to be Irish*) Looka that, now. Arra, whisht,
an' amn't I told it's strange stories you do be tellin' of the
noble things done by your fathers in their days, and in the
old time before them.

2nd Workman (*sinking into a meditative mood*) When
less than a score of the Fianna brought back the King of
England prisoner, invaded Hindostan, an' fixed as subjects
the men of all counthries between our Bay o' Dublin and
the holy river that gave to holy John the holy wather to
baptize our Lord.

Poges (*astonished*) I never heard that one before.

2nd Workman (*with murmuring scorn*) An' where would
th' like o' you hear it, man? That was in the days o' Finn
Mac Coole, before his hair was scarred with a hint o' grey;

337

the mighty Finn, I'm sayin' who stood as still as a stone in
th' heart of a hill to hear the cry of a curlew over th' cliffs
o' Erris, the song of the blackbird, the cry o' the hounds
hotfoot afther a boundin' deer, the steady wail o' the
waves tumblin' in on a lonely shore; the mighty Finn
who'd surrendher an emperor's pomp for a place with the
bards, and the gold o' the King o' Greece for a night asleep
be the sthream of Assaroe!

Poges (*solemnly*) A great man, a great man, surely; a great
man gone for ever.

2nd Workman (*sharply*) He's here for ever! His halloo can
be heard on the hills outside; his spear can be seen with its
point in the stars; but not with an eye that can see no
further than the well-fashioned edge of a golden coin.

Poges (*moving back a step – a little awed*) You see these
things, do you?

2nd Workman I hear sthrange things be day, an' see
sthrange things be night when I'm touched be the feel of
the touch of the long-handed Lugh. When the Dagda
makes a gong o' the moon, an' th' Sword o' Light shows
the way to all who see it.

Poges Aah!

2nd Workman Then every rib o' grass grows into a
burnished fighter that throws a spear, or waves a sword,
an' flings a shield before him. Then Ireland crinkles into a
camp, an' kings an' sages, queens an' heroes, saints an'
harpers stare me in the face, an' bow, an' pass, an' cry out
blessing an' vict'ry too, for Heber's children, with the
branch of greatness waving in their hands!

Poges (*sadly*) And there it ends!

2nd Workman (*giving Poges a drowsy glance*) I'm thinkin'
it might have been well for some if the end an' all was

there; but it sthretches out to the sight of a big dim ship
with a followin' fleet in the great dim distance, with a
stern-fac'd man in the blue-gold coat of the French Armee,
standin' alone on th' bridge of the big dim ship, his eyes
fixed fast on the shore that was fallin' undher the high-
headed, rough-tumblin' waves o' the sea!

Poges (*awed into interest – murmuringly*) A big dim ship
and a following fleet, carrying a man in the blue-gold coat
of the French Armee – who was he, and when was that,
now?

2nd Workman Th' man was Wolfe Tone, and the time
was yestherday.

Poges Yesterday!

2nd Workman The man was there, but the fleet was a
golden dhream, always comin' in an' ever goin' out o' th'
Bay o' Banthry!

> O'Killigain has come in at the commencement of the
> 2nd Workman's musing, unnoticed by the dreaming
> worker, and barely noticed by the interested Poges,
> listening intently to what is being said, and a little awed
> by the influence of the 2nd Workman. O'Killigain
> comes softly over, and stands a little behind but close to
> the dreaming workman.

Poges (*bending towards the 2nd Workman*) And who was
the man in the blue–gold coat of the French Armee?

2nd Workman He was a great Irish soldier and a great
Irish friend to the people of no property in Ireland.

O'Killigain (*very softly*) And there are others.

2nd Workman (*softly too, but not so softly*) And there are
others; for through the roads of the four green fields goes
Shane the Proud, with his fine head hidden, waving away

339

his more venturesome friends from the horns of a bull, the hoofs of a horse, the snarl of a dog, an' th' smile of an Englishman.

Poges (*going back a step*) The smile of an Englishman!

2nd Workman (*unheeding the interruption*) An' in the midst of them all is Parnell standing still; unheeding he stands with a hand on his breast, his white face fixed on the East, with his wine-coloured eyes flashin' hathred to England.

O'Killigain (*very softly*) And there are others.

2nd Workman (*with a glance at O'Killigain*) They came later, an' haven't wandhered fully back to where they cleared a way for a gropin' people, but they will come, an' stare us into the will to take our own again.

Poges (*detaching himself from the spell*) And do none other of those you know, good man, see the things that you see?

2nd Workman Barrin' a few an' O'Killigain there, they see these things only as a little cloud o' purple dust blown before the wind.

Poges That's very sad.

2nd Workman Barrin' O'Killigain there an' a few, what is it all now but a bitther noise of cadgin' mercy from heaven, an' a sour handlin' o' life for a cushion'd seat in a corner? There is no shout in it; no sound of a slap of a spear in a body; no song; no sturdy winecup in a sturdy hand; no liftin' of a mighty arm to push back the tumblin' waters from a ship just sthrikin' a storm. Them that fight now fight in a daze o' thradin'; for buyin' an' sellin', for whores an' holiness, for th' image o' God on a golden coin; while th' men o' peace are little men now, writin' dead words with their tiny pens, seekin' a tidy an' tendher way to the end. Respectable lodgers with life they are, behind solid doors with knockers on them, an' curtained glass to keep the stars from starin'! (*The 2nd Workman stoops, lifts the shafts of the barrow, and is about to go out.*)

Poges (*to 2nd Workman – placatingly*) My own great-grandfather was Irish, I'm told, and my grandmother was a kind of a Scotswoman.

2nd Workman (*going out with the barrow slowly*) That's not such a lot, an' you're not sure of any of it either.

Poges What a strange, odd man! I couldn't get half of what he was trying to say. Are there many like him?

O'Killigain Millions of them, though few of them have tongues so musical.

Poges He rather took to me, I think, and looks upon me as a friend.

O'Killigain (*ironically*) He looks upon you, and all Englishmen, as a rascal, a thief, and a big-pulsed hypocrite.

Poges (*indignantly*) Good God, but that's pure ignorance. Where would the world be without us?

O'Killigain The giddy globe would wobble, slow down, stand still, and death would come quick to us all.

Poges (*a little puzzled by this remark*) Eh? Quite. Well, no, not so bad as that, you know, but near it, damned near it.

Souhaun runs in with a look of dark annoyance on her face.

Souhaun Oh, look at you standing here still, and so much to be done – (*her voice rises*) – so much to be done, so much to be done! I asked you to get the roller away from

the door an hour ago, and here's Barney after twisting his
wrist trying to climb over it standing in the same old place!
(*She catches him by the overall.*) Come, for God's sake,
and take the damn thing out of the way!

Poges (*pulling her hand away from the overall –
angrily*) Oh, have some decency, order, and dignity,
woman! Can't you see I'm having a serious discussion
with O'Killigain? (*He turns swiftly on O'Killigain*) We,
sir, are a liberty-loving people, and have always striven
to preserve perfect – perfect, mind you – freedom of
thought, not only in our own land, but throughout the
whole world; but that anyone should be permitted to
hold opinions such as are held by that lunatic just gone
out, and are apparently held by you, sir, too, is a perfect
scandal and disgrace!

Souhaun Oh, there's no use of you trying to ride your
high horse here in Clune na Geera!

Poges (*stormily*) I'm not trying to ride my high horse
here in Clune na Geera! What is said in Clune na Geera
is a matter of very little importance indeed. But every
right-minded man the world over knows, or ought to
know, that wherever we have gone, progress, civilization,
truth, justice, honour, humanity, righteousness, and peace
have followed at our heels. In the Press, in the
Parliament, in the pulpit, or on the battlefield, no lie has
ever been uttered by us, no false claim made, no right of
man infringed, no law of God ignored, no human law,
national or international, broken.

O'Killigain (*very quietly*) Oh, for God's sake, man, don't
be pratin' like a pantaloon priest!

Souhaun (*trying to push Poges from the room –
impatiently*) Go out and get the garden roller!

Poges (*loudly*) I say, sir, that Justice is England's old nurse;

Righteousness and Peace sit together in her common-
room, and the porter at her gate is Truth!

O'Killigain (*quietly, but sarcastically*) An' God Himself is
England's butler!

Poges (*roaring with rage*) That's a vile slander, sir!

O'Killigain Whether it is or no doesn't matter much, for
in a generation or so the English Empire will be
remembered only as a half-forgotten nursery rhyme!

Poges (*fiercely as Souhaun is pushing him out*) An opinion
like that deserves the jail!

Souhaun (*giving him a last strong push out into one of the
back entrances*) Oh, go on! (*She goes over towards
O'Killigain and stands looking shyly and a little archly at
him.*) What a naughty man you are to provoke him into
such a tantrum! (*After a slight pause.*) I hear terrible things
about you, Mr O'Killigain.

O'Killigain Oh!

Souhaun That you are a great man for the girls!

O'Killigain A pretty girl shows me a sign that God is
smilin'.

Souhaun (*archly*) It's well I need the gay an' youthful gloss
of pretty Avril, or its shelterless I'd be from all your stormy
moods!

O'Killigain (*gallantly*) When I look at you close I see you
a week or two oldher than your younger friend, an' when
you go as bright about the house, an' dhress as gay as she
does, you look like an earlier summer kissin' a tardy
spring goodbye.

Souhaun More than twenty years younger than the old
fool Poges I am of course. It's ridiculous for me to be with

him. I have a nice little income of my own now, and it's like a young bird I feel that has just got command of its restless wings. (*She pauses for a moment.*) You really do believe that I am as pretty as Avril? You're not just teasing me, are you?

O'Killigain Not I. You are one o' th' fine sights of this world. (*He lilts.*)

> There are many fair things in this world as it goes,
> The blue skies of summer, th' flushing red rose,
> But of all th' fair, blossoming things that men see,
> A comely-built lass is th' nearest to me,
> A comely-built lass is th' dearest to me!

And you are a comely-built lass.

Souhaun (*coming near to him and stroking his arm*) Your poor arm, wounded for the sake of others. What's your name?

O'Killigain My name? O'Killigain, of course.

Souhaun No, no, your more familiar name; the name your girl would call you by?

O'Killigain Jack.

Souhaun (*lingering over it*) Jack. What a dear name, Jack! What a dear name – (*She suddenly stands on tiptoe and kisses him.*) – Jack!

She is running out by the entrance on the right when she bumps into Poges laboriously pulling in a gigantic roller as high in diameter as he is tall. The heavy iron side-discs are vividly painted in panels of red, white, blue, green, and yellow. When the roller is pulled into the room, it can be seen that the 1st Workman is pushing it behind.

Poges (*angrily, as Souhaun bumps into him*) Eh, eh, there, look where you are going, can't you?

Souhaun (*amazed at the size of the roller*) God bless us, Cyril, what on earth's that you're carting into the house?

Poges (*petulantly*) Can't you see what it is? The roller you told me to bring through here to the back. The roller, the roller I bought to roll the lawn.

Souhaun But it's too big, man.

Poges No, it isn't too big. The man who sold it to me said that the bigger it was, the more effective it would be.

Souhaun But you'll never be able to pull a mighty thing like that.

Poges And what's to prevent me from pulling it? Amn't I pulling it now? A child of ten could pull it, the man said; well balanced, you know, the man said. Easy to pull, and easier to propel, the man said.

Souhaun You've just been taken in, Cyril. The thing's altogether too big. (*To the 1st Workman*) Isn't it?

1st Workman It looks a size too large to me, ma'am.

Poges The grass in this district needed a special big roller to level it, the man said, and this was the roller to level it.

1st Workman Sure, that roller ud level a hill.

O'Killigain The grass'll give way undher that, right enough.

Souhaun The cheek of declaring that a child of ten could pull it like a toy.

1st Workman G'way, ma'am, an' did he really say that now?

Poges One pull over the lawn with that roller would be enough for the season, the man said.

O'Killigain An', faith, so it would, an' for every season afther too.

345

1st Workman Sure, an' wouldn't a specially powerful horse himself wilt undher a thing like that! Whoever gave you that, man, musta taken it off an oul' steam-roller.

The 3rd Workman appears at entrance to right and proceeds to take an enjoyable interest in what is happening.

3rd Workman Mother o' God, looka what he's after buyin' be th' name of a roller! Isn't it a shame, now, to have imposed on a poor, simple, inoffensive man with a vehicle like that!

Poges (*defiantly*) It's a bargain, I know it's a bargain; the man said it's a bargain.

Souhaun (*mockingly*) The man said, the man said – ay, and you swallowed everything the man said.

O'Killigain (*to 1st Workman*) Give Mr Poges a hand to take this machine out of the sight of mortal man.

Poges (*obstinately*) I'll take it myself, thank you all. Once you got the knack of balancing it, the man said, you could turn it with your little finger, and I believe what the man said.

O'Killigain (*to 3rd Workman*) Here, you go on back to your work; go on, off you go!

He follows the 3rd Workman out of the room. Poges gives a mighty push to the roller, propelling it slowly to one of the entrances at the back. The 1st Workman goes over and helps him to push it.

Poges (*fiercely – to 1st Workman*) Let go, you! I'll manoeuvre it myself. Let go, I tell you!

1st Workman (*as fiercely – to Poges*) Can't you see, man, the declivity runnin' down the passage that'll lead you, if the roller once gets outa hand, into God knows where?

Poges (*with a roar into the face of the 1st Workman*) Let go!

The 1st Workman, startled, suddenly lets go his hold on the roller and the roller shoots forward down the declivity, Poges going with it, like a flash of lightning.

(*Heard as he is careering down the passage – with anguish in his voice*) Help!

There is a pause of a few moments, then a thud is heard, followed by a rumbling crash of falling bricks and mortar; then silence again.

Souhaun (*with vehement rage – running out*) The blasted fool! He has rocked the house and killed himself and hasn't made his will!

1st Workman (*staring down the passage*) Right through the wall he's gone! (*He runs to where the hole is in the ceiling, gets a seat and stands on it. Calling up to the hole*) Eh, Cornelius, eh, quick!

The face of the Yellow-bearded Man appears at the hole, and he thrusts down his head as far as it will go.

Yellow-bearded Man Well, what's up now?

1st Workman (*excitedly*) The oul' man, the oul' fool, has gone right through the wall with the roller, an' shook the house – bang!

Yellow-bearded Man Didn't I think it was an earthquake! (*Testily*) An' don't be tellin' me these things while I'm up here. Can't you wait till I'm down in th' world o' men, and can enjoy these things happenin'!

He angrily takes his head out of the hole. The 1st Workman gets down from the seat and runs out by entrance on right.

1st Workman (*running out*) Mr O'Killigain, Jack, eh, Jack!

Souhaun returns, followed by Cloyne and Barney leading in the frightened Poges, powdered with the dust of the falling mortar. Souhaun arranges a mattress for him on which he squats, supported by pillows.

Souhaun You were warned, you were warned, and you would have your own way. It's fortunate you are, indeed, that none of your bones is broken.

Poges (*moaningly*) Brandy, get me some brandy.

Barney goes out and comes back with a glass, brandy, and soda-water. He fills out a glassful and gives it to Poges.

(*After he has drunk the brandy – to Cloyne and Barney*) Go way, you two, and don't stand there gaping at me!

They go.

(*Musingly*) What a rascal that man must be who sold me the roller! In this simple country, among a simple people, where the very air is redolent with fairy lore, that such a dangerous and materialistic mind should be lurking!

Souhaun For God's sake, man, talk sense.

Poges (*shaking his head sorrowfully*) A gay and charming people, but irresponsible, utterly irresponsible.

O'Killigain appears at the right entrance with a cloudy look on his face.

O'Killigain Look here, that Basil of yours is goin' about the grounds carrying a fully-cocked gun at a dangerous angle. He'll do harm. Send someone to take it off him, or I'll twist it out of his hands myself! And you'll want to be more careful yourself, or you'll have th' oul' house down!

Poges (*indignantly*) Oh, what a conceited fool that fellow is – going about to do dangerous damage for want of a little common sense and caution. I don't believe he ever fired a gun in his life. (*To Souhaun*) Go out, dear, and take it off him, before he shoots somebody – and go quick!

Souhaun runs out by the entrance on the right, and O'Killigain is following her when Poges speaks to him, and halts him at the entrance.

Oh yes, Mr O'Killigain, a word please. (*He drinks some more brandy.*) Er, just a word. People are saying – there's a rumour going about that you and – and Miss Avril are – are, well, seen together at times.

O'Killigain Well?

Poges Well? Damn it, man, she's a lady. Mr Stoke's a gentleman, and you're only a – a tradesman!

O'Killigain Well?

Poges Well? Oh, don't be welling me! The week she was away from here was bad enough and very suspicious. She had the damned cheek to say she was with you.

O'Killigain So she was.

Poges So she was, was she? Well, it's dishonourable, and it will have to stop.

O'Killigain And who'll stop it?

Poges (*firmly*) I and Mr Stoke will stop it.

O'Killigain (*quietly*) You pair of miserable, old, hypocritical, wizened old getts, I'd like to see you trying!

Poges (*choking with rage*) Get out of the house, and come here no more! I'll write to your parish priest! I'll –

A shot rings out in the grounds outside.

Good God, the fool has shot somebody!

> *O'Killigain goes off in a hurry. There is a pause. Then the yellow-bearded face is thrust through the hole in the ceiling as far as it can go, and shouts down at Poges sitting like Buddha on the mattress.*

Yellow-bearded Man (*down to Poges*) He's shot her, shot her dead, the poor little innocent creature! Th' charmin' little thing full o' gaiety an' go!

Poges (*very frightened, up to the Yellow-bearded Man*) Shot who, shot who, man? Is it the young lass?

Yellow-bearded Man Without warnin' he done it, without a flicker of an eyelid he sent her into the unknown!

Poges (*murmuring in agony*) Avril! Oh, my God, little Avril. The curse of the Irish thorn-tree is on us! The little lass gone. (*Near swooning*) Cut down like a coloured bubble! The fairies must be manoeuvring, and they'll get me next, maybe. Sweet little Avril the first to go!

Yellow-bearded Man (*savagely*) Twenty-five pounds, an' not a penny less, he'll pay for it, or I'll have the heavy law on him. I'd ha' let you have her at first for the twenty, but in some compensation for th' agony of seein' the poor thing sink down into death, I'll have to get the other five, or I'll have the heavy law on him!

Poges (*sitting up suddenly*) What are you talking about, man? What's shot, who's killed?

Yellow-bearded Man Be th' way, you don't know that that lean, skulkin' friend o' yours has shot dead me poor little innocent, poor little cow! (*Sarcastically*) He thought it was a bull!

Poges (*bewildered*) Oh, what a terrible country to have anything to do with! My precious vase is gone, my beautiful bowl is broken; a wall's demolished, and an innocent animal's shot dead; what an awful country to be living in! A no-man's land; a waste land; a wilderness!

Curtain.

Act Three

Before the room appears, the sounds of falling rain and swishing winds are heard; and these go on, at intervals, throughout the scene.

The same as in the preceding Act; but some more articles of furniture have been added to the room. Between the entrance to the right at the back, and the right wall, stands what is said to be a Jacobean china-cabinet, filled with old pieces of china. At each side of the larger entrance on the right stands an armoured figure, comical-looking things, with long sharp points protruding where the man's nose (if a man were inside the suit) would certainly be; each figure, standing stiff, holds a long halberd well out from his body. Over these are, crossed, pennons, green and blue, fixed on the wall.

A blazing fire is in the fireplace. No one is in the room. After a moment Poges, dressed in his jazz-patterned overall, with a paper in his hand, runs in and rushes over to the telephone.

Poges (*into the mouthpiece – hurriedly*) Get me – Oh, good evening, good evening. This is Mr Poges, Ormond Manor. Get me St Paul, London: 123. The house is getting on all right, thank you. Be quick, please. (*Warmly*) There's no – seems – in it; I am in a hurry. Oh, the ladies are quite well, sir. No, no, no; I don't want to go to an all-night dance to hear Irish songs sung! I want St Paul! Eh? No, St Peter won't do; please don't try to be funny; I am on very serious business. Get me the number I want at once! (*He takes the mouthpiece from his mouth and gives vent to a roaring growl of anger.*) Whether it won't matter a

hundred years from now isn't the point, sir. (*Shouting*)
Damn it, get me St Paul! (*Bursting with rage*) No wonder I
use bad language. Is this the way business is done here?
No wonder this country's as it is. What's wrong with it?
(*roaring*) Everything's wrong with it! You what? You hope
my stay here will help to civilize me a little!

> *He looks stupefied; then he slams the receiver on the
> hook. Almost instantly the 'phone rings. He whips off
> the receiver again and puts it to his ear.*

What the hell does this – Eh? Who are you? St Paul? Good
God! This is Poges, Bradford. Oh, it's an awful place.
People helpless, superstitious, and ignorant. I want you to
get me five hundred shares in the Welldonian Cement Co.;
shares are bound to jump, the minute the bombing starts
seriously. They have jumped? Ah. What, a fiver a share,
now? Well, get me two fifty. What? Not one to be had?
(*Clicking his tongue*) Dtch, dtch. Run on them, eh? One
wouldn't imagine there'd be so many trying to cash in on
splintered bodies. The world, the world, Bradford! Yes,
yes, of course; if there's any going, snap them up. Righto.
Goodbye.

> *He hangs up the receiver. Barney appears at the
> entrance on the right.*

Barney Canon Chreehewel would like to speak to you, sir.

Poges Right; send the Canon in to me.

> *Barney goes; and, in a second or so, the Canon comes
> in. He is inclined to be portly, has rather a hard face,
> head bald at the front, with bushy greying hair at the
> back of his head and over his ears. He is wearing a soft
> hat, sodden with rain, which he puts on the end of the
> table when he comes in; and a long dark cloak,
> glistening with rain too. He comes over eager – to
> Poges, with a smile on his face, and outstretched hand.*

Canon Ah, my dear friend, I'm so glad to have a chance of a word with you. How are you liking Clune na Geera?

Poges Splendid, though the weather has been cold and very wet. Take your cloak off.

Canon (*taking off his cloak. When his cloak is off, it can be seen that his clothes fit nicely*) Isn't it a nuisance; and we're in for more of it, by all accounts. If it goes on much more, the district will be a dismal swamp.

Poges (*indicating a seat*) Sit down, Canon, sit down. Glass of sherry?

The Canon sits, and Poges sits too, opposite the Canon.

Canon No, thanks. I drink rarely. (*Apologetically*) Good example, you know. Well, welcome, my dear sir, to our district. You have a very beautiful house here. An old house, but a fine one. It is almost a sacred thing to keep an old thing from dying, sir; for whatsoever things are just, whatsoever things are honest, whatsoever things are pure, whatsoever things are lovely and of good report, are invariably found close to, and, sometimes, intimately enclosed in the life and being of ages that have passed, and in the life of men and women who have gone away before us.

Poges (*gratified*) I wholeheartedly agree with you, reverend sir. I feel it, I know it.

Canon With all its frills, its frivolities, its studied ceremonial, however gaily coloured its leisure may have been, the past had in it the core of virtue; while the present swirl of young life, I'm saying, with its feverish sthrut of pretended bravery, its tawdry carelessness about the relation and rule of religion to man, with all its frantic sthretching of pleasure into every second of life, contains within it a tawny core of fear that is turning darker with every chime of the passing hours!

The rain and wind are plainly heard.

Poges (*leaning towards the Canon – eagerly*) We must lengthen our arm back to the past and pluck back some of the good things that haven't gone away as far from us as the dead who knew them.

Canon A worthy enterprise, dear sir, and I hope you and your good people will be a help to us here to bring some of the slow movement of the past into the reckless and Godless speed of the present. (*He leans over towards Poges till their heads nearly touch.*) You and yours can do much to assist the clergy to keep a sensible check on the lower inclinations of the people, a work which should be near the heart of every sensible and responsible man with a stake in the country.

Poges I'll do all I can. (*Leans back with an air of business importance.*) From the practical point of view, how am I to help?

Canon (*dropping a little into the idiom of the district*) Help us to curtail th' damned activity of the devilish dance halls! Open a dance hall, and in a month or less the innocent disthrict becomes worse than your Leicester Square in London when the night has fallen. If the dance halls are allowed to go ahead without the conthrol of the clergy an' responsible people, God will go from Clune na Geera!

Poges (*shocked*) Good God! Such a condition of things among a simple, charming, and pastoral people amazes me.

Canon (*warming to it*) Arra, wouldn't it sicken you, when the hot days come, to see fools of oul' men an' fools of oul' women too, settin' a bad example, goin' about nearly naked, in their coloured shorts, an' brazen-fac'd lasses mixed among them in low-cut bodices, defiant short skirts,

or shorter trousers, murdherin' modesty with a restless an'
a reckless hand!

Poges A lamentable state of affairs entirely, sir.

Canon (*rising and going over close to Poges – intensely*)
An' like Eden, sir, we've a snake in our garden too!

Poges Oh!

Canon O'Killigain!

Poges Ah!

The wind and the rain are plainly heard.

Canon Guard your womenfolk from him, for no woman
is safe with that man. He publicly defends the wearing of
low-necked blouses by brazen hussies; he stands be the
practice of courting couples walking the highways and
byways be night. Why, one moonlight night, meetin' my
curate dhrivin' home a lasciviously minded girl, O'
Killigain tore the stick from the curate's hand an' smashed
it into pieces! A dangerous man, my dear sir, a most
dangerous man.

Poges (*a little nervously*) I'm what you'd call a foreigner
down here, and so couldn't interfere with O'Killigain
personally; but what I can do to help you, I certainly will,
in any other way.

Canon Thank you – I guessed you would. Your fifty
pounds have helped a lot already. And now I've taken up a
lot of your time and must go. (*He takes up his hat.*) By the
way, how's the workman I sent you getting along?

Poges Which one?

Canon The one doing your electric light – a yellow-
bearded fellow.

Poges (*emphatically*) Oh, he's getting along splendidly!

Canon I'm glad to hear it. A good fellow – a Knight of St Columbus.

Poges Well, now, I never knew Columbus was a saint.

Canon (*smiling indulgently*) Oh yes indeed; a great Irish saint.

Poges I always thought he was an American.

Canon An American; who?

Poges Christopher Columbus.

Canon (*smiling*) Oh, there were two Columbuses, one Irish and the other – er – American.

> *As the Canon is about to move away, Avril, followed by Souhaun, dances into the room from an entrance at the back. She is dressed in a low-cut blouse, short tailor-made skirt, and soft leather high boots moulded to her calves and reaching to just below her knees; and looks, indeed, a very tempting and desirable young hussy. She has a mackintosh over her arm. Souhaun, too, is dressed in very short shorts of a vivid crimson and a black V-necked jersey, looking as enticing, in a more mature way, as young Avril herself. Poges is a little embarrassed, but the good Canon does not flicker an eyelid. Souhaun whips off Poges' overall and shows him in a green jersey and brown shorts.*

Souhaun You mustn't receive the Canon, dear, in an overall!

Avril I say, Cyril, old boy, when are we going to get that damned bathroom? It's a bit thick trying to have a bath in a basin. (*She sees the Canon and stops to gaze at him.*)

Poges (*introducing her*) Mr Stoke's – er – wife – Miss Avril, Canon. (*Introducing Souhaun*) My – er – wife, Miss Souhaun.

357

Canon (*bowing graciously – to Avril*) My dear young lady.
(*To Souhaun*) Madam, I'm very pleased to know you.

Avril (*nodding to Canon – to Poges*) Well, when are we
going to have a decent bathroom, old cock o' th' walk?

Poges (*deprecatingly*) The Canon's here, Avril.

Canon (*jovially*) Youthful spirits, sir, youthful spirits.

Poges We'll have a bathroom if we can fit one in without
injuring the harmony of the old house. The Tudor period
never saw a bathroom. This generation's getting soft,
Canon; we want hardening.

Avril Bunkum!

Poges (*indignantly*) It's anything but bunkum!
Shakespeare had to do without one.

Souhaun But surely, dear, you must know that the Tudor
people knew nothing about the use of steam?

*Basil now appears at an entrance at the back, and when
he sees the company, he stays there and listens. He is
dressed in a yellow jersey and black shorts. No one
notices him.*

Poges (*petulantly*) Steam! We stand here, in the centre, not
of a house, but of a great civilization, and you mention
steam!

Souhaun In the centre of a hot bath, dear, I can remain in
the centre of your civilization.

Basil (*joining in – looking like a statue in the doorway*)
Not precisely, Souhaun, for it would require, or at least
postulate, a full and concentrated retirement through the
avenues of thought back to the time of which the visible
surroundings are vividly, but quiescently reminiscent. The
conception of the conscious thoughts, interrelating with

the – with the outward and inward action and reaction of all – or most of the bodily senses, incorporating the outward vision of sight with the inward vision of the inward conception of the – of the fragmentary stumuli – er – stimuli, into a perfect and harmonious whole; a thing, if I may be allowed to say so, if not impossible, is at least improbable, sitting down, or indeed even standing up, in the middle of a hot bath.

Avril (*with mock enthusiasm*) Hooray!

Poges (*to the Canon*) Mr Stoke, Canon; cousin to the uncle of a KG, and passed through Oxford.

Canon Really? Well, well, remarkable connections.

In the far distance a faint clap of thunder is heard; the Canon cocks his ear to listen.

I must be off. Bad sign. The soft rain that's falling may change to a downpour, and I've a long way to go.

The Canon puts on his cloak. Barney and Cloyne come in carrying a heavy Jacobean chair between them.

Souhaun Ah, the Jacobin chair. (*Indicating the way*) Out in the entrance hall, Barney.

Poges Let's look at it a second.

Barney and Cloyne pause.

Ah, Canon, old things take a lot of beating.

Canon They do, they do, sir. Well, I must go now.

Poges (*halting him*) One second, sir. (*He goes to the table, writes a cheque, and hands it to the Canon*) Another little trifle to keep things going, Canon.

Canon Twenty-five pounds! Oh, thank you, and God bless you, my very dear sir.

Souhaun You must come to dinner some night.

Canon I will, I will, with pleasure; goodbye all. (*Midst a murmur of goodbyes the Canon goes out.*)

Poges (*indignantly*) Never showed the slightest interest in the Jacobin chair. Ignorance; Irish ignorance! (*Angrily – to Cloyne and Barney, who are holding the chair like a salesman displaying a piece of silk*) Bring the damned thing into the entrance hall, will you, and don't stand there like fools!

> *Cloyne, in her hurry, jerks the chair from Barney's hold and it bumps to the floor.*

Poges Oh, butter-fingers, d'ye want to destroy it? That's a Jacobin chair, man, a Jacobin chair!

Barney (*with a yell as he carries out the chair with Cloyne*) Well, if I let a damned chair fall, I didn't knock a wall down!

Poges Impudent rascal. The more you do for them the less they think of you! (*He bustles into his overall again.*) Now to business. What'll we do first? The rugs?

Souhaun There's no use of trying the rugs till you get your quattrocento bureau in position. Then we'll be able to see if the colour of the rugs suits the bureau.

> *Avril has put on her mackintosh and sidled over to the entrance on right, leading to the hall, and is about to slip out when Basil darts to her side and catches her arm.*

Basil Where are you slipping off to?

Avril I'm going for a brisk walk along the bank of the brimming river. I'm fed up carrying things about to get this foolish old house in order.

Poges In this weather? Nonsense!

Basil A good idea; I'll go with you, darling.

Avril (*with a malevolent look at him*) Wouldn't you like to, eh? Take my advice and don't! (*To Poges*) Ay, in this weather. (*She goes quickly, leaving Basil, undecided, looking after her.*)

Basil (*bitterly*) She's going to go with O'Killigain!

Souhaun Nonsense. She can't be out of your sight for a minute but you imagine the girl's with O'Killigain. The rain'll soon send her back. (*To Poges*) You see about locking the bureau, while I get the men to carry it in for you.

Poges goes by one of the entrances at the back.

Basil (*going towards entrance at back*) I tell you the jade's gone after O'Killigain.

Souhaun (*warningly*) If I were you, Basil, I shouldn't press hard after little Avril; you are a little too consequential to please her always.

Basil (*maliciously – as he goes out*) And you, me lady, are a lot too old to please O'Killigain at any time!

Souhaun stands stiff for a few moments; then she goes quickly to the entrance to the hall and is seen beckoning for one of the workmen.

Souhaun (*calling*) One of you, come here, please.

The 2nd Workman comes into the room and stands near the entrance, looking quietly at Souhaun.

Send Mr O'Killigain in to me, please.

2nd Workman He's gone to the station to see afther a wagon-load o' bricks.

Souhaun (*slowly, after a pause*) By himself?

2nd Workman (*after a pause*) With th' handsome young woman. (*A pause.*) You're a handsome woman yourself; you're Irish too; an' y'ought to be sensible.

Souhaun (*slowly – a little surprised*) Am I not sensible, good man?

2nd Workman (*earnestly*) Your shinin' eyes can always say you are; an' soon you'll tire o' nestin' in a dusty nook with the hills outside an' th' roads for walkin'.

Souhaun I will, will I?

2nd Workman (*with his eyes looking steadily in hers*) Ay will you, an' dance away from a smoky bragger who thinks th' world spins round on th' rim of a coin; you'll hurry away from him, I'm sayin', an' it's a glad heart'll lighten th' journey to a one'll find a place for your little hand in th' white clouds, an' a place for your saucy head in th' blue o' th' sky.

Souhaun (*with a touch of mockery*) Yourself, for instance?

2nd Workman It's waitin' warm, he'll be, to please you, highly, an' show you wondhers of a manly manner.

Souhaun (*laughing, with a little catch in the laugh*) A daughter of the Ormond with a workman!

2nd Workman (*raising his head proudly and looking steadily at her*) An oldher name is an O'Dempsey, an' an oldher glory's in the name than the honour thrown to th' Earl o' Ormond when he crouched for favour at the English feet!

> *The 2nd Workman looks at Souhaun and Souhaun looks at the 2nd Workman for a moment, then she turns and goes slowly out by right entrance at back.*

3rd Workman (*appearing at the back left entrance*) Here, Philib, what'r you doin'? You're to give us a hand to get in the oul' codger's bureau.

> *The two of them go out by the entrance to the left at back. After a second or two, the sound of scuffling and of voices are heard just outside the narrow entrance through which the two men have gone out, then Poges comes in with an anxious look on his face, turns and concentrates his gaze on the entrance. Presently the end of a big gilded desk-bureau comes in sight round the corner, with the three workmen puffing, pulling, pushing, and scuffling it along, each giving orders to the other two, to the concern of poor old Poges. When the bureau comes to the entrance, it can be seen to be a very tight fit.*

1st Workman A little to the ayste, there, a little more to the ayste, can't yous!

2nd Workman No, west, west; can't yous see it'll jam if yous cant it to the ayste? To th' west, I'm tellin' yous!

Poges (*anxiously*) Easy, boys, easy, now; take care, take great care; that's a thing you won't meet every day, you know. I had an anxious time when it was coming over.

3rd Workman (*taking no notice of Poges*) Where th' hell are yous shovin'? Are yous blind, or wha'? No squirming'll get it in that way. (*Recklessly*) Here, throw th' thing up on its hind legs an' let her go!

Poges (*loudly and anxiously*) Eh, there, eh; steady, steady. Careful how you handle that. It's not a thing to throw up on its hind legs. I can't have a precious thing like that scratched and mangled. That's a quattrocento piece of furniture, and there isn't another piece like it in the world.

1st Workman (*to the others*) Hear what the gentleman's

sayin' to yous! Amn't I tired tellin' yous yous ud look long before yous ud find such a piece o' furniture in th' whole o' Clune na Geera? Yous can't fling a thing like this about the way you'd fling about an oul' kitchen chair. (*To Poges*) Amn't I right, sir?

Poges Yes, yes; quite right, my man. Thousands of people would give a fortune to possess a thing like that bureau. So gently, boys, gently. The slightest scratch will do irreparable damage.

1st Workman See, boys, it's a quattrocento lump o' furniture, an' so needs gentle handlin'. (*To 2nd Workman*) You, Philib, there, give it a sudden swing to the ayste, an' while she's swingin' we'll shoot her ahead.

2nd Workman (*angrily*) How am I goin' to give her a sudden swing to the ayste when there's no purchase to get a grip of her? Squattrocento or nottrocento, I'm not goin' to let it whip a slice outa my hand!

3rd Workman (*thoughtfully*) Th' only way to get it in proper is to get a sledge-hammer an' knock down some o' th' archway.

Poges (*indignantly*) Knock down some of the archway! You'll do no such thing! You'll be suggesting that the house should be knocked down next. There's no sledge-hammer to be brought within sight of this precious bureau. (*Leaning over towards the men*) Listen: this is a piece of quattrocento – understand that, the whole of you, please!

1st Workman (*to the others*) There, now, what did I tell yous? Yous hear what the gentleman says.

Poges It ought to go in easily, if you knew your job. The driver of the furniture van looked at this entrance and told me not to worry, that the bureau would slide in without the slightest trouble.

1st Workman (*scornfully*) Is it Larry Lunigan said that, now, did he? Don't mind anything Larry Lunigan says, sir. If your head was split he'd say it was only a scratch, to keep your heart up.

3rd Workman Even if you were dead he'd tell your wife to wait, an' say you never could be sure of anything. An' we're not furniture shifters, sir.

Poges Well, I'm sure of one thing: that bureau is coming into this room, and coming in without a scratch.

3rd Workman 'Course it is.

1st Workman Time an' patience'll do it.

Poges (*looking closely at the bureau – in anguish*) Oh, my God, there's the stone wall eating into its edge! Get it away, pull it out, shove it in, you fools! (*As they shove*) Wait, wait!

1st Workman (*soothingly*) I shouldn't worry, sir; a shavin' or two off is th' worst that can happen to it.

Poges Wait, wait a second. I'll go and get some cushions and pillows to guard the sides from the wall. (*He runs out by the adjoining entrance for the cushions.*)

1st Workman J'ever see such an oul' fustherer in your life? You'd think the thing was on its way to the kingdom of heaven th' way he's cryin' over it.

3rd Workman With a look on his ugly oul' gob like the tune th' oul' cow died of.

1st Workman A quattrocento, mind you, says he.

3rd Workman Seven hundred years an' more old, says he. Well, it's near time it met its death anyhow.

1st Workman Here, let's get it in before he comes back billowin' with cushions. It's well able to take a knock or two.

2nd Workman Here's th' crowbar he wouldn't let us use. (*He lifts up a big crowbar.*) We'll inch it in be main strength. Now, boys, get your shoulders to the quattrocento while I heave with th' bar! (*To the 1st Workman*) Start a shanty, Bill, to give us encouragement.

1st Workman (*chanting quickly, while they all brace themselves*)
What shall we do with th' dhrunken sailor,
What shall we do with th' dhrunken sailor,
What shall we do with th' dhrunken sailor,
Early in th' mornin'?

All (*together – shoving and tugging vehemently*)
Pull away, an' up she rises,
Pull away, an' up she rises,
Pull away, an' up she rises,
Early in th' mornin'!

Poges rushes in with some cushions in his arms. He is frantic when he sees what the men are doing. As he rushes in he is accompanied by a peal of thunder, louder than the last, but still fairly faint. As he comes to a halt near the bureau the peal ends.

Poges (*enraged*) What, in the devil's name, are you trying to do? Do you want to burst it to bits? Oh, why did I ever bring my poor quattrocento to a country like this! Shove it from the wall, shove it from the wall till I put a cushion in!

1st Workman Sure, it won't go far enough away from the wall to fit a cushion, man.

Poges (*frantically*) Do what you're told, do what you're told. (*He drops the cushions, seizes the edge of the bureau and tries to pull it from the wall.*) Here, somebody, help me!

Before he is aware of it, the 1st Workman leaps on to the top of the bureau to cross over to him, his heavy hobnailed boots scraping the top of it.

Poges (*shouting at him*) Get down, get down, man!

1st Workman (*astonished*) Amn't I only comin' across to help you.

Poges (*yelling at him*) That's a quattrocento, that's a quattrocento, man!

1st Workman Sure, I know it is.

Poges Then get off it, get off it – sticking your hob-nailed boots through and through it!

1st Workman (*lifting up a foot so that the sole of the boot can be seen*) Is it that, sir? Sure, th' nails are worn so soft an' smooth they wouldn't mark th' wing of a butterfly.

Poges (*roaring*) Get down, get down at once!

The 1st Workman jumps off the bureau back among his mates.

2nd Workman (*muttering loudly*) It ud be a godsend to some I know if they opened their eyes to th' signs an' wondhers showin'.

Poges Now, no talk; and don't do anything till I give the order.

Men All right, sir; go ahead; we're waitin'.

Poges When I say go, you swing it to the right, while I swing it to the left. Are you all ready?

1st Workman Ready an' waitin' an' willin'.

Poges Go!

They all swing to the left, and Poges' foot is caught

between the bureau and the archway. He lets a squeal out of him.

Poges (*in anguish*) Release my foot, my foot's caught! Why did you all swing left? Don't you know right from left?

3rd Workman You should have said ayste, sir.

Poges Shove it off, shove it from my foot!

1st Workman (*placing the crowbar between archway, against the column, and the bureau*) Now, boys, all together – heave yo-ho!

There is a might heave from them, one with the bar, the others with their shoulders. The bureau moves slowly; a crack is heard; the column snaps with the push of the bar against it and falls over the bureau, which suddenly shoots forward right into the middle of the room, the men stumbling after it. The men look triumphantly at the bureau, the 1st Workman leaning on the crowbar like a warrior leaning on his spear. Poges rubs his foot and contemplates the damage to the bureau and the entrance.

There she is for you now, sir; right where you want her to be.

3rd Workman I knew well patience ud do it in the end.

Poges Oh, look at the bureau and look at the entrance!

1st Workman (*confidently*) Oh, a spot o' cement an' a lick o' white paint'll make th' entrance look as young as ever again.

Souhaun comes in, followed by Cloyne and Barney, who are carrying a rug between them. They leave it on the floor. Basil is wearing very wide plus-fours.

Souhaun We're getting the house into some kind of order at last. (*She sees the damage.*) Oh, who's caused all the wreckage?

Poges (*sarcastically*) Your very clever countrymen, dear.

Basil (*mockingly*) And the high opinion they have of themselves.

2nd Workman There is sweet music in the land, but not for th' deaf; there is wisdom too, but it is not in a desk it is, but out in th' hills, an' in the life of all things rovin' round, undher th' blue sky.

Poges (*angrily and despairingly*) Take this broken column away and be off to your work again. Leave us, leave us, before the house falls!

The Workmen take away the column and go out by entrance leading to the hall.

Souhaun Let us try the rugs, for God's sake! I can't go out o' th' room but there's damage done.

Cloyne and Barney spread on the floor a rug scattered over with brightly coloured geometrical patterns. Cloyne and Barney then go out; the rest stare at the rug.

Rather gay-looking for the floor of a Tudor house, dear.

Basil (*decidedly*) Too bright and too modern.

Poges Where? How? Why?

Basil The Tudors, my dear sir, were a sensible and sober people, and wouldn't tolerate anything that was vulgar or, shall I say, conspicuous.

Souhaun (*with some mockery*) You see, darling, it was taste, and not steam, that was everything in those days.

Basil Quite, Souhaun; taste was the Tudor – er – er – *monumentum aere perennius*.

Poges I don't know everything, my dear sir; but I do know something about the period that this house – er – exemplifies; in fact, the period was so riotous in colour that the men's breeches had one leg blue, the other leg red, or vice versa.

Basil (*with a patronizing laugh*) Ah, old boy, that wasn't the Tudor period.

Poges What period was it, then?

Souhaun The Hiawatha period.

Poges (*indignantly – to Souhaun*) This is no joke, please. (*To Basil*) What period was it, then?

Basil (*airily*) Not the Tudor period, certainly; no, certainly not, old boy.

Poges (*contemptuously*) Pshaw! You don't know it yourself.

From the entrance at back the 2nd Workman appears wheeling a barrow filled with bricks. Passing by the disputants, on his way to the hall entrance, he wheels the barrow over a rug.

(*Shouting at him*) Where the hell are you going with your dirty barrow?

2nd Workman (*dropping the shafts of the barrow and turning to answer Poges*) I'm bringin' a barrow o' bricks to O'Killigain, sir.

Basil Oh, he's back, is he?

Poges What the hell do you think you're doing, man?

2nd Workman Amn't I after tellin' you, I'm bringin' a barrow o' bricks to O'Killigain?

Poges What d'ye mean, trundling your dirty barrow over a handsome rug laid out for inspection?

2nd Workman What d'ye want me to do? Take th' barrow o' bricks up in me arms an' fly over it?

Basil (*with great dignity*) Take it away at once, sir, and don't show impertinence to your betters.

2nd Workman (*eyeing Basil with scorn*) Jasus, looka what calls itself a betther man than me!

   O'Killigain appears at the entrance leading to the hall.

Poges (*earnestly – to the 2nd Workman*) My man, you're cheeking a cousin of a KG whose family goes back to – to – (*turning to Basil*) – William the Conqueror, isn't it?

Basil (*stiffening – with proud complacency*) Further back, old boy – Alfred; the last man of the last family fell at the Battle of Hastings.

Poges (*impressively*) There, you see.

Souhaun (*with a sign of mockery in her voice*) And the ancient gentleman passed through Oxford, too.

O'Killigain (*from the archway*) The city of dissolute might!

2nd Workman (*with mock deference*) D'ye tell me that, now? Why didn't you make me aware of all that glory before I began to speak? Isn't it an alarmin' thing to hear of the ancientology of a being that I took to be an ordinary man! An' what might be the ancient gentleman's ancient name?

Poges Basil Horatio Nelson Kaiser Stoke.

2nd Workman A right worthy name. It mayn't have a musical sound, but it has a steady one. There's no flightiness in that name. An' now, would you like to know mine?

Poges (*amusedly*) Here, be off with you to your work; as if your name mattered much.

2nd Workman Me name's O'Dempsey, of the clan that were lords of Offaly ere his ancient highness here was a thousand years from bein' born; a clan that sthretches back as far as the time before an Englishman thought of buildin' a weedy shelther; an' further back to a day or two afther th' one when the sun herself was called upon to shine. (*He takes hold of the shafts of the barrow preparatory to starting off.*)

Poges (*contemptuously*) You don't look it, my poor man!

2nd Workman (*as he wheels the barrow out*) I feel it; an' th' river's risin'.

Poges (*severely – to O'Killigain*) You really oughtn't to allow, much more encourage, this silly, ignorant, and superstitious conceit among your men; it is something close to scandalous!

O'Killigain (*quoting*) They go their own gait: looking carelessly in the faces of presidents and governors, as to say, *Who are you?*

Poges (*imperatively*) Well, it's not going to be heard in this house! The bobtag and ragtail must be made to keep their free-and-easy manners at a distance. Dignity reigns here.

A louder peal of thunder is heard in the distance, and the room darkens a little.

O'Killigain It's raining.

Poges Eh?

O'Killigain It's raining hard.

Souhaun (*shivering*) And growing cold.

O'Killigain And old things are perishing.

2nd Workman (*appearing at entrance*) We're knocking off, O'Killigain, for the rain is heavier an' the winds are keen.

O'Killigain You do well to knock off, for it is waste of time to try to butthress up a tumbling house.

Souhaun (*over to the 2nd Workman*) The house'll be lonesome without you.

2nd Workman Come, then, an' abide with the men o' th' wide wathers, who can go off in a tiny curragh o' thought to the New Island with th' outgoin' tide, and come back be th' same tide sweepin' in again!

Poges (*mockingly – to Souhaun, clapping her on the back*) There's a high and hearty invitation to you, me lady!

Avril comes in and dances over to Basil.

Souhaun (*gleefully poking Poges in the ribs – to 2nd Workman*) A long sail on the widening waters, no less; what gift is offered when the tide returns, good man!

2nd Workman With firm-fed men an' comely, cordial women there'll be laughter round a red fire when the mists are risin', when th' roads an' fields are frosty, an' when th' nights is still.

Souhaun (*in a mocking voice – to Poges*) There now, dear, is there anything more in the world than these that you can give?

Poges (*with pretended dismay*) He has me beaten; what am I going to do at all, at all?

2nd Workman A portion, too, with them who, ruddy-faced, were first in battle, with crimson cloak, white coat,

an' silver belt studded with splendour by a cunning hand;
a portion, too, with them of paler faces an' dhressed in
dimmer clothes, who, fearless, stepped a straight way to
th' gallows, silent an' darin' in th' midst of a yelled-out
Sassenach song!

Souhaun (*trying to speak mockingly, but developing a
slight catch in her voice; for she has been moved by the
2nd Workman's words*) Where is the lady who would be
slow to give a man with such a coaxing way an invitation
to her pillow?

> *Avril sees her friend is affected. She comes closer to her,
> and touches her on the arm.*

Avril Souhaun, Souhaun, come an' show me your newest
dhresses, an' don't stay listenin' to his thrancin' talk. Don't
leave me alone with them.

Souhaun (*shaking off Avril's hand; falling into the Irish
idiom*) Let me be, girl, for it's right an' lovely listenin' to a
voice that's makin' gold embroidery out o' dancin' words.

Poges (*angry and a little nervous*) It's time to put an end
to all this nonsense.

O'Killigain (*ignoring Poges' angry exclamation – to Avril*)
An' you, young girl, sweet bud of an out-spreading three,
graft yourself on to the living, and don't stay hidden any
longer here. Come where the rain is heavy, where the frost
frets, and where the sun is warm. Avril, pulse of me heart,
listen to me, an' let longin' flood into your heart for the
call of life. The young thorn-three withered away now, can
awaken again, an' spread its fragrance around us. Spit out
what's here an' come where love is fierce an' fond an'
fruitful. Come, lass, where there's things to say an' things
to do an' love at the endings!

2nd Workman Jack has spoken fair, an' there's no

handsome hindrance near to stop yous. What's here but a creakin' grandeur an' poor witherin' talk; salt food without a dhrink to go with it; an' a purple dhryness turnin' timidly to dust!

O'Killigain (*coming close to Avril*) Aren't my words a star in your ear, lass? Haven't you heard them? They've hit your young breast, lass. Come with me, I say; come away from where rich ignorance is a blessing, an' foolishness a gift from God! Come to th' house on th' hill: the door is open, the fire's alight on the hearth, and the table's laid with a clean white cloth.

Avril Let another go in by the door; let another eat at the table; let another sit by the fire. Why didn't you come for me, O'Killigain, before the young thorn-tree had shed its blossom, and before the stems began to die?

O'Killigain I'd other things to do. While you were livin' your lesser life, an' singing your dowdy songs, I was fightin' in Spain that you might go on singin' in safety an' peace. (*He grips her arm.*) I've come for you, now, me love.

Avril (*emotionally and anxious*) I cannot go where things are said and things are done, for love has had no voice in the beginning of them! (*She tries to free her arm.*) Oh, Jack, let me go – you're hurting me!

O'Killigain It's O'Killigain gives the pressure of comfort and of care. D'ye mind th' hurt when th' hurt's th' hurt of love?

Avril (*passionately*) Yes, I do! Oh, no, no; I don't, O'Killigain! I don't, I don't! Your pressure on my arm presses on my heart, too. Oh, go away an' leave me lonely!

She breaks away and runs to Souhaun, who puts an arm around her.

O'Killigain Avril, come out of th' gutterin' candlelight here to where th' wind puts a flush on the face, ruffles th' hair, and brings a catch to the breath; come to th' one you want; come to th' man who needs you!

2nd Workman (*to Souhaun*) An' you, Souhaun, sturdy lily o' Clune na Geera, come into the love that can fix or flutther th' stars o' th' sky an' change th' shinin' moon into a lamp for two. Come to th' one you need; come to th' man who wants you!

Souhaun (*half joking, all in earnest*) If you only had a horse handy, I'd ride away with you!

2nd Workman (*quietly*) He's outside waitin'. A loan from Mr O'Killigain. An animal can gallop glorious the livelong day undher th' sound of a steady voice an' th' touch of a steady hand.

Souhaun (*greatly moved*) N-no!

2nd Workman (*firmly*) Yes.

Basil (*rising out of astonishment – to Poges, angrily*) How long are you ready to stick this, man? Send these impudent fellows away!

Poges (*as if awaking from a stupor – furiously to the two men*) Get out, the two of you! We haven't lived long enough here to be touched with your insanity! Get out!

Souhaun (*to 2nd Workman – gently*) I'll see; I'll do whatever Avril advises. (*To Avril*) Come, dear, till we think out a wonderful answer.

O'Killigain (*to Avril as she is going out*) Be ready: I'll call, and come to take you when the river rises! (*He goes out.*)

2nd Workman (*to Souhaun as she is going out after Avril*) I'll wait outside be th' good gallopin' horse till th' snowy-breasted pearl comes to shimmer on me shouldher. (*He goes out after O'Killigain.*)

Poges (*furious and mocking*) When the river rises! Come with me and be my love! Come into the garden, Maud. Were ever fools so foolish!

Basil (*in angry glee*) And the fellow with the galloping horse outside! Boot, saddle, and away! I never expected to see and hear the like, even in this odd country. (*Slapping Poges on the back – jokingly*) You'd better watch out for the sound of the galloping horse!

Poges (*slapping Basil on the back*) And you keep an ear open for O'Killigain's call when the river rises!

Basil (*in a mock tragical voice*) Beware the sound of a galloping horse!

Poges (*in the same manner*) Beware of O'Killigain's call! (*Poges goes over to the bureau, opens a drawer, takes some papers out of it, and looks at them; then he sits down at the bureau, and arranges things in order to write a letter.*)

Basil And, for God's sake, did you hear that vulgar fellow chatting about making the moon do something or other?

Poges (*arranging things on the bureau*) Poor crazy fool. They're all a bit demented. Must be the climate. Most amusing.

Basil (*gloomily*) Yes, amusing up to a point, but hardly reassuring; no. (*He comes nearer to Poges.*) I don't like it, Poges.

Poges (*a little startled*) Eh?

Basil Well, it isn't exactly comfortable to be living in a community of crazy people, is it? It may even become dangerous.

Poges (*sitting up straight*) That's a serious thought, Stoke. Now that you mention it, I do feel the insidious influence of the place. We might become demented too.

Basil If they allowed us to live long enough.

Poges Good God, what a thought! I must have a talk with you about this when I finish this letter.

Basil You saw for yourself how this influence is even affecting the girls.

Poges (*emphatically*) The girls? There you are wrong, Stoke. No, no, not the girls, man. They were just humbugging the poor fools. Nonsense; not the girls.

Basil (*about to go out*) You watch. Come up to our room when you've finished the letter, will you?

Poges At once.

Basil goes out. Poges takes some paper, and writes the date on the top right corner. Then he pauses, and evidently begins to think of what has happened.

(*Shaking his head slowly from side to side – musingly*) Erin, the tear and the smile in thine eye.

He clears his throat with a cough, and settles down to write. The room becomes darker. He has hardly been writing a minute when a curious face appears round the corner of the entrance leading to the hall. It is the stout little face of a little man dressed in neat black clothes covered with a saturated fawn-coloured mackintosh. Big spectacles cover his eyes. A huge fiery-red beard spreads over his chest like a breastplate, reaching to his belly, and extending out from his body like a fan turned downwards. He wears a black jerry hat. When he speaks he is found to have a little voice. He carries a blackthorn stick in his hand. As he peeps round he sees

*Poges at the bureau, and pulls in his head again. He
thrusts it forward again, steps out, and comes into full
view. He pulls his coat straight with a jerk and
smoothes his trousers, and then comes with a trot into
the room, right over to Poges, bends over towards him,
and greets him in a hearty manner. He is the Postmaster
of the village.*

Postmaster An honour it is, sir, to meet the owner of such
a fine house. A house with a histhory. A house where the
genthry joined themselves to merriment and danced th'
stars to sleep! (*He dances clumsily round the room,
singing*) See me dance the polka, see me dance the polka,
see me dance the polka, as I have done before. (*He
suddenly stops and comes close to Poges.*) I hope I see you
well, sir? I bear a message from the Postmaster.

Poges (*amazed*) I am well, thank you; and what is your
message from the Postmaster?

Postmaster When I was outside, an' heard you coughin',
it's well I knew be th' sound of th' cough that the cough
was th' cough of a gentleman.

Poges (*impatiently*) Yes, yes; but what is your message?

Postmaster Well, as genuine gentleman, you'll be th' first
to agree that a Postmaster with a small wife an' a large
family, an' hardly any salary – I near forgot to mention
that – hardly any salary at all, if the thruth was told, as a
thrue gentleman, you'll agree that a man like that is
handicapped, an' has a claim on a gentleman's sympathy.

Poges But I can't make his wife bigger or his family
smaller, can I?

Postmaster Sure, I know you can't, an' that's not what the
Postmaster's complainin' about. (*He leans over Poges.*) But
th' poor man needs sleep, he needs his share o' sleep.

Poges (*humouring him – thinking his visitor is out of his mind*) Yes, yes; of course, the poor man needs sleep. We all need sleep. That's a fine stick you have in your hand, sir; can I see it?

Postmaster (*holding up the stick and stretching it away from Poges*) Ay, ay, a fine blackthorn. There y'are; look at it as long as you like – (*warningly*) – but don't lay a finger on it. There's a stick could give a man a crack a man ud remember!

Poges (*nervous*) Oh? I can't see it well from here; let me take it in my hand for a moment.

Postmaster Sorra a second you're goin' to have it in your hand. That stick has never been outa me father's hand an' it has never been outa mine. D'ye know why?

Poges No, friend, I don't.

Postmaster Guess, now, guess.

Poges (*smiling sweetly*) I haven't the slightest idea, friend; I couldn't guess.

Postmaster This's th' very stick that me oul' fellow made a swipe at Parnell with – th' scandalizer of Ireland's holy name, a swipe that, had it got home, ud a laid Parnell up for a month o' Sundays! Now, as a thrue gentleman, wouldn't you say I was right?

Poges Yes, yes; quite right.

Postmaster Well, havin' settled that, let's settle th' other: amn't I right in sayin' that every man should have his share o' sleep?

Poges Yes, yes; of course.

Postmaster Well, then, amn't I right in sayin' that th' poor Postmaster should have his share o' sleep too?

Poges To be sure. (*Rising from his seat*) Now, I must be going.

> A fairly loud clap of thunder is heard, followed by the sound, first of a trotting horse, then of one going off at a gallop. They listen till the sounds die in the distance.

A horse going off at a gallop. (*He makes a move away.*) I must go to see what's wrong.

Postmaster (*waving him back with the stick*) Wait a minute – I'm not done yet. You've just said the poor Postmaster should have his share o' sleep – didn't you?

Poges (*impatiently*) Yes, yes, friend.

Postmaster I knew you'd say that. (*He stretches out his hand to Poges.*) Lave it there. (*He shakes hands with Poges.*) Now I won't have to be keepin' one eye open an' me ear glued to the bell, for fear of a toll car or a thrunk call, afther ten o'clock at night, an' I settlin' down for a cosy sleep.

Poges (*the truth dawning on him*) Oh, so you're the Postmaster, are you? So it was you who delayed me when I wanted St Paul?

Postmaster Didn't you know that?

Poges The telephonic system here is an all-night one, isn't it?

Postmaster 'Course it is, but that says nothin'.

Poges (*decidedly*) Look here, my man; I'm a business man, and have to make calls at all hours of the night; I can't be thinking of every man having an honest night's sleep.

Postmaster 'Course you can't; it's only the poor Postmaster that you've got to keep in mind.

Poges (*severely*) Look here, my man, as long as I pay for the service, the service will have to be supplied. Good day.

Postmaster There isn't a gentleman in th' whole disthrict ud think, except in th' case o' sudden death or disasther, of givin' a tinkle afther th' hand o' th' clock had passed the figure of half-past nine o' night.

Poges Take yourself and your stick away out of the house, man!

Postmaster (*mimicking him*) Take yourself and your stick away outa the house, man. Is it comin' down here to teach us good manners an' feelin' y'are, an' you puttin' a surly gob on you when you're asked to fall in with the sensible an' thried institutions of the neighbourhood?

While they have been talking together, the room has darkened still more, and Poges sharply tugs the string that puts on the light; the wind has risen and can be heard occasionally blowing through the trees outside, and even shaking the old house.

Poges (*in a rage*) Go on, get out!

As he says this, a long, loud peal of thunder is heard.

Postmaster D'ye hear that? There won't be many thrunk calls goin' for a while, an' th' poor Postmaster'll have a sweeter night's sleep than some I know. (*He bends towards Poges.*) When – the river – rises!

The room has darkened; the wind rises; the one light in the room flickers. The Postmaster and Poges watch it. Then the Postmaster turns to go, but halts when a Figure of a man is seen standing at the entrance leading to the hall. He is dressed from head to foot in gleaming black oilskins, hooded over his head, just giving a glimpse of a blue mask, all illumined by the rays of flickering lightning, so that the Figure seems to look like the spirit of the turbulent waters of the rising river. The

*Postmaster goes back, startled, till he is beside Poges,
and the two men stand and stare at the ominous Figure.
Basil, Barney and Cloyne appear at the entrances at
back, each holding a lighted lantern in his and her hand.
They are very frightened. They too hold up their
lanterns and stare at the Figure.*

Basil The river is rising!

Barney Risin' high!

Cloyne An' will overwhelm us all!

Figure (*in a deep voice*) The river has broken her banks
and is rising high; high enough to come tumbling in on top
of you. Cattle, sheep and swine are moaning in the
whirling flood. Trees of an ancient heritage, that looked
down on all below them, are torn from the power of the
place they were born in, and are tossing about in the
foaming energy of the waters. Those who have lifted their
eyes unto the hills are firm of foot, for in the hills is safety;
but a trembling perch in the highest place on the highest
house shall be the portion of those who dwell in the
valleys below!

*The lightning ceases for a moment; the entrance
becomes dark, and the Figure disappears.*

Poges (*frantic*) What shall we do? what must we do? what
can we do?

Basil (*in anguish*) We're lost!

Cloyne (*sinking down on her knees*) King o' th' Angels,
save us!

Barney (*clasping his hands*) Amen! A nice pass we've
come to when we have to call for help in a Tudor house!
(*To Basil and Poges*) It's the evil livin' of you two buckos
that has brought this disaster upon us!

383

Poges (*bawling*) Souhaun, Souhaun! O'Killigain, help!

Basil (*roaring at Poges*) You made us come down here!

Poges (*roaring at Basil*) You're a liar, it was you!

Postmaster (*bringing down the blackthorn stick with a bang on the quattrocento bureau*) Eh, order, order, law an' order there; steady! Measures o' safety to be taken. (*Thrusting his stick towards Poges – sharply*) Has the highest room in the house a way to the roof – quick!

Poges (*answering at once*) Yes.

Cloyne (*in anguish*) Th' roof – oh, my God!

Postmaster (*rapidly*) Up with us all with bread and wine, with firewood and coal, and an axe. Up!

Poges An axe?

Postmaster To hack whatever suitable furniture we can get into a raft if we're swirled off th' roof. (*Driving Cloyne and Barney before him*) Up!

Poges (*loudly*) Souhaun, Souhaun, where's Souhaun?

Basil (*impatiently*) Come on, and come up.

Avril comes in from one of the back entrances. She is covered with a green mackintosh, and a coloured scarf, peasant-wise, is over her head. She carries a small case. She passes between the two men without a word, and stands still near the entrance leading to the hall, looking out before her.

Poges (*staring at her*) What are you doing here? What are you watching?

Avril stands still and silent.

Where's Souhaun, where's Souhaun?

Avril (*quietly – without looking round*) She's gone.

Poges Gone? How? Where?

Avril (*quietly – still not moving*) Gone with the wind; gone with the waters; gone with the one man who alone saw something in her!

Poges (*raging*) What, with that loud-mouthed, ignorant, superstitious, low-born, half-mad Irishman! Oh, she's nicely rooked me! She was with him on the galloping horse that galloped away, was she? Oh, she's nicely rooked a simple, honest, loving-hearted, foolish man! She's gone, is she?

Avril An' well it would be if I was with her.

Poges You damned slut, are you in your mind as bad as she is?

Avril (*indicating Basil*) The mind that went with him is as bad as the mind that went with you.

Basil (*sneeringly*) You lost the chance you had to get away from it.

Avril He said he'd come when the river rises.

O'Killigain (*outside – loudly*) Avril!

Avril (*with a start of joy*) O'Killigain! O'Killigain!

O'Killigain appears, his trench coat drenched and his hair soaking, at the entrance.

O'Killigain My barque is waiting, love; come!

Avril picks up the case and runs to O'Killigain.

Basil Honest, decent woman, she carries the booty of her friends in her pack!

Avril (*quietly*) I gave more than I got, you gilded monkey.

It's winnowed of every touch of life I'd be if I stayed with
th' waste of your mind much longer. (*She taps the case.*)
Th' thrinkets I wormed out of you are all here, an' here
they stay, for th' wages were low for what was done for
you.

Poges (*sneering*) And gentleman O'Killigain will happier
be with a harlot's fortune!

O'Killigain (*good-humouredly*) Of course he will. Th'
good things of this life are good for all, an' a pretty girl
looks handsomer in arms that are fit and fond to hold her.
You have had your day, like every dog. Your Tudors have
had their day, and they are gone; and th' little heap o'
purple dust they left behind them will vanish away in th'
flow of the river. (*To Avril*) Come, love, to my little house
up on th' hill.

> *He goes out with Avril. After a moment the sound of*
> *oars are heard splashing the waters, and O'Killigain is*
> *heard singing.*

(*Singing; other voices, outside, join in the chorus*)
　　Come from the dyin' an' fly from th' dead,
　　Far away O!
　　An' now, with th' quick, make your home an' your bed,
　　With a will an' a way, away O!

　　Then away, love, away,
　　Far away O!
　　To live any life that is looming ahead,
　　With a will an' a way, away O!

　　Away from all mouldherin' ashes we row,
　　Far away O!
　　Takin' th' splendour of livin' in tow,
　　With a will an' a way, away O!

　　Then away, love, away,

Far away O!
Where th' lightning of life flashes vivid we go,
With a will an' a way, away O!

Poges stands still, listening till the song fades away in the distance. Suddenly Basil clutches his arm.

Basil (*frantically*) Look, the waters are tumbling towards us! Run, man!

He tears up the passage while Poges follows more slowly.

Poges (*going out*) My poor little quattrocento, the waters are about to cover thee! My comfort's gone, and my house of pride is straining towards a fall. Would to God I were in England, now that winter's here!

He disappears down the passage as the green waters tumble into the room through the entrance from the hall.
    Curtain.

COME FROM THE DYIN'

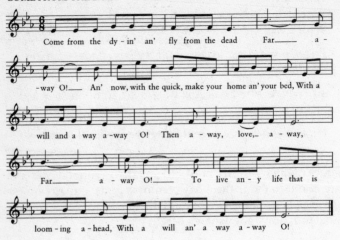

Come from the dy-in' an' fly from the dead Far___ a-
-way O!___ An' now, with the quick, make your home an' your bed, With a
will and a way a-way O! Then a-way, love,__ a-way,
Far___ a-way O!___ To live an-y life that is
loom-ing a-head, With a will an' a way a-way O!

THE MAID OF BUNCLODY

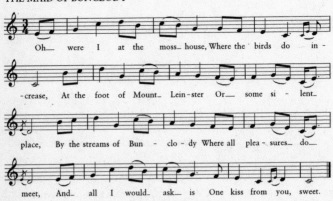

Oh__ were I at the moss__ house, Where the birds do in-
-crease, At the foot of Mount__ Lein-ster Or__ some si - lent__
place, By the streams of Bun - clo-dy Where all plea-sures__ do__
meet, And__ all I would__ ask__ is One kiss from you, sweet.

PURPLE DUST

O'KILLIGAIN'S LILT

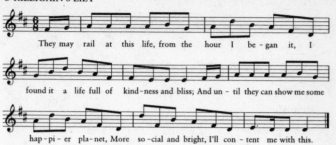

They may rail at this life, from the hour I be-gan it, I found it a life full of kind-ness and bliss; And un-til they can show me some hap-pi-er pla-net, More so-cial and bright, I'll con-tent me with this.

THERE ARE MANY FAIR THINGS IN THIS WORLD

There are ma-ny fair things in this world as it goes, The blue skies of sum-mer, the flush-ing red rose, But of all the fair blos-som-ing things that men see, A come-ly-built lass is the near-est to me, A come-ly-built lass is the dear-est to me.

SEAN O'CASEY

HEY, HEY, THE COUNTRY'S HERE

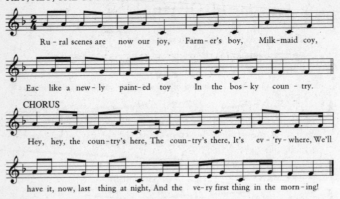

Ru - ral scenes are now our joy, Farm - er's boy, Milk - maid coy,

Eac like a new - ly paint - ed toy In the bos - ky coun - try.

CHORUS

Hey, hey, the coun - try's here, The coun - try's there, It's ev - 'ry - where, We'll

have it, now, last thing at night, And the ve - ry first thing in the morn - ing!

THERE'S LIFE WITH TH' LASSES

Come in or go out or just stay at the door, With a

girl on each arm an' one stand - ing be - fore, Sure, the

more that I have, the more I a - dore, For there's

much slower

life with th' lass - es, says Ro - ry O' More!

390

HALL OF HEALING

A SINCERIOUS FARCE IN ONE SCENE

Characters

Alleluia (Aloysius), the Caretaker of the Dispensary
The Old Woman
The Young Woman
Black Muffler ⎫
Green Muffler ⎬ patients attending the Dispensary
Jentree ⎭
A Lad
The Doctor, the Dispensary's Medical Officer
The Apothecary, the Dispensary's Dispenser
Red Muffler
Grey Shawl, Red Muffler's wife

*The waiting-room of the Dublin Parish Dispensary for the
Poor, on a winter's day. It is a place where the poor, sick,
or diseased are looked at and, usually, rewarded with a
bottle. It is an ugly room, drab, and not too clean. The
few bright spots in it are the posters warning of disease.
Running along the back wall is a bench on which the
patients sit while waiting to go in to the Doctor. A shorter
bench runs along the wall to the left. Beyond this bench is
the entrance door which leads from the waiting-room to
the hall, and thence into the street. In the centre of the
back wall is a window which looks out into the street. Just
to the right of this window, a wooden partition comes
down, somewhat diagonally, through nearly two-thirds of
the room, and then turns to the right, till it is joined to the
side wall on the right. Within this partitioned part of the
room are the Surgery and the Dispensary. A door in this
partition wall, up towards the back, admits one to the
Surgery. Another door in that part of the partition which
has turned to the right, near the right side wall, gives entry
to the Dispensary. To the left of this door is a small
window (shuttered for the moment), with a narrow ledge
in front of it, through which the remedies are handed out
to the patients. On the Surgery door is the word* DOCTOR
*in black letters, and on the door of the Dispensary, the
word* DISPENSER *also in black. On the back wall, to the
left of the window, is a poster on which are the words in
black print,* DIPHTHERIA: BEWARE! *Above the
Dispensary window is another one on which are the words
in red,* TUBERCULOSIS: BEWARE! *The Caretaker,
Aloysius, nick-named Alleluia, is fixing a third one, to the*

right of the window at back, on which are the words in green, CANCER: BEWARE! *Through the window at back, it can be seen that the weather is bad; hurrying flakes of snow are falling in a zigzag way because of the cold wind blowing. At times through the scene, quick and thick flurries of snow pass by the windows outside.*

The patients are all of one patch, immersed in the same uncertainty and want. The lines of care and weariness on their countenances are the same, save that there are more on the face of the old than on the face of the young. The complexion of the younger is starkly pale; that of Jentree a lemon-yellow; that of the Old Woman, a yellowish-brown; that of Alleluia is pale, with a dot of yellow on the points of the cheeks; that of the Doctor a purplish-white; of the Apothecary a pale one, with a bare hint of struggling ruddiness through the paleness. Though differing in cast of countenance, shape and colour of clothing, they all carry in their faces the lines of conscious, or semi-conscious, uncertainty and resignation.

The face of Aloysius is a rather foolish one; his head is narrow at the top, developing down and out to form a square for a chin. His grey eyebrows gather into turned-up tufts at the corners; his tough nose tilts; and, though he has no moustache, a grey spade beard grows naturally, or has been trained, into a tilting tuft too. His mouth is wide, inclined to grin, and is always slightly agape. Whenever he moves across the room, he does so in a movement, half run, half glide, as if he skated on a surface fit only to glide over in places. As he glides he bends his body over and forward, as a stiff-backed bird might do, holding out his arms from his body as he glides and runs along.

Next to the Doctor (to whom he is subservient and of whom he is very much afraid), he is Lord of the Dispensary, dictating to the out-patients, and making things uncomfortable for them; though they try to please him, and follow his humours as well as they can. He wears

*a uniform of dark blue, the frock-coat reaching to below
his knees. It is ornamented with silver buttons. His
trousers are a bit short, coming only to the tops of his
boots. His head is covered with a blue-peaked cap, having
a wide top, and a narrow strap running along the butt of
the peak is fastened on either side by a small silver button.
A fussy old fool. He takes off his coat to tackle the job of
tacking up the poster. He takes up a hammer, spreads out
the poster, and with some difficulty hammers in a tack in
one corner. Fixing the opposite one, he drops the tack, and
curses, immediately ejaculating, 'Mea culpa, mea culpa.'
He fixes that corner, and, in driving the third tack home,
he hits his thumb, exclaims with pain, flings down the
hammer, and thrusts the injured thumb under his armpit,
first giving vent to a yell of agony.*

Alleluia (*pacing about the room, and nursing the injured
thumb*) Ooh! Sacred Heart! Me thumb's desthroyed! May
th' curse o' – (*He checks the profanation by trying to sing
in a woeful way.*) She's me lady love, she is me baby love.
Oooh! (*He again yells in agony, and bends double to
squeeze the injured member tighter under his armpit.*)
Curse o' – (*He checks himself.*) Oh, Holy St
Harmoniumagnus, succour me! (*He sings woefully again.*)
I know she likes me, I know she likes me, Because she says
so – St Serenium, ayse th' pain; ayse it, ayse th' agony!
Preserve me from pain! Today, tomorrow, an' forever
afther! Right on th' tenderest part!

*He goes moaning into the Dispensary, and the clank of
bottles is heard.*
  *Presently, the door leading into the Dispensary
waiting-room from the street is cautiously opened, and
the shawled head of an Old Woman peers into the
room. Then the door is slowly opened, and the Woman
enters. Her back is bent. Her boots are broken, and the
skirt she wears is old and tattered at the hem. Shawl,*

skirt, boots, and all, are mud-coloured. She shivers and shudders as she comes in, slowly rubbing her gnarled hands to promote circulation. She goes over to the bench, and sits down stiffly. She coughs, and then wipes her mouth with the corner of her shawl. The clanking of the bottles stops. She gives another asthmatic cough, and again wipes her mouth with the end of her shawl. The shutter of the Dispensary window is pushed up, and Alleluia's head is thrust out; it looks round the room, and spies the Old Woman sitting on the bench. The head is withdrawn, the shutter pulled down, and Alleluia comes out of the Dispensary, wearing a bandage round the stricken thumb. He goes over with a glide to the Woman, catches her by the arm, pulls her from the seat, and guides her to the door.

Old Woman (*protesting feebly, but submitting calmly to ejection as one to whom it is a familiar part of life*) Ah, now, Mr Aloysius, it's only a bare few minutes from the time of openin'. 'Clare to God, Alleluia, th' weather outside ud perish a body; an' I have within me oul' body a whole kingdom of aches an' pains!

Without a word Alleluia opens room door and leads her out, a look of determined indignation on his face; they can be heard going down the hall. Shortly after, he returns, and shuts the door. He cautiously completes the hanging up of the poster on the wall. He puts on his coat. Then he hurries into the Dispensary, comes out again with a sweeping-brush, and slides it over the floor, pushing whatever may be before it under the bench. While he sweeps, he sings softly, in the rather cracked voice of an old man, the chorus of 'The Rose of Tralee', pausing sometimes, as he pushes the brush, to do a bit of a waltz with it, and picking the song up again from where he left off, when its resumption seems convenient.

Alleluia (*singing*):
> She was lovellee an' fayer as ay . . . rosebud of summer;
> But it wasn't her beautay aylone . . . that . . . won me;
> Aah, no; 'twas they truth in her . . . eyes . . . ever
>   beamin',
> That med me lovev Mary . . . they rose of . . . Thraa . . .
>   lee!

Nearing the end of the chorus, he is near the door of the Dispensary, and, doing a kind of dancing swirl right around, as he sings the last line, he glides into the Dispensary and closes the door behind him.

   After a moment or two, the entrance door opens and Red Muffler, a young man of twenty-five, enters the room. He looks thin and a little careworn. He is very poorly and thinly dressed; his muddy-black trousers are patched with black cloth on one knee. His neck is protected by a thin, red woollen muffler, and a dark tweed cap, dotted with snowflakes, is pulled low down over his eyes. He looks poor, cold, and miserable; but there seems to be some element of grit in his standing. He takes his cap off, and, holding it by the peak, whirls it round to shake the heavier dampness from it; then he replaces it on his head. Between each forefinger and thumb, he pinches together each leg of his trousers, and flicks them in an effort to make them feel drier. The Old Woman's head appears round the edge of the door, peering nervously into the room. Red Muffler sees her.

Red Muffler (*to Old Woman*) Come in, old lady; here is more shelthered than th' hall, an' a heaven from th' sthreet.

Old Woman (*deprecatingly*) I'll do lovely here. If himself seen me, it's out into th' sthreet I'd go again, an' a body pushin' hard to eighty years isn't proof against th' chill o' th' sleet, an' th' chatther of th' interferin' wind outside.

Red Muffler (*irritated by her timidity*) Aw, come in, woman, for God's sake! It's this fear of offendin' that keeps us all so far from th' spice of comfort.

Old Woman (*timidly crossing the threshold*) I wondher if I ought to venthure it? Alleluia 'ill only be shovin' me out again. (*She crosses herself.*) He's a good Catholic, an' maybe he won't now.

Red Muffler (*decisively*) Aw, go and sit down, woman. I'll know how to deal with this Alleluia of yours when he shows himself.

Old Woman (*wandering over to the bench*) Th' docthor before this one gave us a bad habit, always leavin' ordhers to let us in before openin' time, if th' weather was grim, or rain was fallin', or even when the sun happened to be too boistherous.

Red Muffler An' what's wrong with th' present docthor?

Old Woman Aw, he's one o' th' surly specimens. (*She rises stiffly, bending double, and groaning, to come close to him.*) He's partial to th' dhrop. He has th' life frightened outa poor oul' Alleluia. (*She whispers.*) He can't abide you to come on Mondays, because of his feelin' frightful afther Sunday's rest.

Red Muffler Why do you come on Monday, then?

Old Woman It's me one free day. I have to work on all the others.

Red Muffler Is he doin' yeh anny good?

Old Woman Aw, divil a good, so far; but I'm always hopeful he may.

Red Muffler An' is he hopeful?

Old Woman Divil a hopeful. He just says I'm wastin' his

time comin' here; that me back'll never straighten, an' th' ache'll never end. But you can never tell with God.

Red Muffler (*clapping his cold hands against his sides*) An' how much d'ye make outa your work?

Old Woman A shillin' a day, son; five shillin's a week.

Red Muffler Jasus, that's not much!

Old Woman It's something, son. You see, I can do only rough an' heavy work now. Me oul' hands is too shaky for any fancy job. I don't need much. I won't worry if only I can outlast life workin'. (*Anxiously*) D'ye know, I don't really think I ought to stay here – a few more slaps from the flauntin' wind, an' one more scatterin' of rain over me can't do me much harm.

Red Muffler (*ignoring her anxiety*) An' have you no one to fight for you; no childhren to stand up for you?

Old Woman Fight, is it? Fightin' only makes things worse. Of course, I've children, but all married, an' hard set themselves to live. There's one blessin' – I can offer everything up to God.

Red Muffler (*venomously*) Misery isn't much of a gift to give to God, is it?

Old Woman (*shocked and staring – after a pause*) Ah, son, don't say a thing like that! We're too poor to take th' risk of sayin' serious things. We're told God is good, an' we need every little help we can get.

Red Muffler An' th' kind docthor before this fellow come – where did he go?

Old Woman Aw, he went into his grave. Cancer, I'm told. With th' aid o' dhrugs, he kept himself goin' for a year an' a day; then, he was silently seen no more.

Red Muffler (*echoing her*) Silently seen no more! Will this damned doctor never come! Such as us have barely time to glimpse a gleam that's kind before it hurries to the dark again. It's afther ten, and that damned docthor isn't here!

Old Woman (*anxiously*) Why, aren't you feelin' well, son?

Red Muffler Me? Oh, I'm all right. It's our little girl o' nine; our first one. She's been bad a week; she's worse; now, we're afraid she'll soon be something silently seen no more. (*Tensely*) The child is bad; th' child is worse; th' child is chokin'. (*Agonizingly*) Jesus Christ, ha' mercy!

Old Woman (*soothingly*) I wouldn't be fancyin' death for your little one, son. She'll be all right. God is good. They tell us that God's thought is roomy with anxiety for the very young.

Red Muffler (*impatiently*) I know what they tell us, I know, woman; but it's past ten; an' ten's th' hour, an' th' bugger should be here.

The organ is heard playing.

What music is that?

Old Woman An organ in the church next door; every Monday someone plays it: practisin', maybe. When th' wind's this way, you can hear it. The caretaker here dances like a fool, and chants an Alleluia ditty whenever it sounds. That's why we call him Alleluia. (*She comes nearer.*) An oul' fool!

Red Muffler Me feet's numb. It's not good to be left standin' here in these wet things. I'm seepin'.

Old Woman When you're my age, son, you'll be well used to them things.

He stamps his feet heavily on the floor in an effort to give them the feel of life. The shutter on window in

*Dispensary is suddenly pulled up, and the head of
Alleluia, cap and all, is thrust through it. The head peers
around to see who has made the noise, sees Red Muffler,
and the head is pulled in again, while the shutter is
pulled down with a snap. Then the door of the
Dispensary is opened, and Alleluia slides out and over
to the Red Muffler. He takes him by the arm and tries to
guide him to the entrance door, but he is resisted, and
Red Muffler doesn't budge.*

Red Muffler (*shaking off Alleluia's hold*) Here, you –
what's bitin' you?

Alleluia (*a little taken aback by the unexpected resistance*)
You can't stay here. No one's to cross the sthreet door till
th' regulation time o' openin'. (*He snatches Red Muffler by
the arm again.*) Come on, now – out!

Red Muffler (*violently shaking off Alleluia's hold*) G'way,
you fussy, fiddlin' fool!

*A little frightened, and deciding that discretion is
needed, Alleluia side-steps away from Red Muffler,
spots the Old Woman – now cowering in a corner – and
glides over swiftly to where she sits. He catches her arm;
she obediently rises, and he begins to guide her over to
the entrance.*

Old Woman (*timidly apologetic*) I musta strayed in be
mistake, Mister Alleluia – I mean, Mr Aloysius. Th' sleet
an' the bullyin' wind has made th' sthreet unkind, sir. Yes,
th' wind must ha' blew me in, mister. Without me noticin'
either. You'll excuse me, sir; for I've many burdens of
aches an' pains to try to hide from th' blowin' blight of th'
weather.

Alleluia (*decisively*) Yeh can't hide your aches an' pains
here, ma'am. You can't expect to have Alleluia hours of
comfort at your time o' life, or in your circumstances. Th'

last docthor near ruined yous all, so he did, with his scorn
of regulations; with his 'make the bareness brighter', an'
his 'th' most o' them won't last a lot longer'. Had he lived,
he'd ha' wanted cushions for your poor backsides. Th'
waste of it! I'd like to know how we'd fare without th'
regulations.

Old Woman (*meditatively*) Th' last one always had a
winsome word for th' sick an' dyin', so he had.

Alleluia Because he was sick an' dyin' himself – that's
why. Out you go, an' don't put your nose in again, till th'
docthor arrives.

Old Woman (*half turning to glance at Red Muffler*) Th'
gentleman behind us, sir, advised me to shelther in outa th'
weather.

Alleluia (*pushing her out by the door*) Out you go!

*During all this Red Muffler has taken no notice, making
no effort to defend the Old Woman; but has turned his
back on the other two, and is now staring hard at one of
the posters.*

Old Woman (*reaching the door, hesitates, turns suddenly
round, and runs across the room till she is half-way to
where Red Muffler is standing – bitterly*) You went before
me when I was comin' in, but you're not before me goin'
out! You keep your courage secret, you do. (*She makes the
motion and the sound of spitting scornfully towards him.*)
That's your value to this poor oul' woman, you poor
morsel of a man!

*Alleluia has now got behind her with a movement that
is half a run, half a glide, and hastens to shoo her out as
a drover might a cow, adding an occasional shove with
his hand to her back.*

(*As she nears the entrance door – fervently*) Thanks be to

God who spared th' last poor docthor be givin' him death,
an' deliverin' him from th' lousy lot of us!

*She disappears out by the door, Alleluia following
close on her heels. Red Muffler turns slowly away
from the poster, and sinks down to sit on the bench,
resting with his elbow on knee, his head on his hand.
After a pause, the Doctor whirls into the room, fussier
even than old Alleluia, followed meekly by the
Caretaker. The Doctor is of middle height, rather
plump, and widening perceptibly around the belly. His
face – half concealed now by a thick white wool
muffler – is turning to a purplish tinge by hard
drinking. His eyes are small and hard, his eyebrows
thick and shaggy. Had he his black bowler hat off, it
could be seen that he is bald, save for a few reddish-
grey hairs brushed over the crown, in an effort, maybe,
to hide a big expanse of polished skull. He is wearing
a heavy brown topcoat; and his lower legs are encased
in shining black leather leggings; a serviceable
umbrella is in his left hand, a satchel in his right one.
As he enters, he gives a sudden belch, and he
ejaculates, as if to himself, but quite audibly: 'Jasus!'
He catches sight of Red Muffler, and turns to Alleluia.*

Doctor Who's that fella? What's that fella doin'?

Alleluia He's waitin' for you, sir.

Doctor An' how'd he get in before the regulation time?

Alleluia He just came in without by your leave from a
soul. I expostulated with him, but he wouldn't budge for
no one. Wouldn't budge an inch.

Doctor Then th' street door must have been open to let
him in.

Alleluia (*sliding to the left and to the right of the Doctor,* *and back again*) I left it open, sir, for a spessesscific purpose.

Doctor For a what? What d'ye mean, man?

Alleluia (*again sliding to right and left, and around, the Doctor so that the Doctor has to turn to follow what he's saying*) For you, sir; I didn't want you to be fouled with the weather an' you fussin' with th' key for th' keyhole.

Doctor (*impatiently*) Stop that buzzing round me; you make me giddy, man. I'm quite competent to find the keyhole without a fuss. Don't leave that door open again till the regulation time. If I've forgotten the key, I can ring, can't I?

   As Alleluia is silent.

Damn it, I can ring, can't I?

Alleluia Yis, yis; of course you can ring; 'course you can, sir.

Doctor And you're not deaf, man, as well as bothered, are you?

Alleluia Me deaf? (*With a dancing glide before the Doctor*) I'd hear the cuckoo before it came, sir.

Doctor Well, hear the surgery bell when it rings, for I'm not in a waiting mood today. How many are outside, d'ye know?

Alleluia I seen six or seven or eight, maybe nine, when I peeped into the street.

Doctor (*sarcastically*) Are you sure it wasn't ten, now?

Alleluia It might ha' well been ten, for the sleet was fallin' between me an' them. More than ten, maybe, sir.

Doctor Well, you can get them in, and, mind you, no

delay when the bell rings. Immediately one enthers, pop another at the edge of the surgery door to be ready when the bell sounds again.

Alleluia (*doing another gliding dance to the right, to the left of the Doctor*) On their tiptoes; ears cocked; tense with listenin', prepared to spring forward when they hear a tinkle.

Doctor (*thrusting the umbrella under his right arm, and gripping the shoulder of Alleluia with his left hand, which he uses to give him a shake*) Keep still, you rubbered image of desolation! When the bell gives two quick rings, it's you I want, not a patient. And listen: no gossiping while you're on duty – d'ye hear?

Alleluia Gossip, is it? Me gossip? An' on duty? Aw', never! Th' only words I ever uses is expended on expostulations. Never fear, sir; I keep well within th' silences of devotion. Gossip on duty is not good company.

Doctor (*explosively*) Aren't you always at it! Expostulations! Give your expostulations a rest today, and just shove them in to me.

Alleluia You don't know them, doctor; if you did, you wouldn't wondher any. Not a one o' them'll budge without an expostulation.

Doctor (*wildly*) Looka here, if you don't learn to quit yourself better than you do, I'll complain to the Guardians, by God, I will! (*He gives a more violent and sickly belch.*) Ooh, damn it! You're making me worse! If you have me yelling at you today, it'll be th' worse for you. Have you th' Surgery fire going well?

Alleluia (*cheerfully – and beginning to slide about again*) Yissir; oh, ay: it's a beauty; all aglow, an' most enticin'. I'd hurry in to it, an' get them damp things off you.

Doctor They're not damp! (*Near a shout*) I came in a cab!

Alleluia An' a wise man you were, Doctor, to do it.

Doctor (*impatiently*) Get them in, man, and get them out! No dallying today.

He hurries towards the Surgery; Red Muffler rises again from the bench to meet him. Alleluia hurries out by the entrance door, and soon returns followed by the patients, sorry-looking men and women from the tenements. Alleluia stands at the entrance door ushering them in, and waving them to the benches. As they troop in, the organ is heard playing again, and the poor patients seem to fall in with the rhythm of the tune as they drag themselves to the benches.

Among them are Black Muffler; the old bent-back woman; Young Woman of twenty-three, who, behind her hand, gives an occasional dry, hard cough; Mr Jentree, a man of forty-five, dressed in a mode of faded respectability – bowler hat, black, somewhat discoloured; faded brown tweed coat, waistcoat, and trousers; stiff white collar and black tie; and a brown mackintosh. As he enters, his head is shaking, a strained look of anxiety disturbs his face which is fortified by a short beard and moustache. He walks uncertainly with the aid of a stick. He sits down between the Young Woman and the Old Woman. While seated, first his right leg, and then his left one, gives a sudden and spasmodic jerk, signifying a nervous disorder. Among them is Green Muffler, a man of about thirty-five, clad in the rough clothes of a labourer – corduroy trousers, old khaki coat from the remains of the First World War, thick coat of a faded dark blue, and a green muffler round his neck. When he enters, he looks nervously around him, as if asking himself if it were well for him to be there. And when he sits down on the last bit of

bench, he stretches his head forward to look at the
posters. The other patients are but variants of the others
in feature and colour of clothing.

Red Muffler (*going in front of the Doctor before he gets*
to the Surgery door) Excuse me, sir; I want to ask you
about our kid.

Doctor (*brusquely*) What kid? Sit down, sit down, man,
and take your turn.

Red Muffler I'm not ill meself, sir; I've only come about
our little girl who's very bad.

Doctor (*impatiently*) Sit down, sit down, till I'm ready for
you.

Red Muffler (*speaking rapidly for fear the Doctor would*
get away) You seen her a week ago, sir. She's worse, an' th'
missus's afraid for her.

Doctor (*sharply and rapidly*) Oh, sit down when you're
told, man!

Red Muffler (*submissively complying*) Yessir.

The Doctor hurries into the Surgery. Alleluia
obsequiously closes door after him. Red Muffler resumes
his seat nervously, pulling his coat round him; buttoning
it up, and then opening it again.

Young Woman (*coughing behind her hand*) He's in a bad
mood today.

Old Woman When's he any other way? Since the last
doctor's death th' last light left us has gone out.

Black Muffler (*morosely*) What odds? Th' fella taken
away done no more for us than this fella that's left. It's a
new doctor, but it's th' old, old treatment. I dunno that th'
last one was fit to be a docthor at all.

Old Woman (*scornfully*) You dunno! Who're you to dunno? Why wasn't he fit?

Black Muffler Well, ma'am, th' last time he saw me, he said what I needed was betther food, a finer house to live in, an' a lot more enjoyment. An' when I said couldn't you give me a bottle, Docthor, he laughed at me, so that I felt ashamed of me life. An' afther what he had said, d'ye know what he said then?

Jentree (*impatiently*) Then what did he say, what did he say, then?

Black Muffler My good young man, he said, you can't expect to dhrink health into you out of a bottle. Nobody knows how frightened I felt!

Young Woman Wouldn't any sensible one be frightened at th' edge on a remark like that!

Old Woman Poor innocent man – no wondher th' good God took him to Himself!

Black Muffler When he saw th' fright I was in, he put a hand on me shouldher, and said, Looka, says he, if health could be got out of a bottle, says he, I'd be th' healthiest man alive. An' me heart galloped into th' fear that th' poor man wasn't a docthor at all! Unless he was beginnin' to go out of his mind. I've never been th' same since.

Jentree I dunno how life could be lived without some kinda bottles.

Old Woman What if th' poor man did make a slip aself – it's a wise man doesn't. He just had some kind of a kink against bottles.

Meanwhile, Alleluia has gone into the Dispensary, and returns with a stick of chalk. With this he draws a straight line on the floor, half-way between the bench

*and the Surgery door. Just outside this door, draws a
circle. Within the circle, he puts a patient facing the door,
and places another patient toeing the line, facing, too,
towards the Surgery door. The Surgery bell rings.
Alleluia hurries the patient in the circle into the Surgery,
shoves the other patient into it, while another one toes
the line. When the first patient comes out, she goes to the
Dispensary, hands in a bottle, gets it back full, and then
she goes away by the entrance door, shivering with
anticipation at what she will meet outside. This goes on
rapidly till a stream of patients have passed in, come out,
and gone away. Alleluia hurries each in when the bell
tinkles, hurries each to the Dispensary window for the
medicine, and then hurries each out of the place. This is
the common measure of the place, and it goes on rapidly
till Black Muffler passes from the line to the circle, and
from the circle into the Surgery. As each poor patient
comes out to go away, Alleluia waylays him or her,
holding a card out to them, and asking a penny for the
Holy Souls, that Masses may be said for their redemption
from Purgatory. When he gets a penny, he pricks a space
in the card he holds in his hand with a pin. The organ is
heard playing the same tune during the procession of
patients, and Alleluia goes about in a dancing slide to the
tune, chanting, mockingly, 'Alleluia, Alleluia, Alleluia',
waylaying the patients for pennies at intervals,
challenging them with the phrase 'Remember the Holy
Souls in Purgatory'. Black Muffler comes out of the
Surgery cautiously and softly shuts the door behind him.*

Black Muffler (*gesturing back towards the Surgery with
his thumb – in a whisper*) Hunted me out! Lyin' down on
a couch, with th' Dispenser givin' him a cordial. Looks
like a cut-down daisy. We'll be here all day.

Young Woman Maybe it'll give time for the weather to
clear.

Alleluia glides down the room, bends down, hands on knees, before Green Muffler, and stares at him. The patients watch the glide, and Black Muffler – again in the circle – and the rest – except Jentree – turn to watch and listen.

Alleluia (*to Green Muffler*) You're a new customer here, aren't you?

Green Muffler (*staring back at him*) I was never here before, if that's what you mean.

Alleluia An' what are you complainin' of, me man?

Green Muffler Eh? (*Stretching out his right arm carefully and slowly*) Oh, just this arm o' mine – it hurts terrible when I thry to do anything serious.

Alleluia Aah, rheumatism!

Green Muffler (*shortly*) Naw, it's not rheumatism! I know what rheumatism is.

Alleluia (*thoughtfully*) It might be something goin' against th' blood strame.

Green Muffler (*with sharpness and mockery*) Are you th' docthor, or wha'?

Alleluia (*importantly*) I'm next to th' docthor. Where's your bottles?

Green Muffler (*somewhat startled*) Bottles? What bottles?

Alleluia There's no use o' you comin' here if you're not thoughtfully and thoroughly supplied with bottles. Every commencer must have three – one for a draught, one for a liniment, and one for a mixture. You can't go into the doctor's presence unless you are in possession of three comely and commodious bottles.

Green Muffler I didn' know nothin' about bottles.

Old Woman (*leaning forward as far as she can from the bench towards Green Muffler*) You might need only one, son; but, th' nature of your particular throuble might require two; an' in a diversified complaint, three bottles might be called for; so you have to be prepared. Stands to reason, a patient must be provided with a bottle, or two, or three bottles. As likely as not, son, you'll be a three-bottle man.

> *The patients are now more interested than ever in the discussion; the one in the circle of chalk moves out of it to be nearer; and the one toeing the line moves nearer too. Jentree is the only one who is occupied with himself, and takes no notice.*

Alleluia (*not liking the interference – turning towards the Old Woman, with his body still bent double and hands on knees*) If you'll allow me, ma'am, I'd have you notice that this would-be patient is receivin' official attention an' insthruction respectin' any bottles necessary in combination with his ailment.

Young Woman (*coughing behind her hand*) One ud never know, be th' common look of them, that bottles was so important. With every patient, bottles there must be.

Black Muffler Bottles there was, bottles there is, bottles there must be!

Alleluia (*angrily – to the patients in general*) Are yous goin' to have me expostulatin' all th' day! Close your gobs, an' cease from shattherin' me explanations to this man!

Green Muffler Th' whole place seems to be seethin' with bottles. An' where am I goin' to get them?

> *The Surgery bell has been signalling for Alleluia – by giving two quick, consecutive rings – several times; but*

*all are so excited over, and interested in, the bottles that
no one takes the slightest notice.*

Old Woman (*over to Green Muffler*) If you've thruppence
on you, son, you'll get them in some pub: black porther or
green mineral bottles – it doesn't matther, for they're all
good of their kind.

Alleluia (*accompanying Green Muffler out by the
entrance*) An' remember, they must be all rinsed clean so
as to be in a receptionable condition for th' contention of
medicine.

*The bell sounds its two quick, consecutive rings again,
this time with venomous clarity in the now silent room,
startling the patients back into meek and anxious
attention.*

Young Woman (*agitated*) Holy Saint Juniper o' Judaea,
there's th' docthor callin' a patient!

Old Woman (*to the patient who has been standing in the
chalk circle – vigorously*) Off you go; in with you!

Black Muffler (*bewildered by the sudden change of topic*)
Who? Is it me, is it?

Old Woman (*rapidly*) You, you; yes, you. Hop it, man!

Young Woman (*beginning before the Old Woman ends*)
Quick. Yes, you!

Jentree (*beginning before the Young Woman ends*) Before
he's out on top of us, roarin'!

*Black Muffler makes a bewildered rush for the Surgery
door, which he opens. He goes in, but immediately
comes out again, pushed back by the Doctor, who is
angry and furious.*

Doctor (*wildly*) Not you, not you! Aloysius I rang for!

Good God, that fellow'll drive me mad! (*Shouting*) Aloysius!

Alleluia (*sliding into the room again – full of hurry and fear*) Sir, sir; here, sir!

Doctor (*stormily*) Where were you, you dolt! Didn't you hear the bell? You'll quit this very weekend! What were you doing, you deaf oul' ditherer?

Alleluia (*rapidly*) Explainin' regulations to a patient, sir, about bottles.

Doctor (*furious*) You fool, what do bottles matter! My pen – where is it? Pen, pen, man!

Alleluia (*flustered, but smiling*) Pen? Oh, the pen, is it? Oh, yes, the pen. Let me think, now. I remember, yes; th' apothecary got a loan of it, sir.

Doctor (*angrily*) Get it back then, at once. He's no business to touch it! Let him get a pen of his own. This is th' third or fourth time he's pinched it!

Alleluia (*deprecatingly*) Not pinched, sir; oh, no, not pinched it.

Doctor (*roaring*) Pinched, I say! (*He gives a half-belch, ending in a sigh – ejaculating as if to himself*) Oh, God! I'm in a shockin' state! (*To Alleluia – angrily*) Why th' hell d'ye let him take it?

Alleluia (*whisperingly*) Between ourselves, sir, I'm tired expostulatin' with him. You'd want to chain it to your desk, sir.

Doctor Wish I could chain you where you'd be hidden from view! (*Pushing Alleluia from him*) Go, an' get th' pen! (*To Red Muffler, who has risen, and now takes a step towards him*) Oh, sit down, you; sit down!

Crestfallen, Red Muffler does so. The Apothecary's head is poked out of the Dispensary window; the head is completely bald, except for a tiny web of fringe above the forehead; a thick moustache covers the upper lip, and almost hides the mouth; it juts out aggressively at each side of the face. The head twists round in the direction of the voices.

Apothecary's Head (*shouting*) Aloysius; eh, Aloysius!

Alleluia (*running round to the window*) Yessir.

Apothecary's Head (*thrusting out an arm holding a pen*) Here's th' damned pen for him!

Alleluia snatches the pen, and rushes back to the Doctor, who snatches it from him.

Doctor (*indicating with his pen Black Muffler who had stood within the chalk circle*) You there – come in. Come on, come on! (*He goes into the Surgery.*)

Alleluia (*fussy as ever – getting behind the patient, and pushing him along*) Go on, go on, go on!

Green Muffler enters by the entrance door. He is damp and shivery. He carries a porter bottle under his arm, and the neck and shoulders of mineral-water bottles are sticking out from the side pockets of his coat. He sits down, silent and morose, on the end of the bench.

Alleluia beckons the Young Woman, and places her within the chalk circle. He takes another patient from the bench and puts him toeing the line; bending down to shove back a foot that ventures over it, arranging the feet so that they exactly touch the sacred chalk line.

(*Petulantly fixing the foot*) Keep the feet determined toein' the line exact, will you!

Young Woman (*nervously*) I hope I won't be called on to stand too long here – I always feel shaky when I stand for long in th' one place.

Old Woman He'll take a long time between patients today; always does when he's bad from booze.

Jentree (*giving a sudden jerk in his seat*) You know, if I don't get some specific attention soon an' sudden, something terrible's bound to happen. I'll fall, paralysed, from me neck down!

Old Woman (*soothingly*) You're lettin' it, whatever it is, play on you too much, son.

Jentree (*testily*) Aw, for God's sake, woman, talk sense. Can't I feel me legs goin' dead? D'ye imagine I can go on not noticin' things? (*A leg gives a spasmodic jerk.*) Oh! Did yous all see that? (*To Alleluia*) Eh, misther, I'll have to be let in at oncst!

Alleluia (*with a sweeping glide towards Jentree, and a bend down to place his face in front of Jentree's*) You'll wait till th' regulation tinkle of th' bell tells you to go.

Jentree (*as the other leg gives a spasmodic jerk upwards*) Oh! There, did yous all see that one go up? There's no deception, mind yous – I'm really in a desperate condition!

Young Woman (*in the circle*) Poor man! An' what gave you them terrible jerks? What did th' docthor say?

Jentree (*with scorn*) Th' docthors! Th' one before this one, an' this fella, too, said it was because of too much imbibin' of wine.

Old Woman (*startled*) Wine? An' where would you come across th' quantity of wine to give you them sharp an' sudden jitters?

Jentree I was a wine porther, ma'am, but th' little I lowered through th' years couldn't possibly ha' done it.

Old Woman (*realizing the cause, but not willing to hurt*) Looka that now. I wouldn't say all; but it might, it only might, mind you, have had a little to do with it.

Jentree (*getting on to his feet with a shivering jerky movement*) Oh! Th' bottle I get is doin' me damn all of good! An' th' wather I have to dhrink's makin' me worse! Looka, I'm thremblin' all over!

Old Woman (*to the other patients who are now all interested in Jentree*) His mind's sthrayin. (*To Jentree*) Wather? What wather are you dhrinkin', son?

Jentree (*venomously*) Th' wather them getts o' docthors ordhered me to lower – more'n half a gallon a day. (*He sinks back on to the bench.*) Me left leg's lost its motion. Not in a year, mind you, but in a day! I'd like to see him thryin' it himself. (*He jerks up from the bench again.*) I'll have to be carried home, if this goes on! What manner o' mortal man could swally a tank of wather in a single day?

Old Woman Indeed, son, th' boyo inside wouldn't like to have to do it himself.

Jentree I feel close to death when I see the sight of it!

Old Woman Th' sight of what, son?

Jentree (*explosively*) Wather, woman; th' wather!

Alleluia (*coming close to the talkers*) There's only one thing, ma'am, manifested enough to negify th' effects o' wine, an' that's wather; an' th' patient would be well advised to gulp it down, gulp it down with determination, ad lib.

Old Woman (*eagerly – to Jentree*) Hear that, son? Mr Aloysius knows what's good for you! Wholesome stuff is wather. Gulp it down, son, an' it's bound to negify any wine that may be ripplin' round in you still: ad lib's th' only way!

Jentree (*to Old Woman – determinedly*) I'd have you remember, ma'am, that I'm th' custodian of me own ailments, an' am fully endorsed on their concern and their keepin'! (*Indignantly – to Alleluia*) Gulp it down! I wondher would you relish gulpin' cold wather down you till your heart was stunned into stoppin' its beatin'? Would you like to gulp cold wather down you till every vital organ in your poor body was frightened of what was floodin' into them? Negify th' effects o' wine! An' if I go on, what'll I take to negify th' effects of wather?

Old Woman (*to Jentree*) Sure that's the difficulty, son. (*To Alleluia*) If th' poor man has to negify th' wine with wather, and then has to negify the wather with wine, sure th' poor man'll burst himself thryin' to find a solution for his ailment.

Jentree (*to Old Woman*) Sure that's what I'm up against all the time, an' no one'll listen to me! (*Rising shaking to his feet and sitting down again – a little hysterical*) What's keepin' that fella inside! I'm goin' fast. Th' thremors is mountin' me spine. I'll be gone in a minute, if he doesn't hurry to have a look at me!

Young Woman (*from the circle*) Poor man, y'are in a terrible state! Maybe you'd like to take my turn? I'm in no hurry, so I'm not. Indeed, I'd rather wait as long as I can in th' hope th' weather ud be betther when I set out for home.

Old Woman (*to Jentree – encouragingly*) Yes, do; go on, son; take your chance of an earlier overhaul.

She rises, and, with the help of the Young Woman – coughing with the exertion – planks Jentree in the circle. He is shaky, nervous, and leans heavily on his stick. The

*Young and the Old Woman then return, and sit down
on the bench. The Surgery door opens gently, and Black
Muffler enters the waiting-room on tiptoe, a frightened
look on his face. He closes the Surgery door softly, and
gives an admonitory and warning gesture with a
prescription he is holding in a hand.*

Black Muffler (*with a significant wave of a hand*) Husssh!
He's in a murtherin' mood today! Can't sit aysy a second.
Went out once, an' I heard him thryin' to retch. He'll take
ages to get through today. Jasus, we poor have a lot to
bear!

Red Muffler (*rising to his feet – angry and fierce*) An' why
do they bear it! Even with the best docthor in its bosom,
what kind of a kip is this place? I deny that this is all that
God has got to give us! Even with the best music of a
church organ, what betther could we do here but dance a
dance of death! I won't do it; I won't do it! By God, if that
fella inside refuses to come to our sick kid, I'll know th'
reason why!

*He sinks down on the bench again, wiping his forehead
with a soiled rag he has taken from a pocket. After this
outburst, for a little while, there is a dead silence, the
patients, standing and sitting, staring at the fiercely
spoken Red Muffler.*
*Then Black Muffler goes to the window of the
Dispensary, hands in his prescription and a bottle; waits
a moment, then gets the bottle back filled with a rich
yellow fluid. He comes to the middle of the room, and
holds the bottle from him towards the light.*

Black Muffler (*holding the bottle at arm's length*) Oh, a
lovely yella, this time; th' last was blue.

Young Woman Mine was red, so it was.

Old Woman Show us.

He hands her the bottle, and she holds it out at arm's length.

So 'tis – a gorgeous yella! (*She hands the bottle back to him.*) Be th' look of it, son, that should do you a power o' good. This fella thinks more o' bottles than th' other fella did – I'll say that of him!

Alleluia (*down at the entrance, beckoning Black Muffler to go*) Eh, you, with the black muffler, there; you've been fully medicamented, an' you've been handed your documented mixture; (*he glides up to Black Muffler*) so no more chit-chat, but go; but before you go, remember the Holy Souls.

Black Muffler (*ignoring Alleluia's appeal – pocketing the bottle*) I'll enther a new lease o' life when I stoke meself up with this documented stimulant, wha'? I'll renew th' bottle, he says. Well, we'll thry it once more, anyway.

Alleluia slides and glides up to Black Muffler, catches him by the arm, and glides down with him to the entrance door, ushering him out to the street.

Jentree (*becoming more nervous*) What's keepin' him; what's th' fella doin' at all? I'm getting' worse. I'll be down prostrate, numb an' nameless, before th' fella lets me in!

Old Woman (*encouragingly*) Keep calm, son. Take your thoughts off yourself.

Jentree (*turning angrily to Old Woman*) Don't be rattlin' nonsense into me mind, woman, an' me in agony! I need immediate aid to countheract what's comin'. I can't wait. I want help at once; now! (*He totters rapidly over to the Surgery door; kicks it below with a foot, bangs it above with his stick.*) These docthors wouldn't blink an eyelid if a man passed into oblivion! (*He again kicks and hammers* *on the door.*) Eh, eh, you in there, does medical discretion always go disregarded in this place!

As Jentree is hammering at the door, it suddenly opens, and the Doctor, furious with anger, appears. Jentree totters back a little and the patients sit straight and still with respect and a little fear. The patient toeing the line runs off to sit down demurely on the bench.

Doctor (*in an agony of rage*) What's this, my God, what's all this? (*To Jentree*) Was it you who hammered at the door?

Jentree (*smilingly*) Me, sir? I just gave a few quiet knocks, sir, for I was feelin' fit to die.

Doctor (*yelling*) Aloysius! Oh, where's that rambling fool! Aloysius!

Alleluia comes rushing in and over to the Doctor. He grips Jentree and pulls him into the circle again.

Alleluia (*to Jentree*) Stand there; don't budge!

Doctor (*furiously – to Alleluia*) I'll budge you, you Poor Law Guardian's gett!

Alleluia (*ignoring the Doctor – pulling the other patient to toe the line again*) Stand there; don't budge!

Doctor (*talking rapidly, pulling Alleluia by the coat to a place near the Surgery door*) You stand there, and don't budge till they're all in and out again! (*To Jentree*) I told you not to come for a month. I gave you enough bromide mixture for a month. You're not going to die. Be off home.

Jentree Yessir, nosir. But th' delugin' o' wather y'ordhered's doin' me no good.

Doctor Take more of it, then, to weaken the wine in you. Now off you go. (*To the Young Woman*) You're Jenny

Sullivan, aren't you?

Young Woman (*with a prologue of a cough*) Yessir.

Doctor (*to Old Woman*) What do you want – more liniment?

Old Woman Yessir, please.

Doctor Get it then, and go. (*Indicating Green Muffler*) Who's that man?

Alleluia (*sliding into a bending position before the Doctor*) A three-bottle man; a newcomer.

Doctor (*calling down to him*) Eh, you, come on in to me. (*He returns to the Surgery.*)

Jentree (*as he goes out*) Weaken th' wine in me! It's in an ambulance I ought to be, speedin' to a place where a qualified man ud be sacked if he left me out of his sight for a minute! I'll appeal to the authorities, so I will – this very day!

Old Woman Arra, be sensible, son! Let what they give kill or cure us, there's ne'er a one for us to appeal to, bar the good God Himself! The poor who refuse to be patient die young.

Red Muffler (*fiercely*) We've been too patient too long; too damned long; too god-damned long, I'm sayin'! Patience is only th' holy name for suicide!

Alleluia glides along with Green Muffler to the Surgery door, ushers him in, and is about to close the door when the Doctor gives him a note.

Doctor Give that to Jenny Sullivan there, and tell her she can go.

Alleluia gives the Young Woman the note. The Old Woman has crossed to the Dispensary window, handed

*in her prescription and bottle; received her liniment, and
returned to the back to gaze out of the window at the
falling snow.*

Old Woman (*tonelessly*) Th' snowy rain is worse nor what
it was even.

Young Woman Looka what I've got; looka what he's
given me!

Old Woman An' what is it, daughther?

Young Woman (*tonelessly*) A note to the Consumption
Dispensary o' Charles Street. I'm done for now. I feel faint.
I'll lose me job an' all, now. It's me death warrant!

Old Woman (*coming over to her*) Sit still for a few
minutes, an' then we'll go home together. You'll have a lot
more to go through before you'll be done for. There, sit
still, child. I wouldn't say that he wasn't mistaken – th'
fellow doesn't know black from white this mornin'. An'
anyway, daughther, death's th' last thing th' poor should
dhread.

*A Lad of fifteen years of age comes into the waiting-
room, and Alleluia at once glides down to him. The boy
is thinly clad in coat and long trousers too big for him.
His cap, too, is a size too large. He has the mask-like
paleness of the others.*

Alleluia (*to the Lad*) What d'ye want?

Lad (*handing Alleluia a red ticket*) For me mother for the
docthor to call.

Alleluia (*reprovingly*) Sir, sir; don't forget th' sir, lad. Are
you workin'?

Lad I deliver th' papers of a mornin'. I get two shillin's a
week.

Alleluia An' how much d'ye keep for yourself?

Lad Fourpence.

Alleluia Sir, sir; don't forget th' sir – where were you brought up? Don't you know your catechism?

Lad Wha'?

Alleluia Wha'! That's not th' way to addhress a superior. How much o' th' last fourpence have you left?

Lad Tuppence, sir; only tuppence.

Alleluia Ah, that's better (*He shows the Lad the collecting-card.*) Remember th' Holy Souls. Put one o' th' pennies on th' card for th' Holy Souls.

> *After some hesitation, the Lad forks out a penny and gives it to Alleluia, who marks it down by pricking the card with a pin.*

Lad (*earnestly*) Me mother says, sir, she's very sick an' can't stir in th' bed, an' would th' docthor please hurry to her?

Alleluia (*almost shoving the Lad out*) Tell your mother that th' docthor'll go full gallop to her!

> *Green Muffler now comes from the Surgery and goes over to the Dispensary window. He planks his three bottles down on the ledge in front of the hand-out window, and then hands in his prescription to the Apothecary. Alleluia glides over to him, in the hope of collecting another penny for the Holy Souls.*

(*Archly holding collecting-card under Green Muffler's nose*) A penny to help the Holy Souls outa Purgatory, kind man o' th' three big bottles.

Apothecary's Voice (*at the window – to Green Muffler*) Take them bottles away.

Alleluia is startled; lowers card, and listens.

Green Muffler (*startled and puzzled*) Eh? Wha'? What bottles?

Apothecary's Voice (*impatiently*) Them on th' ledge. (*Shouting*) Them on th' ledge!

Alleluia, scenting danger, glides away, and stands as close as he can get to the Surgery door.

Green Muffler I was ordered to bring three bottles. Th' person in authority here said I must have three bottles on me. Bring, says he, three bottles, says he, one for a liniment, one for a mixture, says he, an' one for a draught.

Apothecary's Voice (*impatiently*) Do what you're told, man! (*Shouting*) Take them outa the way! They're no use here!

Green Muffler takes the three bottles from the ledge and deposits them on the floor. After a moment or two, the Apothecary's hand puts a tiny box of pills on the ledge in front of Green Muffler. He is shocked, looking at the tiny box, and then at the bottles.

Green Muffler (*to the patients – who keep a tense silence*) Did yous see what's after happenin'? Did yous or did yous not? Yous all saw me entherin' burdened with bottles, be strict orders forced to spend me last penny to get them. An' when I present them, as sthrictly ordered be a certain person, I'm shouted at to take them away, an' even th' use of one was denied me. (*He extends his hand with the tiny pill-box on its palm.*) Looka what I got; just looka what I got! (*He comes into the centre of the room.*) I'm not dhreamin', mind you. This isn't fairyland either. Yous all seen what happened. After all me huntin' after bottles, looka what's been handed out!

He glares towards where Alleluia is busy totting up

what he has collected on his card – ostensibly unaware
of what is taking place.

Yous all heard what a certain person said to me. You must
have three bottles, he says, one for a mixture, one for a
liniment, he says, an' one for a draught. Three, mind you.
Yous all sung a song about the necessity for bottles. An'
what was the outcome? Yous all seen it yourselves. Yous
all see the bottles scattered about, an' me left with what's
shinin' in th' palm of me hand! I'm not dhreamin', mind
you! Have yous nothin' to say to relieve me feelin's? (*He*
moves towards the door to go.) Jasus, it's a cruel thing to
do on anyone. (*He turns to look towards the patients.*)
An', mind you, that certain person thried to cadge another
penny off me for the Holy Souls! An' what about th'
sufferin' souls here, eh? (*He goes to the door, and turns*
again.) God forbid I'd ever come here again; but if I have
to, I warn that certain person not to mention bottles to
me; for if that certain person does, he'll be a sufferin' soul
in Purgatory himself, without a one to help him out!

He goes slowly out, leaving the bottles on the floor
beside the Dispensary; and, as he goes, he fixes his gaze
on the pill-box.
The Doctor comes from the Surgery, dressed for the
street as he was when we first saw him. He sees the
patients sitting on the bench.

Doctor (*calling*) Aloysius!

Alleluia comes gliding up to him.

Why are these still here? Why haven't they gone home?

Old Woman (*apologetically – to the Doctor*) The Young
Woman here felt faint, an' we were restin' till she got a bit
betther.

Doctor She can't rest here. It's nearly closing time. The best place for her is home. (*To Old Woman*) Do you live near her?

Old Woman Only a sthreet away, sir.

Doctor Well, see her safe home, like a good woman. (*To Alleluia*) Close the house up, Aloysius. (*To Red Muffler who has come close to him*) What is it you want, and speak quick, for I'm in a hurry.

Red Muffler It's me child, sir; me little girl, sir, only just nine years old.

Doctor Yes, yes; what about her?

Red Muffler We're afraid for her. You saw her four days ago; top room, hundhred an' one Hill Sthreet, sir. We want you to come at once.

Doctor I know, I know; everyone wants the doctor to come at once. I'll call sometime tomorrow.

The Doctor makes a step forward towards the entrance door, but Red Muffler makes one too, so that he stands somewhat in the way of the Doctor's passage to the door. At the same time, the Apothecary comes out of the Dispensary. He is dressed for the street – long mackintosh, thick white and red muffler, and a grey trilby hat pulled well down on his forehead. He carries an attaché-case and a walking-stick. He stands outside the Dispensary door and watches what is going on.

Red Muffler (*blocking the Doctor's way to the door*) No, today sir, please; now. She needs you now. Have a look at her, at least. Last night was one of agony to th' missus an' me, listenin' to her losin' her breath. We're afraid soon she'll silently be seen no more. She's bad; she's worse; she's chokin'!

428

Doctor I'll go tomorrow; I can't go sooner. There are others needing attention, you know.

He goes to go, but Red Muffler catches his arm.

Red Muffler (*desperately*) Nine years isn't long enough for a life to live! Damn it, man, if you've none for me, have some thought for th' mother watchin' th' child's rash sthruggles to live!

Doctor (*chucking his arm from Red Muffler's hold*) Oh, man alive, there are thousands of kids like yours gasping for life in the city today.

Red Muffler (*fiercely*) An' no one seems to care a coloured damn about them!

Doctor No living doctor can give them what they need, man. To worry about them would send me to the grave, too.

A young woman appears at the entrance door. Her head and half her body are covered by a grey shawl; her thin skirt is black, fading now to a rusty brown; her boots are old, and are sodden with the slush of the streets.

(*Seeing Grey Shawl – angrily to Alleluia*) Don't let any more in – put that one out!

Alleluia goes gliding down and tries to turn Grey Shawl back, but she pushes him roughly aside and hastens up to Red Muffler.
The Doctor is now half-way down to the door; Red Muffler beside him, a little to his front; Grey Shawl in front of Red Muffler; the Old Woman and the Young Woman have risen from the bench, and stand behind to the left, almost directly in front of the poster warning of diphtheria. The Old Woman has an arm around the young one, though she needs support herself. The

Apothecary stands a little in front of his Dispensary door.

Red Muffler (*to Grey Shawl – frightened at seeing her*) What'r you doin' here? I had to wait to thry to get th' docthor. Who's with th' child? Why th' hell did you leave her?

Grey Shawl (*very quietly*) You needn't throuble th' docthor further, Frank. An' I didn't leave little Sheila, it was her who left me. (*Her hand steals forward to cling to a hand of Red Muffler's, and there is a silence for some moments.*)

Red Muffler (*Quietly*) Well, we've got all we could get here, so we'd betther go. (*To the Doctor*) You might have safely said you'd come, an' kept hope danglin' still in front of us that healin' still was here, an' common goodness. Our little one has had th' charity to save you from a cold an' tirin' journey in th' mornin'. (*Fiercely*) Oh, you blasted fomenter of medicine, you might have listened to what I thried to say!

Grey Shawl (*frightened*) Frank! Do come home, an' don't make a show of us an' little Sheila. I'm frightened she's feelin' lonely wherever she may be now.

Old Woman (*coaxingly*) Ay, do, son, go home. Ah, it's curious how th' old is left to wither on, while th' young often go before they've time to bloom. It doesn't seem right to me. I could ha' gladly gone in the little one's place; for head down an' back bent, what's for me to thry to tarry here a minute longer! God Almighty does odd things at times.

Grey Shawl (*coaxingly*) Come on, Frank, till you see her. She's got all her old good looks back again. (*Brokenly*) Oh, me little one'll be runnin' round frightened, lookin' for her mammy, among the spirits of the blest!

Red Muffler (*to the Doctor*) D'ye hear that? She's got her old good looks all back again. Death has sometimes a kindlier touch than many a human hand.

Red Muffler and Grey Shawl go out followed by the Old Woman and the Young Woman, who pass Red Muffler and Grey Shawl by as Red Muffler turns around at the door with a parting shot at the Doctor.

(*Turning back at the door*) The pair of yous can go home, an' snore away some other buddin' life! Yous are afraid to fight these things. That's what's th' matther – we're all afraid to fight!

Apothecary (*after a pause*) Cheeky boyo, that! Not a grain of gratitude in one of them for all we thry to do for them. Well, I'll be off – good day. It would almost make a man despair of humanity! See you in th' morning.

Doctor Good day. I hope so.

The Apothecary goes off. Alleluia comes gliding down to the Doctor and holds out the red ticket given to him by the young lad.

Alleluia (*holding out the ticket*) Another visitin' ticket, sir.

Doctor (*impatiently*) Put it on my desk, put it on my desk, man!

Alleluia glides off swiftly, with hand extended holding the red ticket; dives into the Surgery; comes out again, and watches the Doctor go. The Doctor pulls the white muffler closer around his neck, settles his hat more firmly on his head, giving a few thick coughs as he does so, and goes out of the waiting-room. Giving a richer belch as he goes out by the door.

Jasus, I'm in a terrible state!

Alleluia shuts the Surgery door and locks it, putting the

key in his pocket. He goes to the Dispensary door and locks that too. He sees the three bottles on the floor that Green Muffler left behind him. He takes them up and shoves them under the bench, singing the chorus of 'The Rose of Tralee' as he does these things. The organ is heard softly playing its old tune; it comes faintly into the room, as if to counterpoint the song sung by Alleluia.

Alleluia (*singing, and breaking off at times, resuming again when his breathing finds it convenient*)
She was lovellee an' fayer as ay . . . rose . . . bud in summer,
But it was not . . . her beau . . . tee aylone that won . . . me;
Ah, no, 'twas they trewth in her . . . eyes fondly beam . . . in',
That mayed me love Mary, they rose of (*He is now at the entrance door; he gives a last look round, then goes out, closing the door behind him. Outside the door*)
Traaa . . . leee!

As the curtain falls.

THE ROSE OF TRALEE

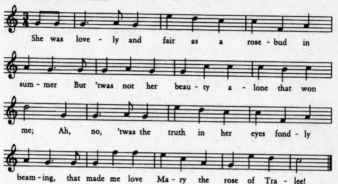

She was love - ly and fair as a rose - bud in sum - mer But 'twas not her beau - ty a - lone that won me; Ah, no, 'twas the truth in her eyes fond - ly beam - ing, that made me love Ma - ry the rose of Tra - lee!

ALLELUIA
Caretaker's Chant

All - all - e - lui - á all - e - all - e - lui - á.

All - all - e - lui - á all - e - all - e - lui - á.